The Optimal Modified 2/1-Club System

Integrating 2/1 with a Strong Club
A New Approach
Using the Optimal Point Count Method

NEIL H. TIMM, PH.D.

Order this book online at www.trafford.com
or email orders@trafford.com

Most Trafford titles are also available at major online book retailers.

Print information available on the last page.

isbn: 978-1-6987-1136-2 (sc)
isbn: 978-1-6987-1137-9 (e)

Library of Congress Control Number: 2022904913

Trafford rev. 03/22/2022

North America & international
toll-free: 844-688-6899 (USA & Canada)
fax: 812 355 4082

CONTENTS

ACKNOWLEDGEMENTS

First and foremost, I want to sincerely thank Patrick Darricades for helping me to better understand the Optimal Point Count (OPC) Method of Hand Evaluation and for the continued support, encouragement, and comments he has provided me with this new bidding system. He has turned my world up-side down. I hope I can do the same for you!

I must also thank the many bridge players for their continued input and suggestions they have provided with my prior books on Precision Simplified and the 2/1 Game Force System.

Finally, I must thank my wife, Verena, who supported me as I sat for many hours in front of the computer typing the material for this book.

The book represents a new approach to bridge that integrates the 2/1 Game Force System with a Strong Club bid into a single new system for both intermediate and experienced players.

Sincerely,
Neil H. Timm, Ph.D.

timm@pitt.edu (please e-mail comments, corrections, and suggestions)
Web Page: www.bridgewebs.com/ocala
March 2022

INTRODUCTION

Contract-Bridge was born in 1925 and refers to new rules, devised by the American H. Vanderbilt, which granted bonus points to a team that bid and made a game contract (9, 10, or 11 tricks) and even more bonus points for a slam contract (12 or 13 tricks).

Numerous American champions became early proponents of the game and the first pioneers to develop bidding systems and tips on the technical play of the cards were H. Vanderbilt, E. Culbertson, C. Goren, M. Work, E. Blackwood, S. Stayman, A. Roth, H. Schenken, E. Kaplan, among others, making the United States the world's dominant nation in Bridge, from 1935 to 1955.

Charles Goren popularized the "Standard American" bidding system in 1949 in North America using Bryant McCampbell's suggestion for evaluating balanced hands using the 4-3-2-1 honor point count method of hand evaluation where an A=4, K=3, Q=1 and J=1 point with 4-card majors in 1915; however, it was Alvin Roth in 1943 who proposed the Two over One (2/1) with 5-card majors which he called the Roth-Stone System.

The game quickly became popular in Great-Britain and France which contributed to advancing the *"art"* of bidding (Acol bidding, P. Albaran's *"Canapé"* bidding, P. Ghestem's *"Monaco"* Relay bidding) and soon after in Italy, whose National Team, the *Blue Team*, made up of 3 pairs, each playing a different strong Club bidding system, achieved unmatched international prominence by winning 12 consecutive World Championships from 1957 on, and then again from 1972 to 1975.

Since the Blue Team's retirement, in 1976, the Americans have re-established their earlier prominence, but many other countries now compete with great champions of their own (Italy, France, Brazil, Poland, Holland, China, Great-Britain, and several others), many of them playing a strong Club bidding system, whether Precision or Modified Precision.

The Two over One (2/1) Game Force bidding system was an improvement over the Standard American (SA) System that has been in effect and played by bridge players for many years. Many claim that the advantage of the 2/1 system allows the partnership to know that game is possible with only a single bid provided one has 13+ points.

As we shall see for suit contracts it is only true if the opening 2/1 bidder has 15 points, not 12/13 points since 25/26 points do not result in game whenever a singleton in one hand finds "wasted honor points" in partner's hand. Yet, most 2/1 conventions call for 13+ High Card Points (HCP).

Another flaw of the 2/1 approach is the fact that opening 1-level suit bids have a wide bidding range (12-21). To eliminate this flaw, the principles of Pinpoint Precision may be implemented with a new and improved hand evaluation method. A major flaw of most Strong Club opening bids is that they are based solely on HCPs with opening bids of 16/17+ points.

To correct these flaws among others, the search for a better hand evaluation method and a better bidding system has been unrelenting. Hand evaluation methods have been popularized by Milton Work, Charles Goren, Marty Bergen (Bergen's Adjust-3 Method) and Petkoy Zar (called Zar Points), and others. All falling short when applied to the commonly used "dialogue" bidding systems.

However, I believe that the **O**ptimal **P**oint **C**ount (OPC), an accurate hand evaluation method unveiled in P. Darricades' book "Optimal Hand Evaluation" (2019) corrects the many flaws of prior hand evaluation methods when applied to any bidding system (e.g., Acol, Standard American (SA), 2/1, or Precision).

In this book many "traditional/standard" bidding practices that do not help to show suit fit and distribution are to be avoided or re-defined. Splinters and mini splinters which show the location of voids and singletons to help locate wasted honors, the XYZ bidding convention, cue bidding, and new bids for the investigation of game and slam are among the cornerstone conventions reviewed in this book.

Newly defined 2 and 3-level bids to show hands with 6/7+card suits are defined to prevent the opponents from finding their optimal contract and to improve upon difficult bidding sequences using traditional bidding strategies. The evaluation of one's Offense to Defense Ratio (ODR), why many well-known bidding sequences must be avoided, and an analysis of several old "standard" bridge laws/rules are reviewed to show why they need not be used to improve one's judgement if one employs the OPC method.

My goal for "The Modified Optimal 2/1-Club System" is to show how to use the OPC method of hand evaluation to improve the dialogue between two players to achieve an optimal bridge contract. The primary objective is to demonstrate how to apply the new system approach to contract bridge by illustrating a more accurate method of hand evaluation.

To quote Alan M. Sontag, an American professional bridge player, who has won six world championships, including two Bermuda Bowl wins; "Some people believe an expert can win using any system. This is simply not true. A player employing an inferior or outmoded bidding system – and bidding is 80 per cent of the game – is at an enormous disadvantage."

What are the most important attributes of a good bridge bidding system? Jan Eric Larsson (2021) in his book "Good, Better, Best - A comparison of Bridge Bidding Systems and Conventions by Computer Simulation", Mater Point Press; found that the best systems include:

(A) Careful point calculation and re-calculation.
(B) Strong club systems are better than natural systems.
(C) Strong NT is better than weak NT.

And that the most important system properties must include:

(1) Constructive precision
(2) Aggressiveness
(3) Communicating information effectively
(4) Giving away as little information as possible
(5) Right-siding the contracts, play-wise and information-wise
(6) Non-symmetry of information value

Finally, these factors must depend primarily on the system itself and are not decided by the players using it.

As you will soon see the Modified Optimal 2/1-Club System satisfies the above criteria: A, B, C and 1-6 above. Weather you currently play Acol, SA, 2/1, or Precision the transition to the Modified Optimal 2/1-Club System should be a natural and rewarding process.

CHAPTER 1

HAND EVALUATION AND OPENING BIDS

Hand Evaluation

The standard deck of cards for the game of bridge contains fifty-two cards. The cards are organized into suits - spades (♠), hearts (♥), diamonds (♦), and clubs (♣). The sequence of suits: spades, hearts, diamonds, and clubs represent the rank order of the suits: spades are higher ranking than hearts; hearts are higher ranking than diamonds, etc.

The major suits are spades and hearts, and the minor suits are diamonds and clubs. A No-Trump (NT) contract is played in no agreed suit.

A bridge contract may be played in a major or minor suit, or in NT. The dialogue between the opening bidder and his partner is used to establish the bridge contract. Bridge contracts are referred to as a Partial Contracts (less than game), Game Contracts, Small Slam Contracts, and Grand Slam Contracts and may occur in either NT or a suit. Hand evaluation and the bidding process are used to find the "best" contract.

There are three common hand distributions: balanced, semi-balanced, and unbalanced.

Balanced Hands are "flat hands" with no singletons or voids. They also have no more than one doubleton. Balanced hand distributions are:
4333
4432
5332

Unbalanced Hands are hands that have a singleton or a void. These hands either have one long suit (6/7-cards) are two suited (55/64-cards) or three suits (4441/4450).

Semi-Balanced Hands are neither balanced nor unbalanced with no singleton or void but have more than one doubleton. The distributions are:
5422
6322
7222 (rare)

Each suit in the bridge deck contains thirteen cards as follows:

A K Q J 10 9 8 7 6 5 4 3 2

The Ace (A), King (K), Queen (Q), Jack (J), and 10 are called honor cards. A bridge hand is created by dealing the fifty-two cards to four players, one at a time, so that each player has a total of thirteen cards. Partnerships at the game are the two persons sitting North-South and those sitting East-West. To evaluate the value of your hand, independent of rank, the standard/ traditional method popularized by Milton Work in 1923 and promoted by Charles Goren in his 1949 book "Point Count Bidding in Contract Bridge" selling more than 3 million copies with 12 printings over 5-years assign values to the Honor "H" cards:

Honor	Value
Ace	4
King	3
Queen	2
Jack	1
Ten	0
	10

The hand evaluation method is referred to as the 4-3-2-1 points and is called the High Card Point (HCP) count method or simply H points. Using this method, one observes that a bridge deck contains a total of 40 H points.

The American Contract Bridge League (ACBL) defines hands based upon H points:

(1) An "Average" hand must have at least 10H points.
(2) Hands with 8H points are termed "Near Average" hands.
(3) Hands with 0-7H points are called "Weak" hands.

To open a hand 1NT or make a natural 1-level suit bid, the ACBL requires a player to have at least 10H pts: an "Average" hand. The accepted practice for most bridge players is to start the bidding with a 1-level suit bid when holding 11/12H pts even though 10 is permitted.

When one makes a 1-level major suit bid, it must contain at least 4-cards (2/1 requires five) and a 1-level minor suit usually contains at least 3 or less cards. If a minor suit bid is made with 0-2 cards and is forcing (partner must bid) it must be alerted, an asterisk (*) is used in this book to denote that a bid must be alerted by partner; however, if the bid is non-forcing (NF) it is merely announced "may be short and non-forcing". No alert or announcement is required if the minor suit bid is "natural" containing at least 3-cards.

A computer analysis of bridge hands shows that the 4-3-2-1 points or H points tend to undervalue aces and tens and to overvalue queens and jacks. Only kings are correctly valued.

According to the Wikipedia Encyclopedia Milton Work in 1927 endorsed the 4-3-2-1- ½ method to compensate for the undervalued 10 but ignored the undervalued A and overvalued Q's and J's.

To compensate for these short coming, Marty Bergen, ten-time national champion, developed his Adjust-3 Method. His 2008 book, "Slam Bidding Made Easier" published by Bergen Books devotes the first 100 pages to his proposed method. However, his adjustments do not adequately account for Fit and Misfits between two bridge hands even though he recommends the use of "Bergen Points" using dialogue bidding practices.

Patrick Darricades (2019) in his book "Optimal Hand Evaluation" published by Master Point Press, has developed a comprehensive system that compensates for undervalued A's and 10's, overvalued Q's and J's and properly evaluates Fit and Misfit hands called the Optimal Point Count (OPC) hand evaluation method.

In his (2020) book "Optimal Hand Evaluation in Competitive Bidding" Darricades illustrates his approach using examples from tournaments seeing both hands – but does not refer to common bridge conventions used to facilitate the dialogue between the opening bidder and his partner. Therefore, my primary goal in this book is to improve the dialogue between the opening bidder and his partner both with and without interference using his OPC method.

Patrick Darricades (2021), "21st Century Relay Bidding Method - Optimal Precision Relay", Tellwell Press shows how one may play Precision using relay methods and transfers to create what he terms "monologue" bidding sequences that are used to replace the more familiar dialogue bidding sequences used by many Strong Club partnerships.

While many current bridge partnerships use bridge laws (e.g., The Law of Total Tricks or "Working Points" or the Losing Trick Count (LTC) method to estimate the trick taking potential of two bridge hands, or rules (e.g., 17/19/20/21/22/15 etc.) to "improve" bidding bridge judgement, these rule or gadgets and are not needed when using the OPC method.

The OPC method relies on three attributes: Honors (**H**), Length (**L**), and Distribution (**D**).

For the OPC method, aces are worth 4.5 points and not 4.0 points and the opening bidder's hand without an Ace is reduced by one point as are hands without any K's or Q's. To distinguish between H values defined by the tradition (4-3-2-1) method from the value of honors defined by the OPC method a bold **H** is used in the text.

The value of a 10 depends on its association with an honor (A/K/Q/J). An isolated 10 or a 10 with an Ace has no value. However, a 10 with an associated K is worth 0.5 points, and with a Q/J is worth 1 point, a J10 combination is worth 1 point, and the Q10 is worth 2 points.

Singleton honors are valued one point less while Q's and J's doubletons are worth HALF a point less than their normal value (e.g., Qx=1and Jx=0). And one point must be deducted for the honor doubletons: **(AK/AQ/KQ/QJ)** excluded are (AK/KJ) doubletons.

Honor Points (H)

Ace: 4½ pts   K: 3pts   Q w/A, K, J: 2 pts   Qxx: 1½ pts   Qx=1pt

J w/A, K, Q: 1pt   Jxx: ½ pts   Jx=0 pts

Value of **10s** vary: 10K=½, 10A=0,   10J=1, 10Jx=2, Q10=2

No Aces = -1-point (Only Opener) No Q =-1 No K=-1 (all hands) with a Max=-2

3Ks = +1 point, 4Ks = +2pts, 4Qs = +1pt

For 3 honors (A/K/Q/J **suit quality-Q**) in a 5-card suit add +1 point and in a 6-card suit add +2 pts.

For a Singleton Honor or for Honor doubletons (AK/AQ/KQ/QJ), one deducts -1 pt. DO NOT deduct a point for an AJ/KJ doubleton since they are better than Ax and Kx.

Length Points (L)

Long suits with at least a 3-honor count have increased value in both Suit and NT contracts.

For a suit headed with at **least 3 points** (QJ/K) and 5-cards add +1 point and for 6-cards add +2 pts for suit length.

For a 6-card suit without 3 points one adds only +1 point.

Add +2 pts for **each point** from the 7th-card on in any 7+ card suit since suit Length alone has value.

For the OPC method HONOR (H) and LENGTH (L) POINTS apply to both No-Trump (NT) and Suit Contracts.

This is a fundament difference between the OPC method and Work/Goren/Bergen/Zar point count approaches.

Distribution Points (D)

The Work/Goren 3-2-1-point count for a short suit (void-singleton-doubleton) is quite inaccurate and must be replaced by the **4-2-1-0** for a void, a singleton, two doubletons, one doubleton:

Suit (without a fit)

VOID = 4pts Singleton= +2 points **TWO** doubleton=+1 pts **ONE** doubletons = 0 pts

4333 distributions = -1pt

NT

4333 distributions = -1point. Honor singleton (A/K/Q) in a NT contract deduct -1 point.

H+L+D points are added together to obtain the value of all opening hands, represented as **HLD** points or **"Starting Points"** for the Optimal Modified 2/1-Club approach.

Responder hands use primarily **H+L** points, with no more than **2L points. However, the subtraction of -1 "D" point for flatness (4333) may be included and then additional D points are added once a suit fit is established.**

Honor singletons and honor doubletons points apply to all hands and all contracts.

A hand with 12-17 starting points is opened at the 1-level for suit contracts (spades, hearts, and diamonds). Responders use only HLD pts with no more than 2Lpts and the only "D" may be -1D for flatness for suit contracts. In NT, responder counts HLD points.

A fit is defined as at least a known 8-card suit fit in all suits for both Suit and NT contracts.

One cannot address Fit (**F**) Points, Distribution Fit (**DF**) Points, Misfit (**MF**) Points, Semi Fit (**SF**) Points, Wasted Honor (**WH**) adjustments, or Mirror Hand/Suit (**MHS**) adjustments until the auction begins; these points are abbreviated by the tuple: **HLDF.**

The primary purpose of hand evaluation is to (1) to assess the number of tricks one can be expected to generate (trick-generating potential NOT just trick-taking potential) and (2) to communicate one's **trick-generating potential** to your partner.

Counting an opening hand using the traditional methods of H or HL (L=Suit Length) or HD (D=Distribution) points only evaluate's "trick-taking potential" because the **trick-generation** potential of a hand depends on not two but three attributes of the hand: **HLD. Why?** The distributional structure of a hand depends on both Length and Distribution and not just one or the other to improve upon trick-generation!

To accurately evaluate the total potential of a hand, distribution points must be added to Honor points and to Length points. This is the fundamental philosophy of the OPC method and a fundamental short coming of prior methods.

The OPC method as developed by Patrick Darricades does not rely on Quick Tricks or controls (i.e., 2 A's where an A = 2 controls and a K=1 control) to open a hand.

The first step at the bridge table is for all players to evaluate their hands; the process begins by the person designated dealer. To open 1♥/1♠/1♦* requires 12/17HLD points; there are exceptions called preemptive bids, the strong 1♣* bid and the 1NT bid to be discussed later.

For the Modified Optimal 2/1-Club System: Open a bridge hand 1♦*/1♥/1♠ with 12-17HLD Starting Points.

As the auction progresses, the value of a bridge hand may increase or decrease depending upon what one learns from your partner and your opponent's using the bidding dialogue between partnerships.

Another facet of the game one must consider when bidding is vulnerability. In general, there are four situations. The two pairs are non-vulnerable, two pairs are vulnerable, one pair is vulnerable, and the other pair is non-vulnerable. The number of tricks won or lost is more critical when vulnerable. When one is vulnerable the penalty for not making a contract is -100pts/trick and when not-vulnerable the penalty is -50pts/trick. And if a contract is doubled by the opponents, these values are doubled. In addition, interference by the opponents complicates the bidding process. More on this later.

Let's now look at a few opening hands using H, HL, and **HLD** points.

Hand 1	Hand 2	Hand 3	Hand 4	Hand 5
♠AKQ105	♠AK9	♠AJ7	♠A104	♠K78
♥10982	♥KJ3	♥KQ54	♥10543	♥AQ9852
♦6	♦J105	♦Q7	♦KJ67	♦A109
♣J67	♣5678	♦J678	♣K10	♣A

Hand 1: 10H & 11HL – In OPC: 16.0 **HLD** [♠: 4.5+3+2+1+2Q+1L, ♥: 0, ♦: 2(SD), ♣: 0.5]

Hand 2: 12H & 11HL – In OPC: 11.5 **HLD** [♠: 4.5+3, ♥: 4, ♦: 2, ♣: 0 & -1point for 4333 and -1 point for no Q]

Hand 3: 13H & 13HL – In OPC: 12.0 **HLD** [♠: 4.5+1, ♥: 5, ♦: 1.0, ♣: 0.5]

Hand 4: 11H & 11HL –In OPC: 11 **HLD** [♠: 4.5, ♥: 0, ♦: 4, ♣:3.5, - 1 for no Q)

Hand 5: 17H & 18HL – In OPC: 21.5 **HLD** [♠: 3, ♥ 6.5+2L, ♦: 4.5, ♣: 3.5 +2D for singleton]

Using Bergen's adjust-3 method, the hands have respectively 12, 11, 12, 12, and 20 points as shown in Timm (2021, pp. 4-5).

Counting traditional H points (HCP), one would have opened hands 2, 3, and 5; using Bergen's method, one opens hands 1, 4 and 5.

Using the OPC method one would open hands 1, 3, and 5 at the 1-level. As we shall soon see, the bids would be 1♠, 1♦*, and 1♣*.

More examples of the OPC method.

Hand 6:   ♠J2 ♥QJ76   ♦A872   ♣A76   11**HLD** (-1 for No K)

Hand 7:   ♠532 ♥AJ107   ♦KQ103   ♣75   12.5**HLD** (2 pts for 10's with Q/J)

Hand 8:   ♠A532 ♥Q8   ♦KQ1032 ♣96   13.5**HLD** (1-point for2 doubleton)

Hand 9:   ♥76 ♥AJ3   ♦32   ♣KQ10654   14.5**HLD** (6-card suit +1 point for 2 doubletons)

Hand 10: ♥AQ76 ♥Q107654 ♦KJ   ♣4   16**HLD** (6-card suit, but w/o 3H pts +1)

All the above hands, except hand 6 would be opened at the 1-level using the OPC method.

To see that counting H or HL points do not result in accurate hand evaluation, consider the following hand:

O: ♠ A10652 ♥ K1054 ♦ 7 ♣ K98

Counting **HLD starting points**, the hand has 13.0points [4.5 (A10) + 1(Length) +3.5 (K10) + 2 for (singleton) +3 for K -1 for no Q]

Hence, one would open this hand 1♠. Using "standard" methods one would not open the hand with 10H or 11HL points. Goren count = 12HD, 2 for the singleton. Standard methods tend to undervalue unbalanced, distributional hands. To correct this, some have suggested using Zar points proposed by Petkov Zar (2003) "Aggressive Hand Evaluation".

Zar Points (ZP) were developed to assess the "total" value of a hand, including its distributional value, more accurately than the Work/Goren point count but was proposed to assess **unbalanced** hands, **not** balanced hands. It is a statistically derived method for evaluating bridge hands using a formula. The formula incorporates **hand strength** and **distribution** follows.

Zar Points = HCP + Control Points + (Longest – Shortest Suit) + (Two Longest Suits)

Where HCP are 4=A, 3=K, 2=Q and 1=J and Control Points are A=2 and K=1. A bridge hand is opened if the number of ZP/2 = 12.5 rounded to 13+ Zar points.

The method is like that proposed by the Four Aces in the 1930's where H pts are defined as 3=A, 2=K, 1=Q, ½=J; and you then add the length of your longest suit, to half the difference in length of the second and fourth longest suits.

To translate the Zar formula to Work/Goren pts, one must **divide by two** the total of the honor points and the distribution pts. i.e., 52 ZAR pts are needed for a major-suit game = 26 Goren points.

However, as shown by Darricades (2019, p. 145), Zar points do not accurately translate the "true" value of a hand; That is because the point differential between each distribution – 4 4 3 2, 10 pts, 5 3 3 2, 11 pts, 5 4 2 2, 12 pts, etc. – is much too small: half-a-point only, once divided by two. As a result, the more **unbalanced** a bridge hand is, the **less accurate** the Zar distribution count becomes. As an illustration – consider the following two hands:

	♠ A K Q J x	♠ A K Q J x x
	♥ x x	♥ x
	♦ A K Q	♦ A K Q J
	♣ x x x	♣ x x
Zar:	25 H + 1 + **11** D	26 H + 1 + **15** D
	37 pts = 18 Goren pts = **7** tricks	**42** pts = 21 Goren pts = **8** tricks!
OPC:	**22 HL** pts: **8** tricks	**28 HLD** pts: **10** tricks

The above hands show that the ZAR point count, already **3** points **short** of what it needs on the first hand, is **10** points **short** on the second hand!

The ZAR point count has the following crippling flaws:

- It only applies to **unbalanced** hands and therefore requires the use of **another** point count for balanced hands.
- It severely **under**values Queens, Jacks and Tens and, furthermore, gives them a fixed, constant value.
- Its distribution (D) points severely **under**value the difference between distributions.
- It does not count "**synergy**" points for 3 honors in a 5-card suit.
- It does **not** factor in "*wasted honor points*".
- Most importantly, it does **not** count **Fit** pts for an **8**-card fit!

The OPC hand evaluation method is far superior to the ZAR point count and is the one endorsed in this book.

Points Required for a Game, Slam or NT Contracts

A suit fit is defined whenever the opening bidder and his partner have found an 8-card fit in the first suit bid by the opener, called the trump suit. The total points between the two hands are represented by **HLDF** points. **In NT there is no trump suit; however, the dialogue between partners may identify suits with an 8-card fit so final NT contracts are also represented by HLDF points.**

Based upon an analysis of 6,875 contracts, the following values represented the **optimal (about 50% for games and small slams, 70 % for grand slams)** chance of success where the minimum number in the range was only about 40%-45% for games).

Optimal Pts	Game/Slam	Range
26 **HLDF** pts	NT game	25-27
27 **HLDF** pts	Major suit game	26-28
30 **HLDF** pts	Minor suit game	29-31
33 **HLDF** pts	Slam in a Suit	32-34
34 **HLDF** pts	Slam in NT	33-35
36+ **HLDF** pts	Grand slam in a Suit	35-36+
37+ **HLDF** pts	Grand slam in NT	36-37+

A primary goal of the OPC method of hand evaluation is to accurately evaluate fit and distribution to bid a game or slam contract requiring 10+ tricks, it is far more common for two hands to only generate 7, 8, or 9 tricks. The ranges for these partial contracts are:

1NT contracts require about 19-21 points and 7 tricks
2NT contracts require about 22-24 points and 8 tricks

1-level Suit Contracts require about 17-19 points and 7 tricks
2-level Suit Contracts require about 20-22 points and 8 tricks
3-level Suit Contracts require about 23-25 points and 9 tricks

Opening Major Suit Bids

Playing the 2/1 game force method, with a five-card or longer major suit, one should bid one of a major with a non-balanced hand (semi-balanced/unbalanced). If one has two five-card majors, the higher ranking major (spades) is opened, not hearts. Ideal hand patterns for major suit opening are hands with the patterns 5-5-x-x, 5-4-x-x, and 5-3-3-2.

When making a 1-level major suit bid one has 12**HLD** Starting Points. A fit is defined as at least eight cards for the partnership; the best fit between two hands is 5-3, or 4-4; however, 6-2 fits also work. In general, it is usually better to play in a 4-4 fit than a 5-3 fit since this allows one to trump in either your hand or dummy (responder).

We next illustrate, using several examples, on how to count OPC points by applying the **HLD** rules formulated above.

M1: ♠AK432　　♥K107　　♦1082　　♣Q2

Hand M1 has 13**HLD** Starting Points (7.5+1L +3.5+1) and is opened 1♠ with 5-spades.

M2: ♠KJ98　　♥AQ976　　♦J2　　♣Q2

Hand M2, you are 5-4 in the majors with 13.5**HLD** Starting Points (4+6.5+1L+0+1.0+1D point for two doubletons); open the hand 1♥.

M3: ♠A1054   ♥A897   ♦A5   ♣Q75

You are 4-4 in the majors and the number of points is 14**HLD** Starting Points (4.5+4.5+4.5+1.5 -1 for no K) and open 1♦*.

M4: ♠A108   ♥A4   ♦AK10876   ♣103

You again do not have a 5-card major and with 19**HLD** Starting Points (4.5+4.5+4.5+3.0+0.5+2L +1D for two doubletons -1 for no Q) points open 1♣*,

M5: ♠8   ♥987   ♦AQ105   ♣AQ987

You do not have a 5-card major, but with 16**HLD** Starting Points (2+0+7.5+6.5+1L-1 for no K) points open 1♦*.

M6: ♠A105   ♥A10897   ♦A54   ♣A7

You have a 5-card major with 4 A's worth 18 points + 1 for suit length -2 for no K/Q or 17**HLD** points so open 1♥.

When opening a major suppose you have two of unequal length, then the longest major is bid first; however, if they are of equal length 5-5/6-6, the higher-ranking major is bid first.

So far, we have only discussed how to evaluate an opening hand with a 5-card major. We next turn to the responder's responses to the bid of an opening hand called dummy/support points.

Dummy Hand Evaluation

Opening bidders use **HLD** points when opening a hand. These points are called "STARTING POINTS". Hands with 12-17**HLD** points are opened at the 1-level for suit contracts. Responder hands count only **HLD pts with no more than 2L pts** and **"D" points only include -1 point for Flatness** when responding to a suit bid. They will add **D** points once a fit is found.

In response to a NT opening – the responder must count **HLD points since except for Flatness or singleton A/K/Q,** opener does not account for count "D" points when opening a hand in NT.

When partner opens one of a major and you have three-card support, you have found a fit, at least 8-cards in the major. With a major suit fit, responder have in addition to **HL** points now adds additional **D** points and all Fit (**F**) points or **HLDF** points.

The dummy hand reevaluation process is used when partner opens a hand. If opener opens a minor and partner (responder) bids a major, opener must reevaluate his Starting Points with a major suit fit (now with at least 4-card support). Thus, the reevaluation process may be done by responder when opener opens and a fit is found or by opener when opening a minor and partner bid a major (with 4+ cards) and opener has a four-card major, a fit has also been found. **The "dummy" re-evaluation process may be employed by opener or responder.**

Recall that **D points are calculated without a fit:**

VOID = +4 points
Singleton= +2 points
ONE doubleton= 0 points
TWO doubletons = +1point
4333 distributions = -1point all contracts

Singleton in NT contract = A/K/Q valued at 1 point less.

Fit Points (F)

The correct assessment of Fit points is one of the most critical elements of accurate hand evaluation – yet it is perhaps the most misunderstood and may be the most "mistreated" of all point count elements since it has never been "taught" properly. Fit assessment consists of THREE elements:

1) Fit points for the number of cards in a suit.
2) Honor card points in any suit with a Fit.
3) Distribution points for short side suits with a trump Fit.

1. **Fit points:** In their 1995 book on Hand Evaluation, J-R. Vernes and B. Charles, two renowned statisticians, observe using statistical analysis that going from a 7 to 8 cards fit increases the average number of tricks made in any suit by 0.45 tricks, and by 0.55 tricks when going from 8 to 9.

Translating their findings into points means that 1 fit point should be added for an 8-card fit, and 2 fit points should be added for a 9-card fit, etc. Furthermore, these fit points apply to all suits, not just the trump suit, and to all contracts, including NT contracts.

This is at variance with most traditional point count methods which attribute only one additional point for a 9-card Fit and only in the trump suit, and none for any 8-card fit.

2. **Honor "card" points:** 1 point should also be added for a King, a Queen, or a Jack, including K10x, QJx, Q10x and J10x, in each suit that has a Fit of 8-cards or more.

And here too, adding these additional points applies to all suits, not just trumps, and to all contracts, including NT contracts.

This is at variance with the Work/Goren/Bergen method which adds +1 point for these honors for only the trump suit.

Let's look at an example:

Opener	Responder
♠98	♠AJ5
♥357	♥A10
♦AK2	♦QJ987
♣AQ763	♣K48

Using Work/Goren HCP (4-3-2-1), opener has 14HL points and Responder has 16HL points. Using the Optimal Point Count (OPC) method, opener has 15**HLD** points and Responder has 17**HLD** points.

However, we must also add one point for the 8-card ♦ fit + 2 points for the 8-card ♣ fit with the King which gives these 2 hands a total of 35 **HLDF** points (34 points without the "wasted" ♠J). The points for a 6 NT slam.

In the above example from a recent tournament, not a single pair found the 6NT contract and only three pairs bid and made 6♦.

3. **Distribution-Fit points**: In his 1966 book, Modern Competitive Bidding, J-R. Vernes states: "Statistics show that the distributional value of a short suit in a hand Bidding, J-R. Vernes states: "Statistics show that the distributional value of a short suit in a hand with a trump fit varies depending upon two variables:

A) the number of cards in the short suit (doubleton, singleton, or void), and

B) the number of trumps held in that suit (2, 3 or 4 cards) allowing one or more ruffs. Thus, the trump support hand should count its distribution fit points as the difference between its number of **trumps** and the number of cards it holds in its **shortest** suit".

These distribution Fit points must be added to the Fit points and to the Honor card points.

Therefore, a doubleton in the support hand with 4 trumps counts 2 points, not one, and a void counts 4 points, not five. This is again at variance with the Goren/Work method which employs 5-3-1 points for the same short suits.

To illustrate consider the example:

Opener	Responder
♠KQ987	♠A1032
♥A765	♥K42
♦A	♦J87
♣J98	♣765

Half the field missed the game in spades since the bidding went:1♠ - 2♠ - Pass.

However, adding 2 points for the 9-card spade fit and 2 points for the heart doubleton with four trumps, Responder should bid 3♠ not 2♠ and game would be reached. Using the OPC method, one has three types of "Fit" Points.

In addition to length, honor support is also critical with an 8+card fit. Thus, one adds +1 for honor(s) in suit(s) with a fit when the total honor (AKQJ10) points < 4 points. An overview of Fit Points follows:

Summary of Fit (F) Points

8/9/10 card fit = +1/2/3 pts (all suits)
+1 for honor(s) in suit(s) with a fit when honor(s) are < 4 points (i.e., K10, QJ, Q10 and J10, K, Q, J).

The fit points count for all suit and NT contracts.

Major suit Distribution Fit points in a support hand requires, 2, 3, or 4 trumps and is defined as the difference between the number of trumps held by the responder and the number of trumps in the support hands shortest suit. In addition to trump suit support, suit shortness in other suits enhance trick-generation by ruffing.

In the hand with 2-card support: a doubleton counts for 0 points (2-2), a singleton for 1 point (2-1), and a void for two points (2-0). Similar calculations apply for 3 and 4 card trump support as shown in the following table.

Distribution Fit (DF) Points

Number of trumps	4+	3	2
Void	4pts	3pts	2pts
Singleton	3pts	2pts	1pts
Doubleton	2pts	1pts	0pts

These calculations **do not apply to any hand having 5-card trump support** since it is considered a long suit whether partner has 4/5 cards in the suit. This means that the hand should only count the distribution points that apply to an opening hand i.e., 2 points for a singleton and not the difference between 5 trumps and the short suit.

A void is worth 4 points without a trump fit. With any 8-card fit it remains +4; however, with 3/2 card support it is reduced from +4 to +3/+2, respectively.

The value of a singleton varies: It is increased to +3 with a 4-card Fit or reduced by 1 with only 2-card support.

In a NT contract deduct -1 point for a singleton.

**Two doubletons are worth 1 point and one doubleton = 0 points:
however, with 4/3/2 trumps each doubleton is worth 2/1/0 points.**

One has a "semi fit" when a hand has an honor doubleton, other than an Ace, for any 8+card fit. This observation applies to both hands whether a response to opener's bid or a rebid. The Ace doubleton does not need to be upgraded since we have already assigned it 4.5 points; however, upgrades do apply to the K, Q and J doubletons.

Semi Fit (SF) Points

Add +1 if you hold an honor doubleton Kx/Qx/J10/Jx doubleton (other than the Ace) in partners long suit (5+cards). Responders must make the +1-point adjustment with a 2-card honor doubleton suit support and a 5-2 fit revealed during the bidding process.

Misfit (MF) Points

Opposite a known long 5-card suit, one must deduct -3/-2/-1 points for a void /singleton/ doubleton WITHOUT AN HONOR (A/K/Q/J). Fit, Semi Fit, Distribution Fit and MF Points are called HLDF points.

Returning to our prior example,

O: ♠ AJ652 ♥ K1054 ♦ void ♣ KJ87
R: ♠KQ107 ♥A2 ♦5432 ♣ AQ6

The opening bidder has 17**HLD** starting point [5.5(AJ) +1(Length) +3.5 (K10) + 4(void) +4 (KJ) -1for no Q]. And responder has 17**H** points.

However, with a 9-card spades fit one must add +2 for the spade fit and + 2 for the doubleton heart with 4 trumps or **21HLDF** The two hands have 38**HLDF points,** or enough for perhaps a grand slam which one may never find using the Work/Goren/Bergen/Zar approach to hand evaluation.

Let's look at a few examples, when your partner opens 1♠ and you hold the following hands. Recall that without a fit one calculates **HL where L≤2 and includes -1 "D" for flatness';** however, with a fit one calculates **HLDF points** fit which included **F, DF, SF (Semi Fit), and MF (Misfit) points/adjustments.**

Hand A: ♠ AJ62 ♥ 6542 ♦ void ♣ AK987

(5.5AJ + 0 + 4void + 7.5AK+ 1L - 1 no Q) = 17**HL** +2F =19**HLDF** points

Hand B: ♠ AQ67 ♥ 678 ♦ AK10432 ♣ void

(6.5AQ +0 + 8AK10 + 2L +4 for the void) = 20.5**HL** +2F =22.5**HLDF** points.

14

Hand C: ♠ KQJ32 ♥ 1098 ♦7 ♣ J987

(6 + 1 for 3 honors in suit +1L +0+2 for singleton+0.5J) = 10.5**HL** + 3**F** (add 3 for the 10-card major fit) = 13.5**HLDF** points.

Hand D: ♠ 9876 ♥ AK ♦ K7 ♣AQ1084

(0+ 7.5AK - (-1 for 2 honors doubleton) +0+3+ 7.5 +1L) = 18.0**HL** + 4**DF** = 22.0 **HLDF**.

Hand E: ♠ 10986 ♥ K ♦ 753 ♣ Q9432

(0 +2K (3-1) +0 +1.5) = 3.5**H** + 2**F** + 3 for singleton = 8.5**HLDF**

Hand F: ♠ 102 ♥ Q64 ♦ KQJ ♣ KQ1098

Hand F: (0 + 1.5Q+6KQJ + 6KQ10+1L) = 14.5 **HL** -1**MF** (for doubleton without an honor opposite opener's 5-card suit) = 13.5**HLDF** points.

As the responder/opener gains knowledge about each other's hand using the bidding dialogue, one must adjust points as the bidding progresses.

Mirror Hand/Suit (MHS) Point Adjustments

If one can determine from the bidding that the partnership has two "mirror" hands (i.e., two perfectly identical hand patterns) one deducts -2 points.

For two mirror suits (i.e., 4-4, 3-3) that are not trump one also deducts -1 point.

Mirror hand patterns and opposite balanced suits in both hands, like singletons in NT, reduce the trick-generation potential of two bridge hands.

A final critical factor that must be consider with or without a fit in **suit contracts** is the effective value of honors (excluding the Ace) opposite a singleton (S) or a void (V) in partner's hand since honors then lose value (have wasted value) and must be downgraded.

Conversely, a suit without an honor opposite a singleton or void has NO wasted value and must be upgraded.

Wasted Honor (WH) Point Adjustments

K/Q/J Honors (excluding the Ace) opposite a S/V = -2/-3 points
Not a single Honor opposite a S/V = +2/+3 points
Axx (without any other honor) opposite a S = +1 point

where S=Singleton and V=Void

Example follows: Partner opens 1♠ with 12**HLD** points and you hold the following hand:

♠K1082 ♥ 532 ♦ KQ962 ♣6

Using the Work/Goren method you have 12 dummy points; since Goren adds 1 point for the trump honor and counts 3 points for the singleton with 4 trumps using OPC you have 15.5**HLDF** points [3.5+5+1L+3D+2F].

However, the continued bidding dialogue may yield wasted honors (e.g., "wasted honors" opposite the singleton club, and additional fit points if the opener bids diamonds).

In any case you will not miss your spade game using the OPC method.

Opening No-trump (NT) Bids

Having sufficient Starting Points to open, the first goal is to describe your hand to your partner. When you open, you may have a balanced hand, an unbalanced hand, or a semi-balanced hand. A hand with a singleton or a void is unbalanced (35.5%). The patterns that do not contain a singleton or a void are 4-4-3-2, 5-3-3-2, and 4-3-3-3 (47.5%) are called balanced hands; semi-balanced hands are hands with the following patterns: 5-4-2-2, 6-3-2-2, and 7-2-2-2 (16.5%).

The most common hand patterns are: **4432** (21.5%), **5332** (15.5%), **5431** (13%), **5422** (10.5%), and **4333** (10.5%) accounting for over 70% of the hand patterns. However, 5-5 hand patterns are less frequent than those that contain at least one 6-card suit and hands that contain at least one singleton, or one void occur in about 33% of the hand patterns.

When you open the bidding, you first want to communicate to you partner whether you have a balanced or non-balanced (unbalanced or semi-balanced) hand. If the semi-balanced hand has honor cards (AKQJ) in two of its doubletons, it may be considered balanced. When hands are balanced, one usually opens the hand with an opening no-trump (NT) bid.

The ACBL currently requires a first bid of 1NT with a range that does not include 15 to be alerted and that all other ranges to be announced (e.g., 15-17 and 15-18). Any range that includes 15 is considered a **strong** NT and any range that does not include 15 points is a **weak** NT bid. Why is this important? When competing against NT bids, the conventions one use often depends upon whether the bidding range is weak or strong.

Contracts may be played in a major suit, NT, or a minor. A game in NT only requires taking nine tricks. A major suit game (four spades or four hearts) requires making ten tricks. A minor suit game (five clubs and five diamonds) requires making eleven tricks, book plus five; almost, the same as a small slam (one trick short of twelve).

Effective Aug 1, 2016: Unbalanced 5-4-3-1, 6-3-3-1, and 4-4-4-1 hand patterns may be opened 1NT, provided the singleton is either an A, K, or Q with no more than one doubleton. **Not allowed** are shapely 5-5-2-1, 6-4-2-1 or 7-2-2-2 hands.

Even though the ACBL has changed the structure for hands for 1NT bids, it does not mean that the change is a good or preferred practice.

When opening 1NT, opener has 15-17**HLD** Starting Points. Ideal no-trump hands are those with balanced, flat hand patterns: 4-3-3-3 and 4-4-3-2 distributions. Semi-balanced minor suit hand patterns: 2-2-4=5 or 2-2-5=4 and 2-2-3=6 or 2-2-6=3 is also opened 1NT.

Playing "traditional" 2/1 the NT range commonly used is 15-17 but when opening a major, the opening point count range is very wide (12-21). So many recommend opening 1NT to communicate a strong hand with a narrower range instead of opening 1M with a 5-card major.

Playing the Optimal Modified 2/1-Club System, the major suit opening point range has been reduced to 12-17**HLD** pts. the preferred approach is to open 1M and not 1NT to try to locate a fit.

Another reason given for opening a hand 1NT rather that 1M is that many hands create severe rebid problems playing traditional 2/1. For example, Larry Cohen suggests opening the hand: ♠Q10 ♥ AQ1042 ♦ KJ2 ♣KJ3 1NT rather than 1♥. His question is How do you show this hand if you open 1♥ and partner next bids 1♠? "If you rebid 1NT you are showing 15 points and if you bid 2NT you are showing 17 points and the hand has 16H points"!

Using the OPC method the hand has 18.5**HLD** [♠: 2 ♥: 8.5, ♦: 4.0, ♣: 4.0] and this hand would be opened 1♣*, this avoids Larry Cohen's rebid problem.

Playing the Modified Optimal 2/1-Club, **any hand with 18+HLD points is opened 1♣* with any distribution, and most semi-balanced and unbalanced hands without a 5-card major are opened 1♦*, 1NT openings use the 15-17 range, and 5-card major suit opening bids use the range 12-17.**

These simple modification helps to avoid many bidding problems playing "standard" 2/1 or Precision as shown by Jan Eric Larsen (2021), "Good, Better, Best - A comparison of Bridge Bidding Systems and Conventions by Computer Simulation", Master Point Press.

We next illustrate OPC evaluation methodology with a few examples.

Example N1	Example N2	Example N3	Example N4
♠ K J	♠ K J 6	♠K 9	♠9 8
♥ A Q 4	♥ A 10 4	♥A Q 5	♥A K J 2
♦ A 10 8	♦ A Q 8	♦K 8	♦10 2
♣ Q 10 8 5 4	♣ A K 9 6	♦K 10 9 8 7 4	♣A K J 4 2

Hand N1: 16H & 17HL In OPC: 17.5**HLD** [♠: 4 ♥: 6.5, ♦: 4.5, ♣: 2.5]

Note one does not count 1 L point for the 5-card suit since it is not headed by 3H points.

Hand N2: 21H. In OPC 21.5**HLD** [♠: 4, ♥: 4.5 ♦: 6.5, ♣: 7.5 -1 for 4333]

Hand N3: 15H & 17HL In OPC 20**HLD** [♠: 3, ♥: 6.5, ♦: 3, ♣: 3.5 +2L+1 for 3 K's + 1 for two doubletons]

Hand N4: 16H & 17HL In OPC 19.0**HLD** [♠: 0, ♥: 8.5 ♦: 0, ♣: 8.5+ 1 for 3 honors in a suit + 1L + 1D for two doubletons -1 for no Q]

Using traditional 2/1 methods, except for hand N2 all hands would be opened 1NT; hand N2 would be opened 2NT. However, using the OPC method, only hand N1 would be opened NT playing a strong 1NT = 15-17**HLD,** the other hands are opened 1♣*.

Consider the hand:

N0: ♠A105 ♥A10897 ♦A54 ♣A7

You have a 5-card major with 4 A's worth 18 points + 1 for suit length- -2 for no K/Q 17**HLD**.

Look at the following hands:

N5: ♠Q98 ♥KQ7 ♦QJ5 ♣KQ52   N6: ♠AK7 ♥QJ4 ♦K3 ♣A5432

Using H points, hand N5 has 15H points with Q's and J's and hand N6 has 17H points with A's and Q's. Some may say hand N5 is a "weak NT hand" while hand N6 is a "strong" NT hand. The problem is that the evaluation process is flawed.

Hand N5 has [1.5 + 5 + 2+1+ + 5 -1 (no Ace) -1 (4333)] =12.5**HLDF** points.

Hand N6 has [7.5+3+3+4.5+1L] = 19**HLDF points** so that neither hand would be opened 1NT!

Using your expert bridge "judgement" and subtracting for flatness, hand N5 has 14HD points and counting length, hand N6 has 17 HL points. Using the OPC method you do not have to be an expert when doing hand evaluation.

With 18 Starting Points some may open a hand 1NT (if partner is a passed hand). **With the OPC you must open the hand 1♣*.**

What would you open the hand N7 ♠AQ8 ♥K97 ♦65 ♣A9852?

Playing a strong NT which requires 15-17 points with either 13H point or 14HL points,

most would not open the hand 1NT! However, using the OPC method the hand has 15**HLDF** points and should be opened 1NT (4.5+2+3+4.5 + 1L) = 15**HLD** points.

Another example: Hand N8 ♠65 ♥AQ45 ♦A32 ♣KQ104?

Using traditional methods, one has 15H points, but using the OPC method the hand has 17**HLDF** where again we have a "strong" NT hand and not a "weak" NT hand.

With a singleton, one does not normally open a hand 1NT; however, the ACBL now allows one to open 1NT with a singleton A/K/Q. Even if one may open such hands 1NT due to past bad behavior, it is in fact totally absurd.

N9: ♠A ♥KQ4 ♦K832 ♣KJ1078

This hand has 15H points with a singleton Ace. However, one must deduct 2 points, not 1, for the singleton Ace if NT was bid by that hand so the hand has only 13H points and should never be opened 1NT. In OPC: 17.5**HLDF** (3.5 for the honor singleton and +5 + 3+6.0); however, in a suit contract we do not deduct for the singleton but add +2 points so we have 19.5**HLDF** points and would open 1♣*.

When considering NT hands most attention is given to Aces and less than 10's. This is a mistake. To see this more clearly consider the following two hands.

O: ♠KQ108 ♥K7 ♣K54 ♣QJ102   R: ♠567 ♥QJ103 ♦QJ103 ♣K9

Observe that both hands are Ace less; however, they contain many 10's which are ignored by traditional methods. Counting only H points O has 14H and R has 9H points for a total of only 23 points. However, by the OPC method, O has 16**HL** points (6+3+3+4+ 1 for 2 for 3K's -1 for no A) and R has 11**HL** points or a total of 27 points for 3NT. Yes, enough for 3NT.

What about Q's and J's? Js and Qs to have reduced value unless they are associated with honors.

The following hands O: ♠A987 ♥A32 ♦K54 ♣A92 and R: ♠K2 ♥K79 ♦A98 ♣109832

are rich in A's and K's. O has 15H points, but only 14.5**HLDF** points (4.5 + 4.5 + 3 + 4.5 -1 4333 -1 no Q) and R has 10 HL points but only 9.5**HL** points (3+3+4.5 - 1 for no Q). Using traditional methods, one might end up in 3NT, but this would not be the case using the OPC method. As we shall soon see we would open 1♦ and pass a bid of 1NT.

In NT contracts, tricks are only won with a suit led. To establish tricks in no-trump, you want to take advantage of long suits since these are the source of tricks. One may not use trump to ruff losers.

You have the following hand: ♠KQ ♥A10 ♦AKQ10753 ♣KQ and your contract is 3NT. In this hand, you have one heart trick, seven diamond tricks, or 8 sure tricks. And you hope you can develop an additional trick in clubs or spades for your contract and make 3NT.

In duplicate bridge, 3NT is worth 400 points if your side is not vulnerable and 600 points if your side is vulnerable. Each overtrick is worth a score of thirty. The same 10 tricks in a suit contract are worth 420 and 620.

Let's assume Opener and Responder the hand N7 and N8 hands previously discussed.

O: ♠AQ8 ♥K97 ♦65 ♣A9852
R: ♠65 ♥AQ45 ♦A32 ♣KQ64

As we saw O has 15**HLDF** points and R, counting only **HL** points has 16 points, clearly enough for a 3NT contract. But is there more given the 5-4 minor suit fit? As we shall soon see the answer is yes using the OPC method and adding "suit fit" and conventions to the evaluation process.

A problem hand frequently encountered is the balanced hand with a 5-3-3-2 pattern when one has sufficient values for opening 1NT, and you are 5-3 in the majors. Do you open it with one of a major or with sufficient values 1NT? While there are special circumstances when opening 1NT is better; in general, one would almost always prefer to open the hand one of a major. In this book, opening 1 NT with a 5-card Major is never considered. However, you may not always get a top score. Making 4NT is better than making four of a major since 430/630 is better than 420/620 called Match Points (MPs) scoring. In team games one uses International Match Points (IMPS) scoring where the strategy is to bid the safest game, because there is little difference.

Consider the following hand:

O: ♠A105 ♥A10987 ♦A54 ♣A7

Using only "H" points some may be tempted to open the hand 1NT.

However, you have a 5-card major with 4 A's worth 18 points + 1 for suit length and deducting 2 for no K/Q = 17**HLD. Open the hand 1♥**, a safer contract. Why? Suppose partner has the following hand:

R: ♠KQ32 ♥54 ♦KJ10 ♣10542

with 9**H** points (5+0+4+0) or using traditional methods most would increase the hand by 1 point for the 2 10's for 10H points and bid 3NT. 10HL points with 2 10's.

A 3NT contract that is doomed to fail losing 3 clubs and 2 heart tricks! A heart contract is clearly superior.

Generally, you will score better by playing a 4-3-3-3 hand pattern opposite a 4-3-3-3 in no-trump than in a 4-4 major suit fit. A 3-3-3-4 pattern opposite a 5-3-3-2 pattern is better in no-trump and not the 5-3 major suit fit! To find these hand patterns require advanced bidding methods. For now, my advice is to always open the hand one of a major given the choice.

An opening bid of 1NT usually shows stoppers in at least three suits where a minimum stopper is defined as Qxx. However, one rarely opens a hand 1NT with Jxx and seldom with a worthless major suit doubleton (xx).

A final example, which of the following hands would you open 1NT?

a) ♠KJ8643 ♥AK ♦K76 ♣J7
b) ♠KJ8642 ♥AK ♦76 ♣K87
c) ♠K8642 ♥AQ7 ♦QJ ♣QJ7

Using the 4-3-2-1 system, all 3 hands have 15H points! However, using the OPC method

a) 18.5**HLD** (3+2+2L+7.5-1(AK doubleton) +3+3K's -1 no Q)
b) 17.**5HLD** (4+2L+6.5+3+3 -1 no Q)
c) 15.5**HLD** (3+1L+6.5+3-1(QJ)+3)

We would only open hand (c) 1NT.

Opening Minor Suit Bids

Playing 2/1 using "traditional" methods one opens 1♣/1♦ with at least 3-cards (called better minor openings); however, you do not know if the length of the bid suit is 5+, 4, or 3. Furthermore, game in a minor is often more difficult to make since it requires 11 tricks and not 10 as for the majors. For this reason, the bids have been revised using the OPC method.

The bid of 1♣* following, Jack W. Hawthorn (2021), "Transfer-Oriented Pinpoint Precision (TOP3) – The Ultimate Power Club," is used to open any hand with 18+**HLD** points and any distribution and is a forcing bid. The bidding zones for the club bid are defined as:18-20, 21-23, 24-26, 27+.

The bid of 1♦* is defined by 12-17**HLD** points like the major suit bids with two bidding zones 12-14 and 15-17; however, the bid is **artificial** and may be short in diamonds having 0-2 diamonds and is forcing for one round.

Partner knows from the 1♦* bid that you do not have a 5-card major, that your hand may be balanced or unbalanced with 4-clubs or 4/5+diamonds, that it may have a 4-card major or be 4-4 in the majors, and that it may be 5-4 clubs and diamonds or even a 4-4-4-1/ 4-4-5-0 hand.

As with a major suit bid without a fit the **D** points are defined:

VOID = 4pts, Singleton= +2 points, **TWO** doubleton= +1 pts, **ONE** doubletons = 0 pts

Difficult hands like: ♠ Q54 ♥ A376 ♦ K5 ♣ AJ97 with 14.5**HLD** points

                ♠ 7 ♥ Q76 ♦AKJ7 ♣ Q5432 with 13.5**HLD** points

would be opened 1♦*.

The bidding goals have a hierarchy: (1) Major suit fit, (2) No-trump, and (3) Minor suit fit.

Opening Preemptive 2-Level Bids, 2NT* and 3NT*

Majors

The ACBL defines a weak 2-level bid as a 6-card suit as weak, near-average (intermediate), and strong if it contains at least 8H, 10H, or 15H pts. The ranges used are respectively: 5-11, 11-14, and 14-17.

A common practice among bridge players is to open any 2-level major suit bid as a pre-emptive bid to show a 6-card suit with a point count range that is less than 12H points: 6-10 and 5-11; however, some using the "rule of 20" (where the sum of the two longest suits +H pts=20 or the rule of 22 adjusting for quick tricks) may open a hand with only 11H pts.

However, a statistical study performed by J-R. Vernes showed that preemptive opening major suit bids with a point range of 7-10H points often lead to negative results, and with such a weak range they are not preemptive, and that they often cause more harm than good in two respects: (1) they communicate too much information to the opponents and (2) they often lead to poor results because they may preempt their partner.

The primary purpose of a preemptive bid is to force the opponents to begin bidding at a higher level; however, if the point range is too high it is less likely the opponents own the hand.

How may one correct for these shortcomings? Recall that J-R. Vernes' statistical analysis has shown that "safety bidding ranges" are defined in zones: (7-9/10-12) (12-14/15-17) (18-20/21-23) – Low-Middle-High.

What is the best option?

Change the range of the preemptive bid 2-level major suit bid to the lower 12-14HLD zone of the 1-level bid.

The new range is not too strong or too weak. It is weak enough that the opponents may want to enter the auction but strong enough that if they do enter the auction, they may get too high.

Examples:

    (1) ♠ KJ10987 ♥ 789 ♦ QJ10 ♣ 7

        12**HLD** (5+2L+4+2-1 for no Ace)   Open 2♠*

    (2) ♠ QJ10456 ♥ K9 ♦678 ♣ Q5

        10.0**HLD** (4+2L+3+1+1 for 2 doubletons -1 for no Ace)   Pass

(3) ♠ 7 ♥ AQ6789 ♦ K765 ♣ J8

13.5**HLD** (2 +6.5 +2L +3 +0 for J doubleton)   Open 2♥*

Whenever the opponents compete over a preempt, be happy. Their auction will likely contain a substantial amount of guesswork, so there's a reasonable chance they'll guess wrong, providing you with a good result. Your primary goal is to interfere with the bidding auction and not win the final contract.

To make a 2-level contract requires 20-22 points for 8 tricks, 23-25 points to make 9 tricks, and 25-27 points to make 10 tricks. With 0-7**HLD** point, responder would pass.

With 8-10 points, we have 20-22 (2-level contract); 11-13 points, we have 23-25 (3-level contract); and with 14-16 (4-level contract) we have 26-28.

Furthermore, this new range is less likely to preempt your partner since he knows you have 12-14**HLD** points and a 6-card suit and may choose to enter the auction with as few as 11**HL** points since 13 (average of 12/14) + 11 = 24 (a 3-level contact) Or, with a 2-card fit may bid 3 of the Major opened.

To illustrate suppose partner opens hand (3) above 2♥* and you have the following hand:

♠ KQ2 ♥ K542 ♦A984 ♣109

18.5**HLDF** (5+3+4.5+3 for 10-card heart fit + 1 for the ♥K + 2 point for the ♣ doubleton 4 trump)

Knowing partner has 12-14**HLD** points, add 12+18.5 =30.5 and bid 4♥.

Without an eight-card fit in partner's bid major, but with values the other suits and having

12/13+**HL** points may bid 2NT which asks partner for a **feature** if he has an outside entry (usually an A/K). The responses are:

Rebid of the Weak-2 suit with 12/13**HL** (might have a "feature" as well).
Rebid in a new suit with 14**HL**, with a "feature" in the suit bid.
Rebid of 3NT with 14**HL** and a solid suit (2 of the top 3 honors)

The responses to the 2NT asking bid must always be alerted. If it is not alerted, you must always ask for the meaning of their response; do not assume you know!

Example: From BBO – Neither vulnerable South Deals

	♠ Q		
	♥ 108		
	♦ QJ75		
	♣ AQ10973		
♠ K765		♠ AJ982	
♥ J42	N	♥ K3	
♦ A9842	W E	♦ 1063	
♣ 5	S	♣ J86	
	♠ 1043		
	♥ AQ9765		
	♦ K		
	♣ K42		

The Bidding:

South	West	North	East
1♥	Pass	1NT*	Pass
2♥	Pass	3♥	Pass
Pass	Pass	Pass	

South has 13.5**HLD** and opens 2♥*. North without a heart fit with 10x in hearts has 12.5**HL** (-1 sig. honor +1 for ♥10+3+4.5+2+1Q+2L) bids 2NT. And South bids 3♣ to show a feature. With a club fit, North has 15.5**HLDF** (2pts for singleton + 1F) and bids 4♥.

An analysis of 3-level major suit preemptive bids by J-R, Vernes revealed that they did not generate favorable results when compared to a pass if the preempt bid did not prevent the opponents from making their own contract, led to a large penalty, or caused their partnership to miss their own game – a pass was often more advantageous than the bid.

If the contract was won, it was often found to be more advantages for the partner to play the hand to avoid leads coming through the stronger hand. As a compromise, the range for 2-level major suit bids will remain 12-14**HLD**. Since majors take up bidding space and it is desirable to play in 3NT. A preemptive 3-level major suit bid will require 12-14**HLD** points and a 6/7-card suit. So, partner with 13**HLD**F, may bid 3NT.

3♥*/3♠*   =   shows 7-card suit and is preemptive with 12-14**HLD**.

Minors

Recall that the bid of 1♣* shows any hand with 18+**HLD** points; hence, the bid of 2♣* is no longer a strong club bid and must be alerted. We define the 2 and 3-level bids:

2♣*   =   15-17**HLD** points with 5/6-card club may have a 4-card major

3♣*   =   12-14**HLD** points with 7+card club suit

When bidding clubs, the lower the bid, the higher the hand value. Higher level bids imply fewer points.

One of the primary goals for weak 2-level major suit bid was to interfere with the opponents and to increase the range for the "weak" bid to 12/14**HLD**.

Because a "weak" bid of 2♦* provides little interference, we shall reverse the "traditional meanings" of 2-level and 3-level bids for diamonds.

3♦*   =   12-14**HLD** with 6-diamonds **not 7** and is preemptive

2♦*   =   15-17**HLD** with 7+diamonds

Why?

(1) Responder knows immediately opener's suit length and the point zone.
(2) It reduces the frequency of the 1♦* opening bid, an opening highly vulnerable to overcalls.
(3) It allows the rebid of 2♦ after the opening bid of 1♦ to show 5♦-4♥ in the 12/14 zone, a difficulty with "standard" 2/1 bidding since the bid of 2♥ is a reverse showing 17+ points. See Chapter 5 for more on preempts.

2NT* and 3NT*

Playing the Optimal Modified 2/1-Club System the opening 2NT* bid does not show a balanced 20–21-point hand since this type of hand is shown using the artificial 1♣* opening bid. This allows an opening bid of 2NT* to have a special meaning as allowed by the ACBL.

2NT* is used to show a two suited (5-5/5-6/6-6/7-6) minor suit hand with 12-14**HLD** points.

Responses to 2NT*

This bid is like the unusual 2NT bid playing 2/1. The responses go:

All 3-level bids are to play except 3♥* which is an asking bid.
Over 2NT*=12-14 what follow are the responses to the 3♥* asking bid.

3♠*/3NT*	12/13-14
4♣*/4♦*	6♣-5♦/6♦-5♣ min=12
4♥*/4♠*	6♦-5♣/6♦-5♣ max=13/14

4NT*/5♣	6♦/6♣ min/max with singleton ♥
5♠*/5NT*	6♦/6♣ min/max with singleton ♠
5♠/5NT*	7♣-6♦/6♣-7♦min
6♣	7♣-6♦/6♣-7♦max

Example:

O: ♠87 ♥ - ♦ QJ9876 ♣ QJ1087   12.0**HLD** (-2 no A/K)

R: ♠KQJ10 ♥QJ10985 - ♦K3 ♣A   20.5**HL** (7+4+2L+3+3.5)

O	R
2NT*	3♥
3♠* =12	3NT

While some may open 3NT with 25-27 **HLDF** points, this will not be the case in this book. We will use the Gambling 3NT* bid. Playing the Modified Optimal 2/1-Club the Gambling 3NT* bid shows a solid seven-card minor suit and denies holding an ace or an outside king. Responses to 3NT* will be covered shortly. However, some may use the Acol 3NT* in the 4th seat since it may include an outside ace/king honor. Or some may use the Kanter Gambling 3NT* bid which show a strong single suited major. These bids must be alerted so don't assume you know the meaning of the 3NT* bid.

3NT* is a preemptive 7+ minor suit hand headed by the AKQ and 17-21**HLD** with 8-9 playing tricks.

Sample Hands follow:

♠Q105 ♥K7♦7 ♣ AKQ9752 and in the 4th seat: ♠A6 ♥K54♦K10 ♣ AKJ10872

Responses to 3NT*

Pass: To play. Shows stoppers in both majors.

4♣   Shows weakness and desire to play in opener's minor suit. Opener passes or corrects to 4♦.

4♦   Asks for a singleton. If opener has a singleton major, they bid it. If opener has a singleton in the other minor, then bid 4NT. If opener does not have a singleton, their minor is bid at the 5-level.

4M: To play.

5/6/7♣:   Desire to play in 5,6, or 7 of opener's minor. Opener should pass or correct to 5, 6, or 7♦.

Responses to gambling 3NT* (for a long minor) as suggested by Marty Bergen follow - Be Careful, there are many other proposed methods.

4♣ says let's play in a part Score 4♣ or 4♦

4♦ usually played two ways:

>   (a) Asks opener to bid a singleton: responses are 4♥=Heart singleton, 4♠=Spade singleton, 4NT=minor suit singleton and 5♣=no singleton.
>   (b) Expert Gerber ace asking (see below).

Depending on the location of the singleton and your hand, responder is usually interested in playing in a game, 5♣/5♦or a slam, 6♣/6♦.

Example: Responder has

>   Spades: AKQ x   Hearts: xx   Diamonds: AKQx   Clubs: xxx

With a heart singleton, you want to play in 6♣ clubs otherwise you would bid 5♣.

4♥ and 4♠ are 6-card suits. Opener must pass.

4NT is invitational to slam (Quantitative), asking opener to bid a minor suit slam

Example: Opener has a hand like

>   Spades: xx   Hearts: x   Diamonds: Qxxx   Clubs: AKQJxxx

5♣ signoff play in club game or correct to 5♦; not slam interest.

5♦ signoff by responder, responder knows that the opener has long diamonds and wants to play game from his side.

5NT is a grand slam try, to play in 7♣/7♦. Responder has no losers outside the trump suit but is usually void of the trump suit and is afraid of a trump loser. Opener bids 7♣/7♦ with a suit like A-K-Q-J-x-x-x or A-K-Q-x-x-x-x-x. With A-K-Q-x-x-x-x-x, opener would sign off in 6 of the suits.

6♣ is to play slam in 6♣/6♦, opener is to pick the suit. Again, a bid of 6♦ by responder is to play slam in diamonds, responder knows that it is the long suit.

How do you defend against the 3NT* bid?

X	=	strong and balanced
4♣	=	both majors
4♦	=	one major (6+)
4M	=	5-card bid major and a 5+ card minor

4NT = suit asking bid: bid your 5-card suit at the 5-level (♣♦♥♠) and 5NT = you pick the suit, usually the other minor

5m = to play, in the other minor

Pass the double if the opponents run and you are 3-suited and short in their minor; otherwise bid your longest major.

What do you lead against the 3NT* bid?

An ace if you have one, fourth best with a 5-card major and without a long major, your shortest major; try to find partner's major.

Summary of 1/2/3-Level Bids

Bid	HLD Points	Description
1♥/1♠	12-17	5+cards
2♥/2♠	12-14	6-cards
3♥/3♠	12-14	7-cards
1♣*	18+	any distribution
2♣*	15-17	5/6 cards (may have 4-card major)
3♣*	12-14	7+cards
1♦*	12-17	May be short in diamonds (0-2)
2♦*	15-17	7+cards
3♦*	12-14	6-cards
1NT	15-17	Balanced/Semi-balanced
2NT*	12-14	5+-5+ in Minors
3NT*		7+card Minor with AKQ

An alternative ace asking version of Gerber is the "1430 style Gerber Convention", also called Expert Gerber. The convention is used in a competitive auction after opening 1♣* and re-bids of 2NT/3NT by the opener.

The 1430 Style Gerber Convention (Expert Gerber)

4♦   shows 1/4 aces

4♥   shows 0/3 aces

4♠   shows 2 aces with 15 points (min)

4NT   shows 2 aces with 16/17 points (max)

The follow up bid of 5♣ is the specific king ask bid not the number of kings.

In chapter 4 we will discuss 1430 Roman Keycard Gerber (RKCG). It is used after one has agreed on a major and then bids NT.

CHAPTER 2

Responses to Opening Bids and Preempts

Responses to One-level Major Suit Bids

Forcing Responses

When responding to a major suit opening, recall that 26-28 points will produce a major suit game. When opening major, one has at least 12**HLD** Starting Points. If you have a fit (at least three cards) and upon reevaluation of your hand have at least 15**HLDF** you have the **optimal** number of total points for game. A game force bid forces partner (opener) to bid.

Observe that if the opening bidder has 15-17**HLD points** and partner has 12**HLFD** points, we have game values at the optimal **27** point-level. If the opening bidder has 12-14**HLD** points, responder needs 13/14**HL points** to invite game but with 13**HL** points may pass.

Recall that the **optimal points** for 2, 3, and 4--level **suit** contracts **21, 24, and 27** subtracting 12 from each the ranges are: 8-10/11-13/14-**15**-16.

Also recall that the **optimal points** for 1, 2, and 3-level **NT** contracts are: **20, 23, and 26,** and subtracting 12 from each the ranges are: 7-9/10-12/13-**14**-15.

From these observations, one may conclude that **responders need** the following points for contracts to succeed.

1M	7-9**HLDF (with <7 PASS)**
2M	10/12**HLDF**
3M	13-15 **HLDF**
4M	16+ **HLDF**
1NT	7-9**HLDF**
2NT	10-12**HLDF**
3NT	13-15**HLDF**

When opening 1NT, the opener only counts **HL** type points (except for flatness); F points are added as fit points are found from the bidding dialogue between partners. Because a contract is based upon **H, L, and D points**; responder may have to consider "**D**" when partner opens 1NT as we shall soon see.

In "traditional" 2/1, a game forcing response by responder is accomplished by showing a new suit at the two- level without jumping or skipping a bidding level. After a major suit opening, and the opponents have pass and you are not a passed hand, the "traditional" 2/1 game force bids are:

2/1 Game Forcing Responses

Opening bid	2/1 Game Forcing (GF) Responses
1♠	2♣/2♦ (4+cards), 2♥ (5+cards)
1♥	2♣/2♦ (4+cards)

Note that the bid of 2♠ as a response to an opening bid of a 1♥ is not a 2/1 game forcing response. In addition, the response of 1♠ to 1♥ is not a 2/1 game forcing bid but is forcing for one round.

While traditional 2/1 methods suggest that one make a 2/1 bid with 13+H points, the bids do not consider the potential for wasted honors. To overcome this problem, one needs 15+H points.

The point zones for traditional 2/1are: 0-6 (7-9/10-12) (13-14/15-17)18+. Using the OPC method, the zones are 7/9, 10/12, 13/14, 15-17, 18-20, 21-23, 24+

If one cannot make a traditional 2/1 bid, the bid of 1NT is used as a temporary bid.

Using the "Traditional bidding Paradigm" the bid of 1NT* (forcing/semi-forcing) is an ambiguous bid that says we do not have a fit and have about 6/7-12H points (not enough for a 2/1 bid). Responding to 1NT*, some may pass or rebid their major or make an ambiguous bid like 2♣/2♦ forcing responder to bid yet another suit or pass. WOW – Not exactly optimal bidding!

Is there a better and more efficient bidding sequence superior to the traditional GF responses, which require 3 bids, playing the OPC method with dialogue bidding?

Yes, but before we present a better approach using the OPC method recall that responder knows partner has 12-17**HLD** points and that game in a major requires 27**HLDF**, so partner needs 15**HLDF points** to make 10 tricks.

As we saw, opener's hand may be divided into two zones: 12-14/15-17. Thus, what is needed is a bid that asks opener to describe his hand by zone by bidding 1NT* (Motivated by Gazzilli-Timm's New Forcing bid). **Because the 1NT* bid requires only 13+HL it is NOT forcing to game.**

1NT* Forcing Convention

Over 1♠	1NT* (13+**HL/HLD=flatness**)
2♣*	Minimum hand 12/14
2♦	5♠ - 4♦ 15/17
2♥	5♠ - 4♥ 15/17
2♠	6♠ 15/17
2NT	5332 balanced 15/17
3♣	5♠ - 4♣ 15/17
3♦	5♠ - 5♦ 15/17
3♥	5♠ - 5♥ 15/17
3♠	6♠ - 4♣ 15/17

Responder over the Minimum bid of 2♣* may bid 2♥/2♠/2NT/3♣/3♦ as natural bids
But 2♦* is an artificial shape ask bid with the following responses by the opener

2♥	5♠ - 4♥ 12/14
2♠	6♠ - 4♥ (since 6♠ with 12-14 is a weak 2♠* opening)
2NT	5332 balanced 12/14
3♣	5♠ - 4♣ 12/14
3♦	5♠ - 4♦ 12/14
3♥	5♠ - 5♥ 12/14

Over 1♥	1NT*
2♣*	Minimum hand 12/14
2♦	5♥ - 4♦ 15/17
2♥	6♥ 15/17
2♠	5♥ - 4♠ 15/17
2NT	3532 balanced 15/17
3♣	5♥ - 4♣ 15/17
3♦	5♥ - 5♦ 15/17
3♥	5♠ - 5♥ 15/17
3♠	6♠ - 4♣ 15/17

Responder over the Minimum bid of 2♣* may bid 2♥/2♠/2NT/3♣/3♦as natural bids
But 2♦* is again a shape asking bid as above: Opener responses follow.

2♥	6♥ - 4♠ 12/14 (since 6♥ with 12-14 is a 2♥* opening)
2♠	5♥ - 4♠ 12/14

2NT	5♥332 balanced
3♣	5♥ - 4♣ 12/14
3♦	5♥ - 4♦ 12/14

For both the OPC 2/1 method and Traditional 2/1 the strong NT zone is 15-17; hence, the 12-14 zone may be considered a "weak" NT zone.

If the opening bidder has 15/17**HLD** points after the forcing 1NT* bid, game is likely if responder has **12HLD** points. However, if opener has 12/14 without a majors suit fit, game is less likely if responder has <14**HL** points, so there is nothing to prevent responder from passing.

An example follows:

O: ♠AJ1054   ♥987   ♦KJ109   ♣7   13.5**HLD** with no Q

R: ♠K2   ♥AQ5   ♦A7532   ♣Q94   17.5**HL**

The bidding would go:

Opener	Responder
1♠	1NT*
2♣* (12/14min)	2♦* (shape asking bid)
3♦(5♥-4♦)	5♦ (add 2 F for 9-card ♦ Fit – 17.5+2F+12=31.5)
Pass	Pass

Some may argue that the 1NT bid should be semi-forcing (no alert, but an announcement) as suggested for example by Larry Cohen and other bridge experts over the major suit bids. Some may play it as forcing over 1♠ since opener may have a 4-card heart which may be bid, but semi-forcing over the bid of 1♥.

Some players may scream "I can then never stop in 1NT with 7-9H points without a fit" playing 1NT* as forcing. Respond by saying that there is no advantage to playing in 1NT rather than 1♠ or 2♥ or 2♠ since either responder has a semi-fit in the major or opener has a misfit in the major, with perhaps a singleton, in which case the responders' hand is worth 2 points less with "wasted values" and you will likely be defeated in either contract. Furthermore, if the opponents allow you to play in a 1NT contract they are very likely to have missed out on a 2-level partial score.

With 7-9**HL** points without a fit after the bid of 1♠ responder makes an artificial NF bid of 2♣*. With a minimum opening hand of 12-14**HLD**, opener may pass with 6+ clubs, bid 2♦=5♠-4♦, or 2♥=5♠-4♥, 2♠=5332. Any other higher level big guarantees a maximum point range of 15-17**HLD.**

O: ♠ AK954 ♥ 87 ♦ 65 ♣ AQ67 has 16**HLD** (8.5+1+6.5)

R: ♠ Q3 ♥ K4 ♦ K43 ♣ KJ9854 has 15.0**HL** [1(Qx) + 1(semi-F) + 6 +4 +2L+1 3K's]

The bidding would go:

Opener	Responder
1♠	1NT*
3♣ 5♠-4♣ 15/17	6NT
Pass	Pass

After hearing opener rebid 3♣, responder may add 3 Fit points for his 6-clubs (10-card fit) so now has 18.0**HLDF** points and 18.0 + 15.0 = 33.0 and bids 6NT.

The optimal number of responder points for 1, 2, 3, and 4 lever bids are:

Tricks/Level	1	2	3	4
Responder NT =	8	9	<u>14</u>	
Responder Suit =	7	9	12	<u>15</u>

When responding to a major suit bid, the OPC method suggests the following responding zones:

(1) **With 3-card trump support one needs 7/9 points, for a 2-level bid, 10/12 for a 3-level bid, and 15+ points for game.**

(2) **Without a fit and 13-15HL points one bids 1NT***

(3) **To bid a new suit at the 2-level requires 10+ HLD points.**

(4) **1♠ after partner opens 1♥ requires 7+HLD points.**

When responder's hand is balanced, he will either:

- Show 3-card support for opener's major
- Rebid in NT

When responder's hand is unbalanced with 5+ clubs, he can either:

- Raise at his second turn with a fit
- Bid something other than 2M or 2NT

Consider the following example.

Opener	Hand 1:	♠ AKQ105 ♥ 10982 ♦ 6 ♣ J67
Responder	Hand D:	♠ 9876 ♥ K7 ♦ 75 ♣ AQ1084

Hand 1 has 15**HLD** points and hand D has 15.5**HLDF** points with 4-card spades support.

The two hands have at least 30.5 points; game in the major is certain. However, it is in the slam zone, when you add F pts for the 8-card club fit.

The bidding would go:

1♠	1NT*
2♥ (4♥, 15/17)	2NT* (relay)
3♣ [3♣ = ♦ singleton) investigate for slam* - (Chapter 4)]	

*Finding two aces missing using the methods in Chapter 4, the final contract is 5♠.

Without 4-card support for the major, one may make a 2/1 bid instead of bidding 1NT* or 2♣*. If responder has 14 points, 12+14 = 26 and the point range for NT is 25-27. Hence one may perhaps do better in NT.

Let's look at an example:

Opener	Responder
♠KQ987	♠A1032
♥A765	♥K2
♦A	♦J87
♣J98	♣7654

Opener has 16.5 **HLD** points (5+1 + 4.5 + 3.5 +0.5 + 2 D pts for the singleton) and responder has 11**HLDF** points (8H points + 2 points for 9-spades + 2 points for the heart doubleton with the spade fit -1 for no Q). Knowing that the opener has at least 12**HLD** and adding his 11**HLDF** brings the total to 23**HLDF,** 4 points short of the ones needed for a game; however, opener may have 17 points, so responder invites game by bidding 3♠. Partner would next bid 4♠, a contract that may be missed counting only H or HL points. With the spade fit do not bid 1NT*.

Let's consider another example using Hands 1 and F.

Opener	Hand 1: ♠ AKQ105 ♥ 10987 ♦ 6 ♣ J67
Responder	Hand F: ♠ 102 ♥ Q64 ♦ KQJ ♣ KQ1098

Hand 1 from our analysis has 15**HLD** points and opens 1♠. However, responder has only two spades and 13.5**HLDF** points (-1 for the ♠ doubleton without honor).

Using the OPC method, one makes the 1NT* bid with 13+**HLDF** points to reach the 3NT game finding out that the opener has 15/17 points.

The bidding would go:

Opener	Responder
1♠	1NT*
2♥(5-4 Max)	2NT (relay)

3♣	3NT
Pass	Pass

Rebid by Opener after 1♥ - 1♠

Recall that if partner opens 1♥ (12-17**HLD**) and responder bids 1♠ that the bid is not a 2/1 bid but shows at least 4+spades, is an unlimited bid with 7+**HL** points, and is forcing for one round but not to game.

The sequence 1♥ - 1♠ - 1NT=12/14 and 1♥ - 1♠ - 2NT=15-17

After the bid 1♥-1♠ =7+**HLD** one bids:

1♥	1♠
1NT	3532 12/14
2♣*	Minimum hand 12/14 unbalanced
2♦	5♥ - 4♦ 15/17
2♥	6♥ 15/17
2♠	5♥ - 4♠ 15/17
2NT	3532 balanced 15/17
3♣	5♥ - 4♣ 15/17
3♦	5♥ - 5♦ 15/17

Responder over the Minimum bid of 2♣* may bid 2♥/2♠/2NT/3♣/3♦as natural bids

But 2♦*	**is a shape asking bid**
2♥	6♥ - 4♠ 12/14
2♠	5♥ - 4♠ 12/14
2NT	5♠- 5♥ 12/14
3♣	5♥ - 4♣ 12/14
3♦	5♥ - 4♦ 12/14

Opener   ♠ 54 ♥AQ982 ♦K965 ♣ AQ and 17**HLD**
Responder   ♠ AJ1098 ♥ K ♦ J75 ♣ 10984

Opener	Responder	
1♥	1♠	
2♦*	Pass	No reason to bid 3♦. Responder may pass on 2♦ as he only has 7 **mis**fit pts (-2 for the singleton in partner's suit, -1 for no Q, only 2 pts for the singleton).
Pass	Pass	

36

When is the 2/1 game force off?

(1) If the responder is a passed hand
(2) if responder's Right-Hand Opponent (RHO) interferes with an overcall bid or a double!

1NT* vs. 2NT* Responses

If you were playing 2/1 game force after partner opens a major, a fit is said to occur with a minimum of 3-card support, what happens if you have four-card support? Well, it depends!

Playing "standard" 2/1 most use the bid of 2NT* called the Jacoby 2NT* bid to invite game in the major suit opened. There are many versions and modifications of the Jacoby 2NT* bid. Thus, one should always explain to the opponents the meaning of their bid; and it must always be alerted (do not just say "Jacoby").

I have defined the new forcing 1NT* bid as 13+**HLD** points, an unlimited forcing bid. The bid of 2NT* **is not Jacoby, but a GF bid requiring 16+HLDF** points and cannot be used by a responder if his hand contains a singleton/void.

Requiring 16+**HLDF** points instead of just 13-15 will substantially reduce the frequency of the use of 2NT* raise; however, the advantage is that it is now slam orientated. Others may prefer to instead require only 13-15 points; however, then it is no longer even a Game Force bid because of the potential for wasted honors!

With 0-3 card support for the major, use 1NT* with 13+HLD/13+HLDF points.

Let's look at an example and replace Hand D with Hand G:

Hand G: ♠ 102 ♥K43 ♦ AQJ74 ♣ Q54

Hand G: (0+3.0+ 7.5 +1L+1(Quality) +1.5) = 14**HL** -1**MF** (for doubleton without an honor opposite opener's 5-card suit) = 13**HLDF** points.

With only 2-spades, responder would bid 2♦and opener would certainly find a game in 3NT.

Let's look at two examples where opener bids 1♠ and responder has:

R (1)	♠ Q9874	♥ KJ2	♦ Q107	♣ A6
R (2)	♠KQ106	♥Q654	♦KJ62	♣ 2

R1 has 16.5**HLD** points (1.5 +4+2.5 +4.5+3F for 10 card fit +1 Q honor)
R2 has 16.5**HLDF** points (6+2F (9 card fit) +1.5+4.0+3 for a singleton with 4 trumps and no extras for ♠KQ10 since 6 >4).

While one may bid 1NT* with R1 since 1NT* has no upper limit, it is better to use 2NT* to show 4-card support (details soon to follow); however, with R2 it is better to show shortness over the fit using a full splinter bid (not a mini splinter which has an upper limit of 15 support points).

Hand R1 is too strong to bid 1NT*, hence we would bid 2NT* (details soon to follow); however, with R2 it is better to show shortness over the fit using a full splinter bid (not a mini splinter which has an upper limit of 15 support points) since it shows at least 4-card support for the major and allows one to evaluate a hand for wasted honors.

Partner opens 1♥ and you hold the following hand

   ♠A105   ♥A1089   ♦A54   ♣A76

You have 4-card trump support and 4-aces, or 18**H** -2 for no KQ = 18**HLDF** (+ 2 fit points) and bids 2NT*, a GF bid with slam interest, and you know you have 30+ points, game with slam interest.

Mini Splinter and Full Splinter Bids

The new 2NT* bid is used to reach at least a game contract in a major or perhaps slam. Another type of bid used to investigate game and slam are mini splinter and splinter bids. Both a mini splinter and full splinter require a **4-trump** fit in the major with shortness (a singleton or void) in a non-trump, side suit.

A mini splinter bid has the point range: 13-15HLDF points and a singleton or void somewhere. and is hence invitational. However, a Full splinter bid requires 16+HLDF with no upper limit as is the case for 2NT*. Except now you may have a single or a void.

Recall that the optimal total points between the two hands for game is 27; however, the opener has no honor opposite a singleton, one may add +2 points and opposite a void may add +3 points. The total "working points" become 29-30**HLDF** points with slam interest.

Full Splinters are shown by a **DOUBLE JUMP** in the shortness suit other than partner's major. It is a game forcing raise in the major suit and shows shortness (singleton/void).

Full Splinter bids are defined as follows (*=alert).

1♥ - double jump to 3♠*/4♣*/4♦* shows SHORTNESS in spades, clubs, and diamonds.

1♠ - double jump to 4♥*/4♣* /4♦* shows SHORTNESS in hearts, clubs, and diamonds.

Mini Splinters are defined:

1♥ - single jump to 2♠*/3♣*/3♦* shows SHORTNESS in spades, clubs, and diamonds.

1♠ - single jump to 3♥*/3♣* /3♦* shows SHORTNESS in hearts, clubs, and diamonds.

While shortness is important, it only has value when the information conveyed to the opener allows the opener to evaluate how well the two hands fit, knowing exactly where the shortness resides. An example will help to clarify this point. Consider the two hands:

Opener	♠AKJ83	♥KQ104	♦567	♣7
Responder	♠Q762	♥7	♦AJ42	♣A567

With spades as trump, opener must lose one heart and two diamonds. But suppose we switch the red suits in responder's hand (dummy) and observe the difference.

Switched Hand	♠Q762	♥AJ42	♦ 7	♣ A567

In the first case, opener's heart honors are duplicated by responder's singleton; both parties prevent two heart losers. In the second case, the defenders hold the diamond honors AKQ of diamonds, but only the ace is useful to the opponents. What can one conclude from the above example?

(1) If a singleton or void is opposite high card concentrations (except the Ace), it has less value: -2 points apposite a singleton and -3 points opposite a void.

(2) Not a single honor opposite a singleton +2 points and opposite a void +3 points.

(3) An ace without any other opposite a singleton add +1 point

Let's look at two examples where opener again opens 1♠.

Opener	♠ Q9874	♥ KJ2	♦ K107	♣ A6
Responder	♠AJ106	♥Q6542	♦Q65	♣ 2

Opener has 13.5**HLD** points (1.5+4+3.5+4.5) and responder has 14.5**HLDF** (6.5+2F (9 card fit) +1.5+1.5+3 -1 for no K and no extras for ♠AJ since 6.5 >4).

The bidding would go:

Opener	Responder
1♠	3♣* (mini splinter singleton/void and 13/**15HLDF** points)

A Full splinter should not be used since responder does not have 16+**HLDF** points.

With the Ace opposite the singleton opener adds +1 for "no wasted honors" so now has **14.5HLDF, enough for game (14.5+15 (min)=29.5)**. Follow-up bids are discussed in Chapter 3.

Suppose partner bid 1♠ and you have the following hand:

Responder	♠Q873 ♥542 ♦AKQ72 ♣ 7

You have 19**HLDF** (1.5+ 1 Q +2F +9.5 +1L+1Q + 3 singleton).

Responder has several bidding choices: Full Splinter, 2NT*, or 1NT*? Since he has a singleton, one may not bid 2NT*, a Full Splinter forces game and with weak hearts takes up too much bidding room, even though you have solid diamonds you have very weak side suits for 2/1. The correct bid is 1NT* forcing, the cheapest forcing bid. The forcing bid allows the most bidding room to begin your bidding dialogue.

Questions about Splinter Bids

(1) Can you use a splinter after a 2/1 bid? Yes, these are called delayed splinter bids; for example, 1♥-2♦; 2♥-4♣*. With delayed splinters are direct splinters showing the shortness suit.

(2) Can one splinter with a singleton ace? Yes, but usually not a good idea!

(3) When the opponents splinter, what is the best lead? Lead trump.

(4) With 5+trump support to you

(5) **How do you show a void? Use a Full Splinter showing 5-trump and a void with 16-18HLDF points.**

(6) Can the opener splinter? Yes, for example 1♦*-1♥/1♠; then 3♣* show a Singleton/Void in diamonds with 4+cards in the partner's bid major (mini-splinter).

(7) A splinter bid for partner's suit always takes precedence over auto/self-splinter.

Rebids after 1♥/1♠ -2NT*

Rebids by Opener	Suit Length	HLDF
3♣*	Club Singleton/Void	12-14
3♦*	Diamond Singleton/Void	12-14
3♥*	Heart Singleton/Void	12-14 with Spades as trumps
3♠*	Spade Singleton/Void	12-14 with Hearts as trumps
3♥*	No Singleton/Void	12-14 with Hearts as trumps
3♠*	No Singleton/Void	12-14 with Spades as trumps
3NT*	Spade Singleton/Void	15-17
4♣*	Club Singleton/Void	15-17
4♦*	Diamond Singleton/Void	15-17
4♥*	Heart Singleton/Void	15-17 with Spades as trumps
4♥*	No Singleton/Void	15-17 with Hearts as trumps
4♠*	No Singleton/Void	15-17 with Spades as trumps

After hearing a suit bid that shows Singleton or Void. The following next step sequential bid is called a Scroll asking bidis an asking bid: Is the suit you bid a Singleton or Void?

Examples of Responses to 2NT*

The bidding goes 1♠ - 2NT*. What do you bid?

(1) ♠AKJ84   ♥7   ♦K10987   ♣102

Show your singleton, bid 4♥ with 16**HLD** (no Q)

(2) ♠AKJ84   ♥107   ♦54   ♣QJ108

No singleton/Void bid 4♠ with 15.5**HLD**

(3) ♠AKJ84   ♥K107   ♦1094   ♣76

No singleton/void bid 3♠ with 13.0**HLD**

(4) ♠AKJ84   ♥Q107   ♦QJ4   ♣76

No singleton/Void bid 4♠ with 16.0**HLD**

Game Try bids after 1M-2M

A simple raise shows three or 4-card support and 7-9**HLDF** points where opener has 12-17**HLD** points. To reach game, opener may need help in either a side suit or trumps to reach a game contract.

Help Suit Game Try Bid

There are many games try conventions available to investigate game or to settle on a part score. The Long Suit Game Try (LSGT) is probably the oldest method employed. This is an attempt by opener to tell responder more about his hand. He shows a second suit with the understanding that as responder revalues his hand, he should give extra weight to honors in this suit. However, over the years the LSGT has given way to the Help Suit Game Try (HSGT). The major difference is that the opening bidder may hold fewer than four cards in that suit and usually a good 15 HCP or perhaps less if he is 5-5 in two suits, the major and another suit. Let's look at an example when used by opener, with no interference:

1♥-2♥

3♣*/3♦*/3NT* needs help (ace or king) in clubs, diamonds, spades – bid game

1♠-2♠

3♣*/3♦/2NT* needs help in clubs, diamonds, or hearts - bid game

The method may also be used by responder in the auction 1♣-1♥; 2♥* - (Help suit bid). For responder to use the bid, he should have 10 Dummy Points.

Some prefer the Short Suit Game Try. Using the Short Suit Try (SSGT) approach, a new bid by the opener shows a **singleton**. For responder this means that the ace is probably the only honor in the short suit that will help opener. Of course, this means that honors in the OTHER suits will be what opener needs. Alternatively, one may combine the HSGT and the SSGT bids by using the 2-Way Game Try method. How does this work?

Two-Way Game Try Bid

Instead of using the HSGT method, opener bids the next suit up to tell responder that we are going into "Short Suit Mode". A 3X bid by opener tells responder about shortness.

1♥-2♥-2♠* (asks for shortness) or 3♣*/3♦*/3♥*=spade shortness (tell mode)

- 3♣* = shows shortness in clubs
- 3♦* = shows shortness in diamonds
- 3♥* = shows shortness in spades

1♠-2♠-2NT* (asks for shortness) –or 3♦*/3♥*/3♠*= club shortness (tell mode)

- 3♦* = shows shortness in diamonds
- 3♥* = shows shortness in hearts
- 3♠* = shows shortness in clubs

Shortness is always 1 or 0 cards in the suit.

Kokish Game Try Bid

1♥-2♥-2♠*   (bid cheapest suit where he would accept a GT- deny bid trump suit i.e., a reverse HSGT)

- 2NT* = shows shortness/Axx/Kxx in spades where 3♥ denies
- 3♣* = shows shortness in clubs/Axx/Kxx where 3♥ denies
- 3♦* = shows shortness in diamond/Axx/Kxx where 3♥ denies
- 3♥* = Trump suit GT with honor

1♠-2♠-2NT*   (bid cheapest suit where he would accept a GT – deny bid trump suit i.e., a reverse HSGT)

- 3♣* = shows shortness in clubs/Axx/Kxx where 3♠ denies
- 3♦* = shows shortness in diamond/Axx/Kxx where 3♠ denies
- 3♥* = show shortness in hearts/Axx/Kxx where 3♠ denies
- 3♠* = Trump Suit GT with honor

4M accept GT

While many prefer the HSGT convention since it follows "natural" bidding; Kokish is more flexible. There is no optimal convention.

Responses to One-Level Minor Suit Bids

Playing "standard" 2/1, Mike Lawrence (1987, p.122), "Mike Lawrence's Workbook on the Two Over One System", and Audrey Grant and Eric Rodwell (2009, p. 9). "2 over 1 Game Force", both suggest that the 2/1 bid of 2♣ to 1♦ should be forcing for one round, not to game. Neither Larry Cohen (2012), "Larry Teaches 2 Over 1Game Forcing" (page 35), or Timm (2021), "2/1 Game Force System" support their approach and purpose that the bid of 2♣ over 1♦ is forcing to game. Both approaches are misguided and should now be replaced with the OPC method.

Opening 1♣ playing "standard" 2/1 there is no 2/1 forcing response unless you adopt the Walsh Club Convention discussed by Timm (2021, p. 41) where the 1♦* response initiates a GF sequence.

Playing the OPC method, the bid of 1♣* is used to open any hand with 18+**HLD** points with any distribution and is a forcing bid. To respond to the 1♣* bid responder considers **HLD points** where the "D" only involves deducting -1 point for flatness=4333 distribution and ignores singletons and voids.

Recall that a game in a major has a range of 26-28 with an optimal value of 27. Since 18+8=26 game is possible with only 8**HLD**. For game in a minor suit the range is 29-31with an optimal value of 30.0. Game is possible with 11**HLD**, 18+12=29. For slam in a major suit, the range is 32-34 with an optimal value of 33. Since 18+14=32 slam is possible with 14**HLD** points since 18+14=32.

These observations suggest that the bid of 1♣* must be two-fold with or without a fit. Responder may have 0-6**HLD** points or 13+**HLD** points.

All other 1-level suit bids (1♥ to 2♦are transfer bids). **Opener accepts the suit transfer only if he has at least 3-card support to establish a known suit fit.** Otherwise, bids a natural 5-card suit or NT.

When opening 1♣* observe that 18+7=25 game invite and 18+12=30 slam invites and that 18+9=27 and 18+15=33 for optimal game and suit slam!

Responses to 1♣* (these are not "Precision" Type Bids)

1♦*	0-6**HLD** points or 13+**HLD** pts
1♥*	Transfer bid for 5+♠ with 7-12**HLD** pts
1♠*	Transfer bid for 1 NT 7-9**HLD** pts
1NT*	Transfer bid for 5+♣ with 7-12**HLD** pts
2♣*	Transfer bid for 5+♦ with 7-12**HLD** pts
2♦*	Transfer bid for 5+♥ with 7-12**HLD** pts.

2♥*/2♠*	6+ card suit with 7-9**HLD**
2NT*	10-12**HLD** balanced no 5-card major/minor

The opening bid for 1♦* is 12-17**HLD** points like the major suit bids. However, the bid is artificial and may have 0-2 diamonds (4414/4405) and is forcing for 1-round.

Partner knows you do not have a 5-card major, that your hand may be balanced or unbalanced with 5-clubs or 5+diamonds, that it may have a 4-card major or be 4-4 in the majors, and that it may be 5-4 in clubs and diamonds.

The ranges for a minor suit game with a fit are:

2m	10-12 **HLDF**
3m	13-14 **HLDF**
4m	15-17 **HLDF**
5m	18+ **HLDF**

When responding to a 1♦*, responder may have a weak hand 7-9**HLD**, 10-12**HLD**, 13+**HLD** points. With <7**HLD** responder passes.

Responses to 1♦* Opening (12-17**HLD** and 0-2 diamonds)

1♥ 4+ Cards in suit with 7+**HLD**

    Rebids by Opener

1♠	4+ spades over 1♥
1NT	12-14 HCP over 1♥/1♠
2♣	5+ clubs 12-14
2♦	5+diamonds 12-14
2♥/3♥	4 hearts 12-14/15-17
2♠/3♠	4 spades 12-14/15-17

1♠ 4+ Cards in suit with 7+**HLD**

    Rebids by Opener

1NT	12-14 HCP over 1♥/1♠
2♣	5+ clubs 12-14
2♦	5+diamonds 12-14
2♥	15-17
3M	15-17

1NT	7-10, balanced hand, no 4-card major
2♣	4+clubs GF unless opener rebids 3♣
2♦	4/5+ diamonds GF unless opener rebids 3♣/3♦
2♥	5♥-4♠7-10

2♠	5♠-4♥ 7-10
2NT	11-12, balanced hand, no 4-card major
3♣	4+clubs GF
3♦	5/6+ diamonds GF
3♥	5♥-4♠11-12
3♠	5♠-4♥11-12
3NT	13-15, balanced hand, no 4-card major
4♣	6+clubs 13+
4♦	6+ diamonds 13+
4M	7+ major 13+

As we shall soon see a very good convention to play over the bid of 1♦* is the XYZ convention. **For the Optimal Modified 2/1-Club System, XYZ does not apply over the bid of 1♣* with 18+HLD pts.** Details for the convention with bidding examples is soon to follow in Chapter 3.

Responses to 1NT Opening Bid

When partner open 1NT recall that his hand is balanced or semi-balanced hand with 15-17 **HLD** pts. The bid denies a 5/6 card major but may include two 4-card majors.

When you open the bidding 1NT, your first goal is to find a 4-4 major suit fit. A convention designed for this purpose is the Stayman Convention.

Stayman Convention

After the bid of 1NT, the Stayman Convention uses the asking bid of 2♣ as an artificial bid to inquire whether partner has a four-card major. The convention is so engrained in bridge that it need not be alerted.

Point Count for Stayman

Playing "traditional" 2/1 if partner opens 1NT=15-17HCP and you hold a 4-card major; most bridge books recommend that one have 8H pts to use Stayman. Why?

(a) Without a 4-4 fit, one requires 23H to play in 2NT.
(b) You should not look for game with less than 25H.

This is a serious error, since it ignores Length, Distribution, and Fit points!

When responding to 1NT, responder must evaluate his hand using HLD points and then add "Fit" points. The conventional following Stayman responses which follow assume NO Interference (See Chapter 8 – Bidding over Interference).

As we shall soon see, the Stayman convention is used when responder has at least **8HLD** points. This implies that with 8 points the totals for the two hands is 23-25. Enough for a 2/3 level contract or 8/9 tricks.

Opener's Bids after 2♣

2♦	Denies a four-card major.
2♥	Shows four hearts may have four spades
2♠	Shows four spades, denies four hearts

Responder's rebids after 2♦ by opener

2♥	Shows four hearts and five spades; invitational: non-forcing. (Responder bids the 4-card suit and not the 5-card suit to allow the opener, the strong hand to be declarer.
2♠	Shows four spades and five hearts, invitational: non forcing.
2NT	Invitational: non forcing (8/9 points)
3♣	Shows 5/6 clubs and may not have a 4-card major, invitational non forcing.
3♦	Shows 5/6 diamonds and may not have a 4-card major, invitational non forcing.
3♥*	Shows five spades and four hearts, game forcing (Smolen - Responder bids his short suit at the 3-level, the reverse of the non-forcing 2-level bid). Opener is asked to bid 3♠ with a 3-card spade suit, or 3NT with 2 spades (*=alert).
3♠*	Shows five hearts and four spades, game forcing (Smolen- Responder bids his short suit at the 3-level, the reverse of the non-forcing 2-level bid). Opener is asked to bid 3NT if he only holds 2 hearts or 4 if he has 3 hearts. (*=Alert).
3NT	Signoff
4♥	Signoff.
4♠	Signoff.

Responder's rebids after 2♥ by opener

2♠	Shows four spades, less than four hearts, invitational. Opener can pass, sign-off in 3 with four spades, or bid 3NT.
2NT	Invitational: non forcing (8/9 points)
3♣	Game forcing with at least five clubs (usually 6), denies a 4-card major.
3♦	Game forcing with at least five diamonds (usually 6), denies a 4-card major.
3♥	Shows four hearts invitational.
3♠	Shows four spades, game forcing showing 4 spades and 4 hearts.
3NT	Signoff
4♥	Signoff.

Responder's rebids after 2♠ by opener

2NT   Invitational

3♣   Game forcing with at least five clubs (usually 6), denies a 4-card major.
3♦   Game forcing with at least five diamonds (usually 6), denies a 4-card major.
3♥   Five hearts, game forcing.
3♠   Shows four spades, invitational.

3NT   Signoff.
4♠   Signoff.

Opener has the following hand.

♠A86 ♥AQ65 ♦K1042 ♣K5 = 17.5**HLD Opener bids 1NT**

and suppose two responders' have hand (a) and hand (b)

(a) ♠7 ♥K974 ♦QJ32 ♣10986 = 6H pts
(b) ♠72 ♥K97 ♦QJ873 ♣1098 = 6H pts

Using traditional methods opener has 16H points and would open 1NT; however with only 6H points both responders would pass.

However (a) has **8HLD points.**

Even though hand (a) seems weak, bid 2♣. After partner bids 2♥, responder adds +2 pts for the 8-card heart fit with the K + 3 pts for the spade's singleton with 4-trumps + 6H pts = 11**HLDF** points and after an invite a game is reached with 17.5+11.0=28.5 pts.

For hand (b) opener has 17.5**HL** points, but responder with only 7**HL** decides to bid 2♣. After hearing 2♦, responder next bids 3♦. Opener adds 2 points for a 9-card diamond fit and bids 3NT (19.5+7.0=26.5).

We have said that the responder only counts **HL** and **D** for flatness. This is not the case when responder holds a 4-card major. Instead, responder must bid 2♣ since finding a fit in in a major or when bidding reveals a fit in a secondary suit and since opener did not account for "D-shortness), the total points in the two hands may be increased by 3-5 points.

With at least one 4-card major bid 2♣ with at least 8HLD points and with less pass.

Checkback Stayman

In the sequence 1♥-1♠-1NT-2♣ by responder is called Checkback Stayman. Responder knows you have 5-hearts, and you are trying to find a major suit fit. The responses are:

- 2♦   Denies 3-spades and a good suit
- 2♥   Denies 3-spades
- 2♠   Exactly 5-3 in the Hearts and Spades

Garbage and Crawling Stayman

After a 1NT opening by partner, the bid of 2♣'s is also used to show a weak 3-suited hand, with <8HLD pts. It is referred to Garbage Stayman with 4-4-4-1 distribution and Crawling Stayman with 4-4-x-y in the majors or 3-4-4/5-x or 4-3-4/5-x distribution with 4/5 diamonds.

With Garbage Stayman you pass the bids of 2♦/2♥/2♠.

With Crawling Stayman you pass 2♦ with 3/4 -5-x distribution you bid 2♥ if 4-4-x-y.

This asks partner to pass or correct to 2♠. Hence you may be playing at the 2-level in a major with either a 4-4 or 4-3 fit. However, it is usually better than no-trump.

Some examples hands where you may use Garbage /Crawling Stayman

| (4-4-4-1) | ♠A345 ♥A1084 ♦7892 ♣7 (Garbage) |

(4-4-4-1)   ♠A345 ♥A1084 ♦7892 ♣7 (Garbage)

(4-3-5-1)   ♠Q652 ♥Q43 ♦97652 ♣J (Crawling)

(4-4-3-2)   ♠QJ32 ♥AJ98 ♦978 ♣98 (Crawling)

(4-4-3-2)   ♠Q1053 ♥J1098 ♦1097 ♣107 (Pass)

Garbage Stayman is used when responder has the exact distributions: 4=4=4=1 or 4=4=5=0 and you have 0-6/7 Starting Points. Responder will pass whatever opener bids; some refer to this as "Drop Dead Stayman."

Jacoby Transfers

Jacoby Transfers, developed by Oswald Jacoby, may be employed with a variety of hands. Responder may have a one- suited, two-suited, or even a three-suited hand. Transfers are used with weak, invitational, or strong hands. **Responder's hand is unlimited.**

To use the Jacoby transfer you need a 5/6-card major suit. Not 5-4 or 4-5. Responder clarifies his hand after the transfer suit is **announced** by responder and then accepted by the opener.

For this Jacoby transfer, the bids after 1NT are:

2♦   announce transfer to hearts (♥)
2♥   announce transfer to spades (♠)

Responder's bids after 1NT- 2♦ -2♥

Pass   A weak hand with 5+ hearts. Opposite a strong 1NT, this shows 0-7**HLD** points.

2♠   An invitational, non-forcing hand with 5 hearts and 5 spades. Opposite a strong 1NT, this shows 8-9 starting points.

2NT   A balanced or semi-balanced distribution, 5 hearts, and invitational. Partner can pass, sign off in 3♥ or bid 3NT.

3♣   5+ hearts, 4+ clubs and game-forcing.

3♦   5+ hearts, 4+ diamonds and game-forcing.

3♥   6+ hearts, invitational. Partner can pass or bid 4 ♥.

3♠   Not really part of the original convention but can be played as a singleton/void in spades with slam interest.

3NT   A balanced or semi-balanced (no singletons or voids) distribution with 5 hearts and 10+ points. Partner may pass or correct to 4 ♥.

4♥   6+ hearts, signoff.

Responder's bids after 1NT- 2♥-2♠

Pass   A weak hand with 5+ spades. Opposite a strong 1NT, this shows 0-7**HLD** points.

2NT   A balanced or semi-balanced (no singletons or voids) distribution, 5 spades, and invitational. Partner can pass, sign off in 3♠ or bid 3NT.

3♣   5+ spades, 4+ clubs and game forcing.

3♦   5+ spades, 4+ diamonds and game forcing.

3♥   5+ spades, 5+ hearts and game forcing with slam interest. This is stronger than jumping directly to 4 ♥.

3♠   6+ spades, invitational. Partner can pass or bid 4♠.

3NT   A balanced or semi-balanced (no singletons or voids) distribution with 5 spades and 10+ points. Partner may pass or correct to 4♠.

4♥   5+ spades and 5+ hearts with game values. Partner can pass or bid 4♠.

4♥   6+ spades, signoff.

One may also transfer to a 6+card club suit using the bid of 2♠* with a correction to 3♦ if diamonds is the preferred suit with 6+ diamonds. When the 2♠* bid is made by responder; opener may bid 2NT* which says he prefers diamonds over clubs. Responder may now bid 3♣/3♦.

Help Suit Game Try after a Jacoby Transfer

When using the Jacoby Transfer, one may not be sure of game in a major. In this case, responder may use the bid of 2NT* as a Help Suit Game Try 2NT. After a Jacoby Transfer, responder bids 2NT*, opener's responses follow.

Transfer to hearts

After 1NT - 2♦ - 2♥ - 2NT* (ASK)
Pass – minimum and normally denies 3♥s
3♣ = is a ♣ help suit game try
3♦ = is a ♦ help suit game try
3♥ = sign off
3♠ = is looking for a 5-3 ♠ fit (else 3NT)
3NT normally denies 5♠ or 3♥s

Transfer to spades

After 1NT - 2♥ - 2♠ - 2NT* (ASK)
Pass – minimum and normally denies 3♠s
3♣ = is a ♣ help suit game try
3♦ = is a ♦ help suit game try
3♥ = is looking for 5-3 ♥ fit (else 3NT)
3♠ = sign off
3NT normally denies 5♥ or 3♠s

Let's consider an example.

Opener	Responder	Opener	Responder	Comments
♠ AJ9	♠ KQ876	1NT	2♥ (1)	(1) transfer to spades
♥ AQ104	♥ J3	2♠ (2)	2NT* (3)	(2) normal accept
♦ 85	♦ Q104	3♣ (4)	3♠ (5)	(3) invitational with 5♠
♣ KJ72	♣ 964	pass	pass	(4) can you help in clubs
				(5) No

Four-Way Transfers

Four-way transfers include the Jacoby transfer bids and transfers to the minor suits.

Responder's will again clarify the nature of his hand with subsequent bids. The major suit Jacoby transfers are announced as transfers; however, the minor suit transfers **ARE NOT ANNOUNCED, but Must ALWAYS be alerted=*.**

After the bid of 1NT 15-17**HLD,** responder makes the following bids, promising at least 5+ cards in the major transfer or 6+ cards in the minor suit transfers.

2♦	Jacoby transfer to hearts (♥)
2♥	Jacoby transfer to spades (♠)
2♠*	transfer to clubs (♣)
2NT*	transfer to diamonds (♦)

If opener has a minor suit fit with a top honor (A/K/Q) xx, he makes a bid between responder's transfers call and the actual indicated suit (this is called "bidding the gap") and indicates a "pre-acceptance" of the indicated trump suit:

1NT - P - 2♠* - P - 2NT*=Gap
1NT - P - 2NT* - P - 3♣*=Gap

Responder now knows that the NT opener has a missing high honor and sufficient cards to suggest that the suit will run and then may elect to bid 3NT.

Be careful, some partnerships prefer to reverse the meaning of "bidding the gap" and simply prefer to complete the transfer when the fit is identified and bidding the "gap" when no fit is identified. Arguments can be made for either approach.

We have stressed that whenever one has a 4-card major that one bids 2♣ with **8HLD** points. How does one find a 4-4 major fit using 4-Way-Transfers with a game going hand 17**HL** points?

Playing 4-Way Transfers, the bid of 2♣ by responder does not promise a 4-card major; if opener rebids by showing a four-card major and a fit is found, it is raised (as normal). If opener rebids by showing a four-card major and no fit is immediately found, responder's can easily define their holdings by logical rebids.

Examples (opponents are passing):

1NT-2♣-2♥-3♥	4-4 heart fit
1NT-2♣-2♠-3♠	4-4 spade fit
1NT-2♣-2♥-2♠	Minimum hand with 4-spades
1NT-2♣-2♠-2NT*	May have 4-hearts and minimal hand
1NT-2♣-2♥-2NT*	May have 4-spades or no 4-card major
1NT-2♣-2♦-2NT*	May or may not have a 4-card major

Now 2NT* is alerted (*), because a Stayman sequence (in other treatments) always promises a four-card major.

Four-Way transfers with the Range Ask Bid

The major flaw of Four-Way transfers (2♠* for ♣, 2NT* for ♦) is the use of Stayman to show a minimal hand. Eric Rodwell revised the meaning of 2♠* bid to be range/size asking bid.

The 2♠* bid serves a dual purpose as a transfer to clubs and to invite NT.

2♠* = 6+♣ OR 8HLD without a 4-card major

The responses by opener are:

2NT* = I have a minimum for my range (I would not accept a balanced invite)

3♣* = I have a maximum for my range (I would accept a balanced invite)

By asking opener to show a minimum or maximum immediately, responder can continue with a transfer auction as before.

Hearing a minimum bid responder may pass 2NT or bid 3NT.

When responder has clubs, nothing has changed. All bids continue to mean exactly what they would have meant in the "standard" 4-way transfer structure:

3♣ = 6+♣, signoff
3♦ = 6+♣, short ♦, Game Force (GF) **OR** 6+♣, no shortness, with slam interest
3♥ = 6+♣, short ♥, GF
3♠ = 6+♣, short ♠, GF

All these responses (except 3♣) apply over a 3♣ rebid by the opener as well.

For a discussion on using the range/size ask bid to see the Bridge Winners article by Gavin Wolpert September 11, 2015: bridgewinners.com/4-way-transfers-with-range-ask.

Transfer Bidding Examples

Partner opens 1NT=15-17**HLD** and you hold:

1) ♠789   ♥Q7   ♦K5643   ♣J98

Minimal hand and only a 5-card minor with a flat 3-2-5-3 hand. Pass and let partner play in 1NT. You need a 6-card minor.

2) ♠89   ♥7   ♦7652   ♣J98743

Bid 2♠* as a transfer to clubs, you have a 6-card club suit. Pass openers 3♣ bid, and if he bids 2NT*=Maximum, bid 3♣.

3) ♠K954   ♥67   ♦ K109743   ♣7

You have a 4-card major with 8.5**HL** (-1 for no Q) and a distributional hand, bid 2♣ as Stayman to try to find a 4-4 spaded fit.

If partner bids 2♦, you must pass. If he bid 2♠, you must add 2D + 1 for the K of spades = 11.5**HLDF** points and bid 4♠.

Alternatively, you 6-4 in diamonds and spades, so you may transfer to diamonds and then bid spades. This bidding sequence is a reverse by responder and is a game force sequence requiring 10+ points.

4) ♠J2   ♥K2   ♦J57   ♣AQ10765

You have 14**HLD** (+1 for 2 doubletons) points and no 4-card major. Knowing partner has 15-17, bid 3NT. You have no interest in paying in clubs. 2♠.

5) ♠K2   ♥Q57   ♦KQJ98   ♣1098

With 12.5**HLD**, you should just bid 3NT.

For more information and examples of Four-Way transfers and the expert range ask sequence, see the book by Eric Rodwell (2019) "Bidding Topics Book Two", Baron Barclay, pp 25-42.

Auto/Self-Splinter Bids

Auto/Self-Splinter is a name for a splinter bid when the splinter bidder is setting not his partner's suit, but his own. Again, the bid must be alerted.

Opener	Responder
1NT	2♥ (transfer)
2♠	4♣*(singleton/void)

Responder is setting diamonds as trump.

Opener	Responder
1♦*	1NT
3♥* (Singleton/Void)	??

Opener with the Auto/Self Splinter is setting diamonds as trump. Responder can bid 3NT, 4♦, or show a long club suit.

Opener	Responder
1♥	2♥
3♠*(Singleton/Void)	4♥

Note that the bid of 2♠ would be a reverse so the jump reverse is an Auto/Self-Splinter which set hearts as trump.

Some only play Auto/Self Splinters by the opening bidder when the opener's bid is NOT natural. And others only play them if responder has agreed to openers natural bid by showing a fit. So, discuss these bids with your partner.

Smolen Transfers

Playing 1NT, if responder has a five-card major one may use a Jacoby Transfer bid (responder has an unlimited hand) to transfer into the major, use Crawling Stayman if very weak and 4-4 in the majors. or use Stayman to find a 4-4 major suit with at least one 4-card major; however, when 5-4 in the majors and game going values ns 5-4 in the major one may play the Smolen convention with 10+**HLD** pts.

Playing Smolen, once again one bids 2♣. If partner bids a major, you have found a fit, raise to game. What if partner's bid is 2♦ no 4-card major? Because partner is 5-4, he wants for find a major (5-3) fit and bids as follows (the lower of the two suits):

3♥*   shows 5 spades and 4 hearts \and is forcing to game
3♠*   shows 5 hearts and 4 spades and is forcing to game

Opener may pass or complete the Smolen Transfer to game in a major, although 3NT is allowed.

If the sequence goes:

1NT - 2♣ - 2♦ - 3♥* (5-4) what would the bids 3♠, 4♣/4♦/4♥ mean?
Or
1NT - 2♣ - 2♦ - 3♠* (5-4) what would the bid 4♣/4♦ mean?

These are called **Smolen Super-accept cue bids** and have the following meaning:
After 1NT - 2♣ - 2♦ - 3♥*   and after   1NT - 2♣ - 2♦ - 3♠*

3♠*   3 spades and ♥A   4♣*   3 hearts and ♣A
4♣*   3 spades and ♣A   4♦*   3 hearts and ♦A
4♦*   3 spades and ♦A   4♥*   Smolen Transfer
4♥*   slam interest, with no ace to cue
4♠   Smolen Transfer

Responder hands that may use Smolen after partner bid 1NT are:

♠KJ84 ♥AQ742 ♦43 ♣98   or   ♠QJ987 ♥KJ75 ♦A ♣652

Two-suited Hands (Mini Maxi Convention)

When partner opens 1NT, you sometimes find that you are either 5-5 in the minors or 5-5 in the majors. A simple and straightforward convention to address this distribution is the Mini-Maxi. After the bid of 1NT, one bids (*=alert)

3♣*   5-5 in the minors and <10 Starting Points
3♦*   5-5 in the minors and 10+ Starting Points

3♥*   5-5 in the majors and <10 Starting Points

3♠*   5-5 in the majors and 10+ Starting Points

Because playing in a minor is not usually a goal, some may prefer to replace the minor suit three-level bids with Broken Suit Slam Try bids (since the goal is to play in a major). If you prefer this approach, then one would replace the three-level minor suit bids with the following.

1NT - 3♣*   transfer to hearts 5/6+, indicates a broken heart suit with slam interest with shortage somewhere

1NT - 3♦*   transfer to spades 5/6+, indicates a broken spade suit with slam interest with shortage somewhere

Of course, there are many more options; readers may define their own preferences.

Texas Transfers (4♦ and 4♥)

After opener bids 1NT, suppose you have a six-card major with game going values and have no interest in slam or as a preemptive hand < 8**HLD** pts. Using the principle of fast arrival, one employs the four-level bids of:

4♦#   transfer to hearts

4♥#   transfer to spades

Announced (no alert)

Caution 1NT-4♥ is a transfer. To avoid this problem some may use South African Transfers (SAT). Then 4♣# is a transfer to hearts and 4♦# is a transfer to spades. The primary advantage to these transfers is that they may be easier to remember.

Examples:

(1) preemptive hand ♠842 ♥QJ76542 ♦43 ♣7   Bid 4♦

(2) Invitational hand ♠Q109876 ♥KJ7 ♦A ♣K52   Bid 4♥

Overview of Responses to 1NT (15-17HLD)

Responder Points	Bids	Meaning
0-9**HLD**	2♣	Stayman
	2♦/2♥	Jacoby Major Suit Transfer
	Pass	
10-12**HLD**	2♣	Stayman

(Invitational)	2♦/2♥	Jacoby Major Suit Transfer
	2♠*/2NT*	4-Way Transfers
13+**HLD**	2♣	Stayman/Smolen
(At least Game)	2♦/2♥	Jacoby Major Suit Transfer
	2♠*/2NT*	4-Way Transfers
	3NT	Semi-balanced no 4-card major
	4♦*/4♥*	Texas Transfer

Examples of Transfers After 1NT

We have covered a lot of material, basic, intermediate, and advanced, when responding to the bid of 1NT. To review the concepts discussed, we review more examples.

Your partner opens 1NT, what do you bid with the following hands?

(1) ♠QJ84 ♥10786 ♦8543 ♣A

You are very weak, but 4-4 in the majors; bid 2♣ and pass any two-level bid made by partner (Garbage Stayman).

(2) ♠AKJ8 ♥10765 ♦54 ♣98   or   (3) ♠J10987 ♥109876 ♦54 ♣7

Hands are weak, one is 4-4 in the majors and the other is 5-5, again bid 2♣. If partner bids a major with hand (2), you have 9.5H (no Q but a doubleton), but if partner has a major you would add 1F point for 10.5**HLDF** points and bid 3♥/3♠, and partner would pass or bid game. With hand (3) over a major suit bid you would pass and if partner bid 2♦, you would bid 2♥* asking partner to pass or correct.

(4) ♠AKJ8   ♥J764 ♦543   ♣Q8   or   (5) ♠K1098 ♥A95 ♦Q2 ♣K987

Hands (4) and (5) are invitational. Once again bid Stayman. If in hand (4) partner bids 2♥ or 2♠, you would bid game. Hand (4) has 10H points and with a fit, you would add 1(2) fit points + 2 pts for the doubleton club for 13**HDF** points and 15+13=28 points, enough for game.

However, hand (5) is different; after the bid of 2♠, you would bid 3NT; partner will pass or correct to four spades if he has four.

(6) ♠KJ85   ♥K764 ♦AQ   ♣AJ8   or   (7) ♠AQ4 ♥KQ76 ♦Q4 ♣KQ67

Both hands are strong and contain a 4-card major and in the slam zone, bid 2♣ to try to locate a major fit. Do not bid 4NT.

(8) ♠Q10987 ♥76 ♦7810 ♣432   or   (9) ♠AQ654 ♥KQ72 ♦Q4 ♣67

With the hand (8), bid 2♥ (Jacoby Transfer) and pass partner's bid. This is also the case with hand (9); after partner bid 2♠, do not pass and do not bid 3NT, you have 14.5**HLD** points and 15+14.5=29.5, but 17+14.5=31 in the slam zone; bid 3♥. If you now find a fit in either spades or hearts, after adding fit points (8-card fit=1 +2D pts) may have a slam!

Since you are 5-4 in the majors you could also bid 2♣ to look for a slam in a major using Smolen.

(10) ♠542 ♥Q7 ♦KQ9876 ♣67   (11) ♠542 ♥97 ♦J109876 ♣67

With hand (10), bid 2NT and after partner's response of 3♦, pass. What if he responds 3♣, the super-accept bid? You must next bid 3NT. For hand (11), again use the transfer bid of 2NT; however, with a super-accept, bid 3♦. If partner bids 4♦, then pass.

Opener	♠KQ106 ♥1074	♦Q4	♣AK106
Responder	♠53 ♥AKQ32	♦J10752	♣3

Opener has 15.0**HLD** (6+0+1 +8) and opens 1NT. Responder has 15.5**HLD** (0+9.5+1L +1 Q + 2 for J10 + 2 for the singleton) and bids 2♦ (announced as a transfer to hearts). Opener bids 2♥ with 3. Because the bid is merely a demand response, south does not know yet if a fit exits and next bids his second suit 3♦. Opener knows they have a fit in hearts and adds +1 point for the fit and adds 1D for the diamond doubleton having found a heart fit and bids 3♥. Responder next bids 4♥

North-South, vulnerable and West Deal

		♠	QJ108		
		♥	J9		
		♦	A1076		
		♣	Q107		
♠	K7		N	♠	643
♥	A8643	W	E	♥	K75
♦	85	S		♦	J93
♣	KJ94			♣	9832
		♠	A952		
		♥	Q102		
		♦	KQ42		
		♣	A6		

West opens 1♥ and both North and East pass. With 16.5**HLD** points. South bids 1NT. West passes and North bids 2♣. South bids 2♠, but north has 10H pts (no K) + 1 for the Fit + 2 for the doubleton = 13**HDF** pts. He does **not** invite; he bids game directly since 13 + 15 = 28. Note the appropriate value of 2 pts given to the heart doubleton which limits the opponents to no more than 2 heart tricks. The opening lead is the ♥A. West was end played in clubs and South makes the Spade Game.

Partner bids 1NT. What are your responses with each of the following hands?

(12) ♠KQ97 ♥Q10876 ♦AQ ♣Q9   (13) ♠KQ976 ♥K10975 ♦ 7 ♣A6

With hand (12), you would bid Stayman. Upon hearing the bid of 2♦, playing Smolen you would bid 3♠* to show your 4-5 distribution. Partner must now bid 4♥ with three.

With hand (13), after 1NT, you would bid 3♠*, 5-5 in the majors (Mini-Maxi). After the bid, partner is the captain to bid a major game, no-trump, or investigate slam.

(14) ♠KQJ972 ♥Q106 ♦56 ♣Q2   (15) ♠KQJ972 ♥AQ72 ♦ J7 ♣A

Hand (14) has a six-card spade suit, bid 4♥* (Texas transfer), and do not pass 4♠. Partner knows you have six spades. What if he had the hand: ♠ x x x ♥ A K x ♦ A x x ♣ A K x x 17.5 (no Q, 4333). You must investigate slam. Of course, he will probably pass on 4♥! Most players forget these transfers.

With hand (15) would bid 2♣. If partner now bids 2♦, you will bid 4♦ (Extended Texas Transfer) to show that you are 6-4 in the majors (hearts and spades).

We again consider two hands where opener bids 1NT.

Opener   ♠AJ56 ♥J98 ♦AK4 ♣KJ4
Responder   ♠KQ975 ♥ 7 ♦Q6 ♣AQ765

In this hand, you would transfer to spades and then bid clubs. You cannot use mini maxi.

Extended Texas Transfers

We can combine the Stayman Convention with Texas Transfers when one is 6-4 in the majors. After 1NT -2♣ -2♦/2♥/2♠, one next bid

4♦*   transfer to hearts with 6 and 4 spades
4♥*   transfer to spades with 6 and 4 hearts

If you are 6-5 in the majors, since we are using Mini-Maxi Convention when 5-5 in the majors, we can use Jacoby Transfers to show the long six-card suit and next bid the other major to show the five-card suit. After 1NT

2♦ .   transfers to hearts (♥)
2♥   transfers to spades (♠)

After opener's bid of   2♥   responder bids 4♠* to show 6 hearts and 5 spades
                        2♠   responder bids 4♥* to show 6 spades and 5 hearts

Thus, you simply transfer to the six-card suit and bid the other major at the four levels (the shorter following Smolen) to show 6-5.

Example

North   ♠A62 ♥K75 ♦AQ74 ♣K53
South   ♠KJ9543 ♥AJ32 ♦105 ♣7

North	South
1NT	2♣
2♦	4♥* (Extended Texas)
4♠	Pass

North has 16**HLD** [4.5+3+4.5+2 +3 -1 (4333)] and South has 11.5**HL**. Warning, the convention works provided partner does not pass 4♥

Minor-Major Two Suited Hand

We saw that Smolen may be used when you are 5-4 in the majors and the Mini Maxi Convention may be used if you are 5-5 in the majors or the minors. What is one to do if you are 5-4 in the minors and a major playing 4-way transfers with game going values?

A simple approach is to simply transfer into the 5-card minor and the bid the 4-card major and partner may accept the transfer or bid 3NT.

   1NT - 2♠* - 2♠*/2NT* -3♥/3♠   5♣-4♥/5♦-4♠

Or switching the major suit bids: 3♠/3♥ we have 5♣-4♠/5♦-4♥
Yes, keep it simple!

Example

North   ♠986 ♥AKQ62 ♦J3 ♣AJ5
South   ♠KQ87 ♥53 ♦AK764 ♣K7

North	South
1NT	2NT* (transfer to diamonds)
3♦	3♠ (Natural)
3NT	Pass

Other bridge authors have devised more complicated systems using Quest/Smolen Transfers with super-accepts, but they are more complex. See Terrence Quested (2006), "No Trump Bidding, Stayman and Transfers". Trafford Press.

CHAPTER 3

RESPONDER REBIDS

We have reviewed major, minor, and NT opening bids, responses by partner, and rebids by the opening bidder. In this section, we review responder rebidding with opener continuation bids.

1♦*- Auctions

Recall that the bid 1♦* has the bidding range 12-17**HLD** points like major suit bids (with two bidding zones 12-14 and 15-17), however, the bid is **artificial** and may have 0-2 diamonds, so it is forcing.

Partner knows you do not have a 5-card major, that your hand may be balanced or unbalanced with 4-clubs or 4/5+diamonds, that it may have a 4-card major or be 4-4 in the majors, that it may be 5-4 clubs and diamonds or even a 4-4-4-1/ 4-4-5-0 hand.

Responder ranges are defined:

    (1) Weak with 7-9HLD
    (2) Invitational 10-12HLD
    (3) Strong 13+HLD

XYZ Convention

The convention goes by two names XYZ or Two-Way Checkback and is like but better than Two-Way New Minor Forcing. It is a corner stone convention for the Modified Optimal 2/1-Club System when opening 1♦*= 12-17**HLD**.

In applies to the following bidding sequences:

Opener	Responder
1♦*	1♥/1♠
1NT	?

60

1♥	1♠
1NT	?

1♦*	1♥
1♠	?

The system's basic premise is that bids of 2♣* and 2♦* are both artificial. There are three features to the system

1) The 2♣* response to a 1NT/1♠ rebid is a forced relay to 2♦*
2) The 2♦* response to a 1NT/1♠ rebid is an artificial game force (yes even if partner's opening bid was 1♦). It is usually a Major suit Checkback but is occasionally a prelude to showing a forcing bid in a minor.
3) Jump rebids by responder, in any suit, are forcing. They describe good hands or good suit(s) with good values and long suit(s).

The approach to signing off in a minor is as follows. To sign-off in 2♦ responder bids 2♣* - Opener should alert and explain as a RELAY to 2♦*, either to play or the start of some invitational sequence.

The auction may go 1♦* 1♠

1NT 2♣*
2♦* Pass

This is how responder gets back to 2♦. Remember you can't bid 2♦ directly over 1NT as a preference for it is an artificial force.

1♦* 1♥ (7+**HLD**)	**Responder's Bids**
1NT ? Pass	To play
2♣*	Forces 2♦*
2♦*	GF
2♥	To Play
2♠	Invitational with 4-Spades
2NT	6+ diamonds
3♣	Sign-off in Clubs (5-4)
3♦	5♦-5♥ slam try
3♥	6+Hearts, slam try
3♠	4-Spades and 6+Hearts

follows.

1♦* 1♠ (7+**HLD**)	**Responder's Bids**
1NT ? Pass	To Play

2♣*	Forces 2♦*
2♦*	GF
2♥	5+spades – 4+hearts Opener Pass or bids 2♠ - 3♥ not a possible bid)
2♠	To Play
2NT	6+ diamonds
3♣	Sign-off in Clubs
3♦	Slam try 5-5
3♥	Slam try 5-5
3♠	6+Spades Slam try

Using the XYZ convention the auctions may be weak, invitational, or strong.

Weak	1♦* 1♥	1♦* 1♥	
	1♠ 2♥	1♠ 1NT	
		2♣* 2♦	
Invitational	1♦* 1♥	1♦* 1♥	1♦* 1♥
	1♠ 2♣*	1♠ 2♣*	1♠ 2♣
		2♦* 3♦	2♦ 2♥
			3NT

Slam	1♦*	1♠
	1NT	2♦*
	3♣	3♦
	4♦	4♥
	5♦	7♦

Opener	♠106	♥AQ52	♦J86	♣KQ64
Responder	♠KJ875	♥76	♦AKQ72	♣7

Opener	Responder
1♦*	1♠
1NT	2♦*
2♥	3♦
3NT	

Opener	♠Q102	♥A5	♦K987	♣A872
Responder	♠7	♥KJ10974	♦A52	♣Q73

Opener	Responder
1♦*	1♥

1NT	2*
2NT	3NT

Opener	♠Q62	♥K65	♦AK987	♣72
Responder	♠AK7	♥AQ972	♦52	♣863

Opener	Responder
1♦*	1♥
1NT	2♦*
2♥	4♥

We have seen how useful the XYZ convention is when the sequence is X-Y-Z; however, there are other responses:2-level bids and 3-level bids. In general, 2-level bids are invitational and 3-level bid are GF bids.

The sequence 1♦*- Pass - 1♥ - (1♠) – X = Support Double developed by Eric Rodwell (more on this later, Chapter 9).

Fourth Suit Forcing

Fourth Suit Forcing (fsf) occurs when a partnership bids all four suits in the first two bidding rounds. The fourth suit bid is artificial with game-invitational values 10+**HLD points.** Although some partnerships play it as game-forcing.

Opener	Responder
1♦	1♠
2♣	2♥*(fsf)

Opener	Responder
1♥	1♠
2♣	2♦*(fsf)

Opener's rebids are natural. However, the priorities are:

1. Showing 4-card support for partner's major
2. Rebidding a suit to show extra length
3. Bidding NT with a stopper in the fourth suit
4. Raising the fourth suit with 4 cards in that suit

Playing Fourth Suit Forcing as a one-round-force (not game-forcing), then opener must make jump bids to show extra values and commit the partnership to game.

Opener	♠J93	♥KQ1054	♦A	♣Q42
Responder	♠KQ942	♥A2	♦J32	♣A52

Opener	Responder
1♥	1♠
2♣	2♦* fsf
2♠ (Min)	4♠

Opener has 12.5**HLD** [0.5+6+1L+3.5+1.5] and
Responder has 15.5**HL** [5+1L+4.5+0.5+4.5]

Fourth Suit Forcing is OFF if any of the following conditions apply:

- Responder is a passed hand.
- The opponents overcall or make a double
- The partnership bids all four suits at the 1-level

1♥/1♠ - Auctions

Playing "traditional" 2/1, many partnerships play Bergen raises (e.g., Bergen, Reverse Bergen, or Combined Bergen) because they believe that it is safe to bid to the 3-level with 9 trumps. The idea behind Bergen raises is that, if you are aware of your nine-card fit, you should take up as much space as possible, and bid directly to the 3-level ("your safety level"). Therefore, the bids of 3 Clubs and 3 Diamonds have become the foundation for Bergen's major suit raises.

Larry Cohen (1994, p.15), "Following the Law" states "The Total Number of Tricks available on any deal is approximately equal to the Total Number of Trumps". And Mike Lawrence and Andres Wirgren (2004, p.25), "I Fought the Law of Total Trick" found based upon 1500 deals that only 601 hands or 40.07% of the hands matched exactly the number of tricks. Or approximately a 40% of the time! Why?

Patrick Darricades (2020, p.46-58)," Optimal Hand Evaluation in Competitive Bidding" shows that taking tricks depend on "distribution" not the number of trumps. It is short suits, and their location that determine the effectiveness of the trumps.

Neil Timm (2021, p. 332), "2/1 Game Force System" developed a formula that tried to correct the flawed "Law" that considers hand shape (distribution), double fits, and poor honor combinations.

I agree with Darricades that the solution in the determination of the level of the bid includes trump fit, secondary suit fit, distribution, D-fit, honor valuation, and suit quality is the application of the Optimal Point Count Method. One of the major reasons for this book.

Paulo Brum in his March 20, 2020, Article "Bye, Bye, Bergen" States "The major drawback of Bergen raises is that they are pretty much *incompatible with 2/1 GF*. Yes, you heard me. One of the most popular systems in America right now includes both 2/1 GF and Bergen raises -- and this leaves an enormous, unsolvable gap in your system. When you use the bids of 3 Clubs and 3 Diamonds to support partner, you no longer have them available in their natural sense. This means that any hand in which the primary suit is clubs (or diamonds) cannot use any other route than bidding its suit at the 2-level, or 1NT. But the 2-level new suit is game forcing! And so, we have a huge range of club (and diamond) hands that are shoveled into the forcing 1NT response. (If you play it as semi-forcing, meaning that your partner can pass with a balanced minimum, your problem becomes even worse)".

What is one to do?

(1) Redefine the meaning of 1NT* forcing as defined above.
(2) Replace Bergen bids with mini splinters.
(3) Say bye, bye to Bergen and adopt the Optimal Point Count method of hand evaluation.

What about the Rules of 19/20/22 which state: Count your two longest suits and add to that total your H points; if it adds to 19/20+points open the hand using good judgement. The Rule of 22 uses the same method but also requires adding +2 points for quick tricks (two A's or AK in the hand) for a total of 22 points to open.

Two problems are clear, the honor point values are counted incorrectly, there is no mention of suit quality, and distribution is ignored! You no longer need these misguided rules if you adopt the OPC method.

When partner opens a major responder's primary obligation is to show shortness with a fit with an unbalanced hand. This is done with the aid of mini splinters and full splinters. High card points are great for bidding balanced hands. As distribution enters the picture, the location of cards becomes increasingly important. In general, no single bid describes an unbalanced hand better than a short suit bid. Recall the following over a major suit bid.

Mini splinter - 13-15**HLDF** points with 4-card support
Full Splinter – 16+**HLDF** points 4-card support

1NT* - 13+**HLD** points
2NT* - 16+**HLDF** points 4-card fit no shortness

2/1 Bid with 15+**HLDF** points
2M -7-9**HLDF** points
3M – 10-12**HLDF** points
<7 **HLD** Pass

The structure of the responses to the opening major suit are:

1♥ - 1♠ =7+**HLD**
      1NT*-Invitational, one-round forcing!
      2♣/2♦ - Natural (10/12)

2♥ - simple raise 7-9**HLDF**

2♠*- mini-splinter in spades with 4 hearts, 13-15**HLDF**

2NT* GF – 4-hearts 16+**HLDF**

3♣* - mini-splinter, short in clubs with 4 hearts, 13-15**HLDF**

3♦* - mini-splinter, short in diamonds with 4 hearts, 13-15**HLDF**

3♥ - Natural invite 10-12.

3♠ - full splinter, short in spades with 4 hearts, 16+**HLDF**

3NT – 13-15 3-card support

4♣* - full splinter short in clubs with 4 hearts, 16+**HLDF**

4♦* - full splinter short in diamonds. with 4 hearts, 16+**HLDF**

4♥ - To play

1♠ -   1NT*--One-round forcing

2♣/2♦ - Natural (10-12)

2♠ - simple raise 7-9**HLDF**

2NT*- 4-spades 16+**HLDF**

3♣* - mini-splinter, short in clubs with 4 spades, 13-15**HLDF**

3♦* - mini-splinter, short in diamonds with 4 spades, 13-15**HLDF**

3♥* - mini-splinter, short in hearts with 4 spades, 13-15**HLDF**

3♠ - Natural invite 10-12

3NT -13-15 3-card support

4♣* - full splinter short in clubs with 4 spades, 16+**HLDF**

4♦* - full splinter short in diamonds with 4 spades, 16+**HLDF**

4♥* - full splinter short in hearts with 4 spades, 16+**HLDF**

4♠ - To Play

(1) Your partner opens 1♠ and you hold the following hand.

Responder   ♠1095 ♥ A1032 ♦A106 ♣Q98

You have 9.5**HLD** points (+1 Fit -1 no K and -1 for 4 3 3 3) and would bid 2♠. And if you had 10-12**HLD** pts you would bid 3♠. You cannot bid 2♥ because you hold only four cards.

(2) Your partner opens 1♠ and you hold:

Responder   ♠AQJ762 ♥7 ♦AK983 ♣5

You have great spade support with 27 HLDF pts (7.5 + 2 Q + 2 L + 3 Fit + 2 + 7.5 + 1 L + 2). But you have a singleton and cannot bid 2NT*. Bid 1NT*

DO NOT SPLINTER with 4♥* an absurd bid with two singletons.

How does interference effect major suit opening bids playing Optimal Modified 2/1?

1NT* vs. Mixed Raise (MR)

If the opponents interfere and bid a suit, or if partner is a passed hand what bid may partner now use with or without support?

To illustrate, suppose you have the following hand: ♠75 ♥Q106 ♦AKJ732 ♣72.

Partner opens 1♥ and his LHO bids 1♠, what do you bid?

You have a fit in hearts with 3-hearts and 18 **HDLF** pts (2.5 + 2 Fit pts + 1 D for one doubleton + 8.5 + 2 Q + 2 L). For a mini splinter you need 13-15**HLDF** points with 4-card support, a Full Splinter requires 4-card support with 16+**HLDF** points, and for the bid of 2NT* you need 4-card support with16+**HLDF** points and no shortness. While you may make the 2/1 bid of 2♦, this bid fails to show the heart fit. Some have suggested a Mixed Raise which describes the hand but communicates too much information to the opponents.

The best bid is 1NT* forcing which requires 13+**HLD** points. But what if you have less?

Suppose you are passed with the hand:

♠75 ♥K1096 ♦KQJ72 ♣54 with 11.5**HLDF** [0+3.5+8 +0 +1for 2 doubletons -1 no Ace]

And partner opens 1♥ with interference. Again, bid 1NT*.

The bid of 1NT* may be played in all seats, by a passed hand as well as over interference **with or without a fit**.

In the following bidding sequence, the bid of 1NT* is again made.

LHO	Partner	RHO	You= Advancer
1♦	1♥	1♠	1NT*

When making an opening bid of 1♦*/1♥/1♠ one needs 12-17**HLD** points. However, an overcall bid at the 1 or 2-level is different. Why?

Clearly having cards (3+) in the opponent's suit is bad while having a singleton or void is good and a doubleton is neutral. Thus, one must adjust for holding cards in the opponents' suit when evaluating an overcall bid.

Overcall Suit Adjustments

Deduct -1 point for 3-cards in the opponent's suit

Deduct -2 point for 4-cards in the opponent's suit
Deduct -3 point for 5-cards in the opponent's suit

Add +1 for a singleton in the opponent's suit
Add +1 for a void in the opponent's suit

The opponents open 1♥ open and you hold:

♥xx	No adjustment
♥xxx	-1L point
♥Axx	-1L point = 3.5 points (4.5-1L)
♥Axxx	-2L point = 2.5 points (4.5-2L)
♥Kxxx	-2L point = 1.0 points (3.0-2L)
♥x	+1D so total =3 (2D+1D)
♥ -	+1D so total =5 (4D+1D)

A second factor that effects your hand are **lone honors and honors outside your bid suit and the opponent's suit**. The honors in 3 and 4 card suits and lone honors help to determine whether your hand is more defensive than offensive orientated.

Overcall Honor Adjustments

   (1) Honors in Opponent's Suit

   Kxx/Kxxx (K alone) deduct -1 point (regardless of position) with KJx
   or Kx no adjustment
   K with Q -1 when before opponents' suit
   +1 when after opponents' suit
   Qxx/QJx no adjustment

   J without a 10 -0.5 (e.g., Jxx/Jxxx J alone); otherwise, no adjustment

   (2) Honors in 3/4 card side suits

   Kxx/Kxxx alone -1 point with Q/J no adjustment
   Jxx/Jxxx alone -0.5 with 10 no adjustment

   (3) No other honor adjustments

In summary the Overcall evaluation process requires 3 steps:

   (1) Starting Points HLD
   (2) Adjustments for Opponent's suit length and Honors
   (3) Adjustments for Honors in 3 or 4 suits Outside the Opponents' suit

These points are called **Adjusted Optimal Count (AOC).**

To open 1M requires 12-17**HLD** points; however, to overcall at the one level requires 12-17**AOC** points and 15-17**AOC** points are required for a 2-level bid.

While many will overcall with a 5-card suit, it is best that the suit has not 5 but 6-cards unless the suit is spades. However, hands that are 5-5/5-4 card suits tend to yield more positive than negative results when compared to over calls using only one 5-card suit.

Do not let vulnerability influence your decision or use the commonly used Culbertson's rule of "2 or 3" (i.e., do not go down more than 2 -tricks vulnerable or more than 3-tricks non-vulnerable). Use the Adjusted Optimal Count.

A double of a suit bid normally shows 12+**AOC** points. However, when the opponents open 1♣ a X is a power X which signifies the over caller has 18+**HLD** points and his partner is to respond to the X as if partner had opened 1♣*.

The opponents open 1♥ and you hold the following hand:

♠KQJ65 ♥K87 ♦AJ5 ♣J10

You have 17.5**HLD** [8 +3+5.5 +1] -1L (for 3 hearts) -1 for the lone ♥K= 15.5**AOC** pts.
So, bid 1♠.

♠QJ5 ♥Q87 ♦KQ6543 ♣7

You have 12.5**HLD** [3+1.5+7+2 -1 for no A] – 1L (3 hearts) =11.5**AOC** do not bid 2♦ even though you have 10H points.

1♣*- Auctions

A cornerstone bid for the Optimal Modified 2/1 System is the bid of 1♣* = 18+**HLD** points with any distribution. A hand with as little as 10/11**H** may be opened 1♣* if it is an extremely distributional hand. For example, the hand:

♠QJ5 ♥AKQ9876 ♦--- ♣987 has 22.5**HLD** points [3+9.5+4 void+4L for 7 hearts+2 for 3 honors] not 12H points.

The 1♣* is not the precision club. In Precision this hand would be opened 1♥ (using only H points). And partner with 0-7H points would pass!

If responder had the hand: ♠K64 ♥543 ♦98765 ♣54; responder has **5HDLF** points

[3 -1 for no Q+1 for Heart fit (maybe more!) + 1D for club doubleton] = 27.5 enough for game! Yes, a game missed playing Precision counting only H=HCP.

For the Optimal Modified 2/1-Club System 1♣* is not like the Precision club but goes as follows.

Responses to 1♣*

1♦*	0-6**HLD** points or 13+**HLD** pts
1♥*	Transfer bid for 5+♠ with 7-12**HLD** pts
1♠*	Transfer bid for 1 NT 7-9**HLD** pts
1NT*	Transfer bid for 5+♣ with 7-12**HLD** pts
2♣*	Transfer bid for 5+♦ with 7-12**HLD** pts
2♦*	Transfer bid for 5+♥ with 7-12**HLD** pts.
2♥*/2♠*	6+ card suit with 7-9**HLD**
2NT*	10-12**HLD** balanced no 5-card major/minor

(1) After Negative: 1♦* 0-6 HLD

Opener Rebids after 1♦*:

1♥/1♠/2♣/2♦ Natural forcing one round with 5/6 cards, unbalanced and 18+**HLD**

1NT* 18-20 balanced

Responder Bids

Pass	0-4 **HLD**/Garbage Stayman
2♣	5+**HLD**, Stayman
2♦/2♥	Jacoby Transfer
2♠	The Minors

Opener Bids

2NT	Prefer Diamonds
3♣	Prefer Clubs

2♠* shows 5+cards and 21-23**HLD** or 21+**HLD**, forcing one round

2♥ shows 5+cards and 21-23**HLD** or 21+**HLD**, forcing one round

Responder bids 2♠ (ask)
2NT 22-23 and balanced
3NT 24-26 and balanced
3X = Natural (4/5 cards) with 22+**HLD** and 5+ hearts

2NT* 21-23**HLD** balanced

Responder Rebids

Pass	0-2 **HLD**
3♣	3+**HLD**-Stayman
3♦/3♥/3♠	Jacoby Transfers (5-card suit- H/S/Clubs)
	May correct to 4♦ over 4♣-transfer bid
4♣	Expert Gerber
4♦	transfers to hearts (6-card)
4♥	transfers to spades (6-card)
4♠	transfers to clubs (6-card)
	Or correct to 5♦ over 5♣-transfer bid

3NT* 24+**HLD** balanced

Responder Rebids

Pass	0**HLD**
4♣	Expert Gerber
4♦	transfers to hearts
4♥	transfers to spades
4♠	transfers to clubs (with correction to diamonds)

(2) After Positive Transfer Responses to 1♣* Opening--Positive Transfer Responses **to 1♣*** are 5+ card suits. Opener must have 3+ card supports to accept transfer.

To transfer to a minor, you need **7-12HLD. Opener will accept again with 3+-card support even though he may have a 5-card major.**

Bids of 1NT=18-20, 2NT=21-23, 3NT=24-26 show NO-FIT

(3) After 1♠* (7-9 HLD) === Positive Transfer and relay to 1NT by Opener

After opener accepts the suit transfer responder next tells opener about his controls

First Step 0-1 control (K=1), next step = 2 (1Ace/2kings) etc.

TAB (trump asking bid) Opener may next bid the Trump suit at lowest available level if he wants to ask about responder's trump suit

1st step	Five or more trumps with no top honor (A, K, Q)
2nd step	Five with one top honor
3rd step	Five with two top honors
4th step	Six or more with one honor
5th step	Six or more with two honors
6th step	Five/Six or more with three top honors

CAB (control asking bid) Opener next may bid any non-trump suit if he wants to ASK for controls in that suit

1st step	No Controls (Qxx or worse)
2nd step	Second round Control (K/singleton)
3rd step	First round Control (A/void)

(4) Responder bids 2♥*/2♠*/3♣*/3♦*shows singleton in bid suit (7+HLD)

Opener Rebids:

3♥/3♠	**1430 for bid major**
4♣/4♦	**1430 for bid minor**
4♥/4♠/5♣/5♦	**To Play**

(5) Responder's bid of 2NT* 10-12HLD, balanced/semi-balanced

Opener Rebids:

3♣*   Ask bid

Responder bids 4-card suits up the line (3♦/3♥/3♠) 3NT* show clubs

3♦/3♥/3♠   Natural bids show 5-card suit

3NT*   Asking Bid

Responder bids

4♣*=14 points

4♦*= 15 points

After 4 clubs and 4 diamonds, opener bids 4-card suits up-the-line or bids 4NT (to-play)

4♥*/4♠*/5♣*/5♦*=16+

4♣   Expert Gerber Ace ask

Slam examples are discussed in the next Chapter.

(1) Your partner opens 1♣* and you hold the hand.

Responder   ♠K93 ♥ K7 ♦A1094 ♣Q1075

You have 13**HLD** points (3+3+4.5+2.5). You are near slam (18+13 = 31); without a 5-card suit you must bid 1♦*.

(2) You hold the following hand, what is your bid? ♠AQJ106 ♥A8 ♦QJ7 ♣K98

You have 21**HLD** points. You have five spades and only three hearts, bid 1♣*.

(3) You hold ♠A2 ♥AJ984 ♦AK852 ♣7

Your partner opens 1♣*. What do you bid? You have 19.5**HL** pts and two five-card suits. You have over 13 pts, therefore your bid is 1♦*. Partner now responds 1♠ (forcing for one round). Bid next 2♦, a natural forcing bid. Partner will continue the auction to game somewhere.

(4)

Opener	♠K987	♥A32	♦A76	♣AK5
Responder	♠1092	♥K987	♦KJ54	♣63

Opener has 17.5**HLD** [13.5 for 3 aces-2 pts for 4333D an no Q] and opens 1NT. East has 6**HLD** points [-1 for no Q] and must pass.

At a Regional most bid this hand playing 2/1: 1♣ with 18H points, followed by 1♥; the opener jumped to 2NT with 18H points and Responder with 7 points bid 3NT. Which among the 27 boards played was successful only once!

(5)

Opener	♠QJ10754	♥A32	♦A6	♣A5
Responder	♠K2	♥J107	♦9754	♣K872

Opener has 19.5**HLD** [(no king) points +1 for 2 doubletons] and responder has 7**HL** (no Queen).

Opener	Responder
1♣*	1♠*
1NT	2NT
3NT	Pass

The 1♠ bid is forcing for one round and responder bids 1NT. Responder now knows opener has at least 5 spades and adds +1 Semi Fit point for 8**HLDF** points where now 18+ 8=26 points and next bids 2NT. Opener bids 3NT without distributional values.

At most tables playing traditional methods pairs were either in 4♠ for down one or stopped in 2NT.

CHAPTER 4

SLAM BIDDING

To investigate slam the partnership needs about 31-32 points. To evaluate whether the partnership has the required controls A=2 controls and K=1 control), one uses cue bids and Blackwood Conventions. Blackwood Conventions reveal how many aces and kings for example, while cue bidding or control showing bids reveal where they reside.

The Blackwood Convention

The most used and perhaps the most abused convention in bridge is the original Blackwood Convention developed by Easley Blackwood Sr. because many believe it will handle all situations. It does not. While the convention does not require knowing the trump suit, it does require that one knows whether slam is possible. The convention augments this knowledge by helping one find the number of aces and kings.

The convention should not be used when:

(1) Holding two or more cards in an unbid suit with no ace or king (e.g., xx, Qx, Jx).
(2) Holding a void.
(3) One has a slam invitational hand (e.g., 1NT facing 1NT hands).

To use the convention, the captain bids 4NT which is the asking partner for the number of aces held.

The responses are:

5♣	0 aces or all 4 aces
5♦	1 ace
5♥	2 aces
5♠	3 aces

If two aces are missing, the captain signs off in five of the agreed suits. If one ace is missing, one may bid 6NT or six of the suits. When spades are not trump, the bid of 5♠ asks partner to bid 5NT.

What do you do if you have a void? Do not count it as an ace. With an even number of aces (two or four) bid 5NT and with an odd number (one or three) bid the suit at the six-level. It works. If you have no aces and a void (ignore the void), bid 5♣ since the void may be in a suit in which your partner has an ace.

Knowing you have all the aces, 5NT is the king's ask (without a void response); the responses are:

6♣	0 kings or all 4 kings
6♦	1 king
6♥	2 kings
6♠	3 kings

Having all the aces and kings, one is in the grand slam zone; recall it requires about thirty-seven Bergen Points.

The major problem with the Blackwood Convention is you have no way of knowing about the ace and king of trump and the specific location of aces are unknown. To solve these shortcomings, one uses cue bids and the Roman Keycard Blackwood Convention, which has replaced the Blackwood Convention.

Roman Keycard Blackwood (RKCB) Convention - 1430

The most authoritative book on this convention is by Eddie Kantar (2008), "Roman Keycard Blackwood the Final Word" 5th Edition, Master Point Press, Toronto, Ontario, Canada.

However, the book by Krzysztof Martens (2014), "Professional Slam Bidding" Part 1 and Part 2, and the books by Roger Munger (2014), "KICKBACK Slam Bidding at Bridge" and Patty Tucker (2014), "Slam Bidding Conventions", should also be consulted.

To use the RKCB Convention, one must have agreed upon a trump suit. There are two Roman Keycard Conventions known as 1430 and 3014. When the weak hand asks, Kantar (2008) recommends that one play the 1430 version (marked as 1430 on the convention card); if the very strong hand asks, he recommends 3014 (marked as RCK on the convention card). While Kantar has several criteria to determine which hand is considered very strong and which is the weak hand, because often the hand that asks usually has two keycards (or if not, one with the Queen), **I recommend to always using the 1430 Roman Keycard Convention since it facilitates the queen ask step of 5♦ over 5♣ as we shall soon see and let's not get too complicated.**

When using the RKCB Convention, there are five keycards, the four aces, and the king of trump. Another keycard is the queen of trump. If you do not use kickback (to be explained later), the 1430 RKCB ask is again 4NT. The responses are:

5♣	1 or 4 keycards (the 14 step)
5♦	3 or 0 keycards (the 30 step)

5♥   2 (or 5) keycards without the queen of trump

5♠   2 (or 5) keycards with the queen of trump or holding a 6th trump

When one responds five clubs or five diamonds, the queen ask may be needed. After the response five clubs, the bid of 5♦ is the queen ask (when hearts or spades are the agreed upon trump suit). After the bid of five diamonds, the bid of 5♥ is the queen asks.

Queen Asks

After five clubs and five diamonds, the queen asks are: 5♦ and 5♥ queen asks

Responding to the 5♦ ask

(1) If you **do not** hold the queen, responder returns to the agreed upon suit at the five- level.
(2) 5NT shows the queen, but no outside king!
(3) With both (Q of trump and one or two kings), bid at the six-level of the lowest ranking king.

Responding to the 5♥ queens ask (whether hearts or spades are the agreed upon suit).

If you do not hold the queen, pass 5♥ if hearts are trumps. If spades is the agreed upon suit, then 5♠ denies the spade queen.

1. If responder has a side-suit king, the king is bid at the 6 level, to show king and queen of trump.
2. If responder has no side-suit king, but the queen of trump, bid 5NT.
3. If responder has 4-3-3-3 distribution without a side-suit king or queen, bid 6NT.

Another simple option when hearts is the agreed upon suit is to bid 6♥ if you do not hold the queen, with three key cards and to bid 7♥ holding the queen.

King Ask

Knowing you hold all the aces and king-queen of trump (some players do not require holding the queen); **5NT is the specific king's ask (SKA)!**

The specific king ask is needed for a grand slam try in the agreed upon suit or no-trump.

Responses are:

(1) Return to the agreed upon trump suit at the six-level denies any kings.
(2) With two kings, bid the cheapest at the six-level (below agreed upon trump suit); if the second king is of higher rank, bid 6 of agreed suit. Only bid 6NT if spades were bid or if it was a splinter suit.

(3) With three kings, bid 6NT.

To find a second king below the trump suit, bid the suit. Without the second king, responder bids the trump suit at the six-level. With the king, bid as follows.

(1) Make a first step response, including 6NT with Kxx(x),
(2) Make a second step response with Kxx, and
(3) Raise the ask suit with Kx.

When hearts are the agreed upon suit on does not use 5NT for the king ask; instead, the specific suit ask (SSA) bid is used as discussed later (below).

Playing 1430 RKCB, the standard is to use the specific king ask; however, some still may play the number of kings from "Blackwood" excluding the trump suit –YOU BETTER ASK your partner.

Responding with voids

Using the 1430 convention, and have a void the responses to 4NT are:

5NT = 2 or 4, an even number of keycards with a void (with 0, bid 5♦-- ignore the void)

6 of suit below the trump suit = odd number keycards (1 or 3)
6 trump suits = odd number of keycards (1or 3) with a void in higher ranking suit

Specific Suit Asks (SSA)

We have seen that one may ask for keycards, the queen of trump and having both, ask for specific kings. When searching for a grand slam, one may also need to know about an outside suit (not the trump suit). For example, do you have a queen in the suit, a doubleton, or a singleton? To ask and answer this question, one makes a Specific Suit Ask (SSA).

The specific suit asks is usually done when the captain has the queen of trump after the keycard responses of 5♣ or 5♦.

After 5♣	6♣, 6♦, 6♥, 6♠ is SSA.
After 5♦	5♠, 6♣, 6♦, 6♥ is SSA

Lacking a control (xxx) simply sign-off in the trump suit at the 6-level or pass the 6-level asking bid. With a control: Axx, Kxx, xx, xx, x one jumps to the 7-level in the trump suit.

More complicated responses are:

(1) Make a first step response, including 6NT with third-round control Qx(x), Ax, AQx
(2) Make a second step response with second-round control Kxx(x)

(3) Make a third step response with Kx

(4) Raise the ask bid with KQx and JUMP to the trump suit with a singleton

The SSA is also used in place of 5NT for the king asks when hearts are trumps since you do not want to hear 5♠, going beyond 6♥. Instead of bidding 5NT one bids 5♠ as a SSA.

Following the above pattern, the responses follow.

5NT	=	third-round control, either a queen or doubleton
6♣	=	Kxx(x)
6♦	=	Kx
6♠	=	KQ(x)
7♥	=	singleton
6♥	=	denies K – usually xxx(x) – no controls

Over Interference D0P1-R0P1 or DEP0

When the opponents interfere, most players play D0P1/R0P1. Another option is to use DEP0. While some do not use both, I recommend the use of both which depends on the level of interference and the rank of the suit bid.

If the opponents interfere at the five levels with a bid, use D0P1*,

Pass	One Keycard
Double	No keycards
1st Step suit above	Two keycards
2nd Step up	Three keycards

If the opponents interfere at the five levels with a double, use R0P1*,

Pass	One keycard
Double	No keycards
1st Step suit above	Two keycards
2nd Step up	Three keycards

*Caution – Some use these as RKC responses (0/3 and 1/4) – Partnership agreement.

However, if the bid used by the opponents is higher ranking than you're agreed upon suit you must use DEP0 and not D0P1 or R0P1.

DEP0	
Double	Even Number of keycards (0, 2, 4)
Pass	Odd Number of keycards (1, 3)

The bidding goes 1♥ pass 4NT then 5♠. Since spades is higher ranking than hearts, one must use DEP0: double is even, and pass is odd. You are still at the 5-level and the double may be passed for penalty. If instead, the opponents bid 5♣, D0P1 is used since the bid is of lower rank. Now double is zero and pass is one keycard. A bid of 5♦ hearts shows two key cards and 5♥ would indicate three keycards. If instead, the opponents doubled, one would use R0P1.

If the opponents interfere over 5NT (at the **six-levels**) use DEP0 to show number of kings, not including the trump king. Now double shows zero or two and pass shows one or three. If you play specific kings, you may not be able to show the king and hence may also revert to DEP0.

Overview: Roman Keycard Blackwood 1430

4NT when spades are the agreed upon suit (Keycard Ask)
5♣ = 1 or 4 keycards
5♦ = 0 or 3 keycards
5♥ = 2 or 5 keycards without the queen of trump
5♠ = 2 or 5 keycards with the queen of trump or holding a 6th trump

Kickback
Use four diamonds as keycard ask when CLUBS is the agreed upon suit
Use four hearts as keycard ask when DIAMONDS is the agreed upon suit
Use four spades as keycard ask when HEARTS is the agreed upon suit

Voids
5NT = 2 or 4 an even number of keycards with a void (5♦=0, ignore the void)
6 of suit below the trump suit = odd number keycards (1/3)
6 of the trump suits = odd number of keycards (1/3) with a void in a higher-ranking suit

D0P1/R0P1 Interference at the 5 level **DBL/RE-DBL:** 0 or 3 keycards and **PASS:** 1 or 4 keycards

DEP0 Interference at the 6-level **DBL:** Even # keycards (0/2/4) or **PASS:** Odd # (1/3)
QUEEN ASK: After 5♣, 5♦ is Queen Ask

Responses:
    Denial: Return to the five-level of the agreed upon suit
    6 Level of agreed Suit: With queen and **no** side-suit king or extra trump
    6 Level of Lower King Suit: With queen and king
    5NT: With queen **without** a side-suit king, but trump extra

After 5♦, 5♥ is the Queen Ask
    Denial: If spades are trump, bids 5♠, with hearts pass.
    6 Level of Lower King Suit: With queen and side king
    5NT: With queen **without** a side-suit king, but trump extra
    6NT: With queen **without** a side-suit king and 4-3-3-3 distribution

5NT is a Specific King ASK (NOT NUMBER OF KINGS)

Responses are:

(1) Return to the agreed upon trump suit at the six-level denies any kings.
(2) With two kings, bid the cheapest at the six-level (below agreed upon trump suit); if the second king is of higher rank, return agreed suit at the 6-level. If spades are bid or shown as a singleton/void is shown, bid 6NT.
(3) With three kings, bid 6NT.

SPECIFIC SUIT ASK (SSA) After 5♣: 5♥, 6♣, 6♦ is SSA. After 5♦: 5♠, 6♦, 6♥ is SSA. Make a first step response, including 6NT with third-round control Qx(x), Ax, AQx, xx

Make a second step response with second-round control Kxx(x)
Make a third step response with Kx
Raise the ask bid with KQx and JUMP to the trump suit with a singleton

With NO AGREED upon SUIT, use standard BLACKWOOD CONVENTION for Ace Asking and 5NT for NUMBER of Kings Ask

Slam Bidding with No Agreed Upon Suit

When playing 1430 RKCB, how should one proceed if there is not a prior agreement on the trump suit? Some recommend that (1) it should always be the last-bid suit, some suggest that (2) one should not play any form of RKCB, but instead just use Blackwood as an ace only ask (no keycards), others recommend (3) that RKCB be used only if the last-bid suit is a minor (opener or responder) but not a major and some play (4) that it is the last-bid suit of the responder. What is your agreement?

The approach you use must be discussed with your partner when you make out your convention card. There is no "best" or standard approach. However, let's consider a few examples.

Suppose you open one spade and partner responds two hearts (a 2/1 response), and as opener, you hold the hand: ♠AKQJ763 ♥4 ♦KQ53 ♣7. If you play the last-bid suit, you cannot bid 4NT. You might try three spades and then 4NT, but if partner bids four hearts over three spades, you are back to square one. If your agreement allows you to agree that the last-bid major with a forcing three-level raise or a splinter jump (even a fake splinter jump!) below game and this is not done, the last-bid suit is not the agreed upon suit. In the previous example, a strong case could be made to make spades the agreed upon suit if opener jumps to 4NT over two hearts. The last-bid suit works whenever you have a fit for the last-bid suit. But if you do not, it usually does not work. We consider an example.

Opener	Responder
♠KQ9863	♠A2
♥K10942	♥J7

♦Q8   ♦AK5
♣Void   ♣AKQJ104

The bidding may go:

Opener	Responder
1♠ 17.5**HLD**	2♣
2♥	3♦
3♥	4NT
6♣	7NT

Responder leaps to 4NT to ask for keycards. Since the last-bid suit was hearts, opener bids 6♣ which shows an odd number of keycards, the king of hearts and a void in clubs. Thinking that the one keycard is the ace of hearts, responder bids a grand slam, 7NT. whose fault? The fault was that they lacked a mutual agreement as to what 4NT means when there is no agreed upon suit.

If you play the last-bid suit, you will only survive a 4NT ask when you intend to play in your own suit if you hold the king of the last-bid suit. Partner is forced to answer only aces! In the above example, responder did not hold the king. Because there was no agreed upon suit, one would bid 5♣ (zero keycards). Partner would bid 6NT.

The above example suggests that one use Blackwood if there is no agreed upon suit.

To illustrate, suppose the bidding goes one heart-two clubs-two hearts-4NT. Then, since the last-bid minor suit of responder was clubs, 4NT agrees clubs. If responder wanted to agree hearts, and the partnership plays that a raise to three hearts is forcing, it is easy enough to bid three hearts and then 4NT. If a raise to three hearts is not forcing, then a jump to four diamonds agrees hearts and if partner bids four hearts, 4NT can be bid. If the responder wants to agree spades, he bids two spades or three spades, and then bids 4NT. Thus, if you do not have an agreed upon suit, you can play Blackwood or agree that one may play the last-bid minor suit of opener or responder.

With no agreed upon suit, here are my suggestions.

1. Use Keycard after any four-level bid.
2. All Kickback auctions are RKCB.
3. If two suits are agreed upon, the **FIRST SUIT BID** is trumps for RKCB purposes.
4. When none of the previous applies, use Blackwood as ace only asks.

Double Agreement Roman Keycard Blackwood (DRKCB)

With a double agreement, there are now six keycards (four aces and two kings), NOT FIVE, so we have what are called Double agreement 1430 Roman Keycard Blackwood

(DRKCB). We consider DRKCB responses for some double agreements.

1. Major-Major Agreements

a)	Opener	Responder	b)	Opener	Responder
	1♠	2♥		1♥	2♠
	3♣	3♠		3♠	4♥
	4♥	4NT		4NT	

Then 4NT is a DRKCB ask.

When responding to DRKCB asks, there are now six keycards. And **there are no void-showing responses.** The first two responses (5♣ and 5♦) of DRKCB are the same as 1430 RKCB; however, there are now three queens showing responses:

5♥	2 with neither queen
5♠	2 with lower ranking queen
5NT	2 with higher ranking queen
6♣	2 with both queens

Note that in the second step (5♠), you do not know which queen. However, if partner makes a first or second step response to a DRKCB ask (5♣ and 5♦), unless the asker has both agreed-upon suit queens, the queen situation is unknown. To now ask about queens, the asker uses the next available "free bid" step, excluding the trump suits, but including 4NT for a queen ask. The four-response steps now become:

1st step	2 with no queen
2nd step	2 with lower-ranking queen only
3rd step	2 higher-ranking queen only
4th step	2 both queens

When investigating a small slam using the double-agreement sequence, you are looking to have at least five of the six missing keycards plus at least one queen of the agreed upon suits.

Exclusion Roman Keycard Blackwood (ERKCB) Convention

The convention may be played with a known major/minor suit agreement, and you know you are in the slam zone. For example, after Jacoby 2NT* or splinter bids (direct/ambiguous) and game forcing inverted minor bids. The convention is initiated by an unusual jump to the five levels above game in your void suit. You are asking for keycards for the agreed suit (or last bid suit, if agreed) excluding the void suit. Partner does not count the ace in the void suit bid; now there are four keycards, three aces and a king. **There is really no such thing as 1430 or 3014 ERKCB.**

Responses to ERKCB

First Step	0 keycards
Second Step	1 keycard without the queen
Third Step	1 keycard with the queen
Fourth Step	2 keycards without the queen
Fifth Step	2 keycards with the queen
Sixth Step	3 keycards without the queen
Seventh	3 keycards with the queen

As with 1430 RKCB, the bid of 5NT is again the specific king ask; however, one may also use the bid of 5♠. The next step after a 0/1 or 1/4 step is the queens ask. A negative response is the next step. And with the Queen and no kings, bid 5NT. With the queen and a king bid 6x to show a king. Finally, the bid of any suit that is not the queen ask is the SSA.

What do you do after an ERKCB ask with a void? Most ignore it, but you can again bid 5NT with an even number and bid 6x to show a void and an odd number.

Returning to our Slam 3 example, opener bids 5♣ (ERKCB). Excluding the club suit, responder has one keycard (king of hearts without the Q) and bids 5♥ since 5♦=0. Partner with all the aces and a void in clubs knows it is the king of hearts. Having the queen, what next? He bids 5NT which is again the specific king ask, without the king of diamonds, partner again signs off in 6♥.

While I have stated that there is no such thing as 1430 ERKCB, some do not believe this and will respond to the jump bid as if was 1430 e.g., first step=1/4, next 0/3 etc.

So, ask your partner to review the bids to ERKCB. And I have seen that some only use steps: 0, 1, 2, and 3 keycards.

Kickback or Redwood and Minorwood

When the agreed upon suit is a minor, the use of 4NT as a keycard ask will often get the responses too high. To avoid this problem, one uses Roman Keycard Blackwood with kickback. It works as follows: if clubs are trump, then 4♦ is used to ask. If diamonds are trump, then 4♥ is used to ask. If hearts are trump, then 4♠ and not 4NT is used. When spades are trump, one always uses 4NT to ask.

One responds to the ask using each suit in order. For example, suppose the agreed upon suit is hearts so 4♠ is the asking bid, the responses are:

4NT	1/4 keycards (the 14 step) **1ˢᵗ step**
5♣	3/0 keycards (the 30 step) **2ⁿᵈ step**
5♦	2/5 keycards w/o queen of trump in agreed suit **3ʳᵈ step**
5♥	2/5 keycards with queen of trump in agreed suit **4ᵗʰ step**

What is the queen ask? After 4NT, it is 5♣ and after 5♣ it is 5♦, always the next step. Note that without the queen, you are at the five-level of the agreed upon heart trump suit.

Responding to the 4NT/5♣ Queen ask – (next step)

(1) If you **do not** hold the queen, responder **returns to the agreed upon suit at the five-level (5♥).**
(2) 5NT shows the queen, but no outside king!
(3) With both (Q of trump and one or more kings), bid at the six level of the lowest ranking king.

Knowing you have all Keycards, 5♠ is now the (SKA) when using Kickback for Hearts; the responses are for specific kings:

5NT	spade king (easy to now show higher ranking king)
6♥	0 outside kings
6♣/6♦	1 king (cheapest lower rank)

Some use 5NT for the SKA, so you best ask your partner. However, then you cannot show the higher-ranking king; and 6♥ would show no lower ranking king. Again one may do a second lower ranking king ask.

Asks that are not the Queen or the (SKA) are again used as for the SSA. All extensions follow.

If one uses 4NT for the majors and Only Kickback for the minors, it is referred to as Redwood. An alternative to Redwood is Minorwood for the minors.

The **Minorwood Convention** uses four of the agreed minors for the RKCB ask. For example, in the auction 1♦ - 2♦*, the bid of 4♦ is Minorwood – no alert needed (note some partnerships use 3♦* as Minorwood called 1-2-3 Minorwood – if you do it must be alerted); it is used instead of 4♥, kickback (Redwood). It can also be played in a sequence when kickback may be confusing. If the bid of 4♠ is confusing, an option is to bid four of a 4♣/4♦ instead of using kickback RKCB. I have heard this called the **"Bothwood" Convention.**

Instead of playing **Minorwood,** some play **Crosswood.** The difference is that with **Crosswood,** if diamonds is the agreed upon suit, then 4♣ is the 1430 keycard ask and if clubs is agreed, then 4♦ is the 1430 ask.

With a double fit in either the majors or the minors, some use Double Roman Keycard Blackwood (DRKCB).

Minorwood

Over 4♣

4♦	1 or 4 keycards (the 14 step)	1st step

4♥	3 or 0 keycards (the 30 step)	2nd step
4♠	2 (or 5) keycards w/o queen of trump in agreed suit	3rd step
4NT	2 (or 5) keycards with queen of trump in agreed suit	4th step
5♣	To Play	

Over 4♦

4♥	1 or 4 keycards (the 14 step)	1st step
4♠	3 or 0 keycards (the 30 step)	2nd step
4NT	2 (or 5) keycards w/o queen of trump in agreed suit	3rd step
5♣	2 (or 5) keycards with queen of trump in agreed suit	4th step
5♦	To Play	

Minorwood   (Queen Ask)

As before the Queen ask is initiated by bidding the next step up after showing 1/4 or 0/3 key cards (e.g., 4♥, 4♠, or 4NT).

If you do not have the queen bid the minor suit at the 5-level. With the Queen bid the agreed upon minor suit at the six level.

Minorwood   (King Ask – Specific Kings)

If one has all the Key Cards, one may ask about kings. The King-Ask is **one level higher than the Minor trump suit** (for example 5♦ if clubs is the suit and 5♥ if diamonds is the suit). Then the bid of 5NT – Denies any Kings

With two Kings, bid the cheapest at the 6-level (below the agreed trump suit); if the second king is of a higher rank bid 6NT. With three kings bid 7NT. **Note some play Number of King's Ask (Ask Partner what they Play)**

After 5♦:5♥=0, 5♠=1, 5NT=2, 6♣=3 (partner can bid 7♣ or 7NT)
After 5♥:5♠=0, 5NT=1, 6♣=3, 7♦=3 (partner can bid 7♦ or 7NT

Scroll Bids after 2NT*

Let's look at two bidding sequences:

(A) 1♠ - 2NT* - 3♣*/3♦*/3♥* which shows a singleton or a void in the suit bid.
(B) 1♥ - 2NT* - 3♣*/3♦*/3♠* which shows a singleton or a void in the suit bid.

To determine whether partner has a singleton or a void, one bids as follows.

For sequence (A), one bids: 4♣/4♦/4♥, and for sequence (B), one bids: 4♣/4♦/4♠. A scroll-up bid at the four levels. Do you have a singleton or a void?

Responses become:

Next cheapest bid shows a singleton
(Step 2) shows 1 or 4 keycards with a void
(Step 3) shows 0 or 3 keycards with a void
(Step 4) shows 2 or 5 keycards without the queen and a void
(Step 5) shows 2 or 5 keycards with the queen and a void

Thus, one is easily able to determine singleton and void with Keycard Blackwood. Let's look at an example:

Opening 1♠ and responding 2NT*, suppose partner hears the bid 3♥* that shows a singleton or void in hearts. After hearing the bid of 3♥*, one next makes the next sequential bid 4♥ to ask whether it is a singleton heart or a void (**note, the bid of 4♠ is a sign-off**). The responses follow.

4♠	heart singletons (next cheapest step)
4NT	heart void with 1 or 4 keycards (step 2)
5♣	heart voids with 0 or 3 keycards (step 3)
5♦	heart voids with 2 keycards without the queen (step 4)
5♥	heart voids with 2 keycards with the queen (step 5)

Similarly, opening 1♥, the responses after hearing for example 3♠* (a spade singleton or void), and one would bid 4♠.

The responses follow.

4NT	spade singleton (next cheapest step)
5♣	spade void with 1 or 4 keycards (step 2)
5♦	spade void with 0 or 3 keycards (step 3)
5♥	spade voids with 2 keycards without the queen (step 4)
5♠	spade void with 2 keycards with the queen (step 5)

Note that the asking bids and responses provide all the information required to bid slam or to sign off at the five-level, below slam.

Example: East is Dealer

		♠	J9		
		♥	A984		
		♦	J109		
		♣	Q1086		
♠	K10642			♠	AQ875
♥	10632		**N**	♥	7
♦	AQ	**W**	**E**	♦	K765
♣	A3		**S**	♣	1K42
		♠	3		
		♥	KQJ5		
		♦	6432		
		♣	J965		

North	East	South	West
	1♠	Pass	2NT*
Pass	3♥*	Pass	4♥*
4NT	Pass	5♣	Pass
6♠ Pass	Pass	Pass	

East has 15**HLD** points and west has 18.5**HLDF** (3+0.5+1L+6.5-1AQ+4.5 +1D+2F +1♠K) points and bid 2NT*. The bid of 3♥* shows a Singleton/Void (S/V). The first next step bid asks if it an S/V where the next first step response says it is a singleton. 4NT is 1430 and 5♣ shows 1/4 keycards: with an Ace missing, west bids 6♠.

Slam Bidding Examples

Slam 1
Opener   ♠A7 ♥AQ65 ♦84 ♣AKQ98
Responder   ♠KQ5 ♥ K843 ♦KQJ6 ♣7

Opener		Responder	
1♣*	23.5**HLD**	1♦*	15.0**HL**
2NT		3♦	
3♥		4♥	
4♠		4NT	
5NT		6♦	
6♥		Pass	

The opener has 23.5**HLD** points and responder has 15.0**HL** points and bids 1♦*. Rounding down opener bids 2NT=21-23**HLD** points. Responder next bids 3♦so opener now knows he has 13+points and next bids 3♥. With the 8-card heart fit and the singleton responder has 15+1+3=19**HLDF** points and bids 4♥. Next, the 4♠ bid is kickback for the agreed suit, hearts. 4NT shows one Keycard. 5NT is the SKA and 6♦ says yes, I have the heart king plus the ♦K. Opener next bids 6♥.

Using traditional methods, the bidding went:

Opener	Responder
1♣ =12-21	3NT =13-15
4♣ Expert Gerber	4♥=0/3
4NT	Pass

Slam 2

Opener	♠AJ7 ♥AQJ753 ♦AQ98 ♣ void
Responder	♠K5 ♥ K1084 ♦8765 ♣AK9

Opener		Responder	
1♣*	25.5**HLD**	1♦*	14.0**HL**
2♥		3♥	
5♣		5♥	1 w/o the Q
6♥		Pass	

After you agree hearts, opener cannot bid 4♠ as kickback with the void. Instead, the bid of 5♣ is made or ERKCB for hearts excluding clubs. Responder has one keycard excluding clubs without the Queen and bids 5♥. Opener bids the slam.

Using traditional methods, the bidding may go:

Opener		Responder
1♥	12-21h	2NT*=Jacoby
3♣	S/V	4NT
6♣	1/3 of keycards w S/V in clubs	6♥
Pass		Pass

Slam 3

Opener	Responder	Comments
♠A10732	♠KJ5	
♥A982	♥KQJ63	
♦K2	♦A94	
♣Q7	♣A5	

Opener	Responder	
1♠	2♥	(1) Double Agreement
3♥	3♠ (1)	(2) DRKCB
4♥	4NT (2)	(3) 2 with neither queen
5♥ (3)	6♥ (4)	(4) Q♠ is missing

Slam 4	6♥ (4)	(4) Q♠ is missing
Opener	Responder	Comments
♠A8732	♠KJ5	
♥AQ95	♥KJ632	
♦A2	♦K94	
♣A5	♣Q7	

Opener	Responder	
1♣*	2♦* transfer to ♥	(1) 3-Controls (A/K or 3K's)
2♥	3♦*(1)	(2) Double Agreement
3♠	4♠(2)	(3) DRKCB
4NT (3)	5♥(4)	(4) 2 with neither Q
5NT (5)	6♦(6)	(5) SKA
6♥	Pass	(6) ♦K

Remember to use DRKCB you must have two keycards to begin the DRKC asking bid of 4NT. Queen asks are more easily used with kickback DRKCB sequences. If available, 5NT is the SKA bid.

Slam 5	Pass	(6) ♦K
Opener	Responder	Comments
♠AK1086	♠J2	
♥5	♥A96	
♦A5432	♦Q87	
♣K9	♣AJ1052	

Opener	Responder	
1♣*18.5**HLD**	1♦* 13.5**HL**	(1) 15.5**HLF** points
1♠	2♣	(2) Kickback for Diamonds
2♦	3♦(1)	(3) 2Keycards with Q
4♥(2)	5♦(3)	
6♦	Pass	

Using traditional methods, the bidding may go:

Opener	Responder	
1♠	12-21HCP	2♣
2♦	2♥* fsf	
3♦	4♦	
5♦	Pass	

Slam 6

Opener	Responder	Comments
♠AQ986	♠KJ105	
♥K1054	♥A9	
♦-	♦8765	
♣KJ84	♣AQ2	

Opener	Responder	
1♣* 19.0**HLD**	1♦* 16.0**HL**	(1) 5 controls
2♠	3♠ (1)	
4♥	4♠	
5♦	6♣	
7♣	7♥	
7♠	Pass	

This example is from a tournament where the two players were playing Precision and counting only H points. The bidding went:

Opener	Responder
1♠ 13H	2♠ 14H
3♥	4♣
4♦	4♠
Pass	Pass

Playing "traditional" 2/1 opener has 14HL points and again the grand slam would not be bid.

Slam 7	Pass
Opener	Responder
♠A6	♠105
♥1054	♥AKQ9
♦K8543	♦AQ87
♣AK7	♣Q82

Opener	Responder
1NT 15.0**HLD**	2♣ 17.5**HL**
2♦ no 4-card major	2♥
3♦	6NT Add F points for diamond fit (15+19.5=34.5)

At other tables the bidding went:

Opener	Responder
1NT	4NT = Quantitative
Pass	Pass

Not one pair at the tournament reached the slam playing traditional methods. Note playing the Modified Optimal 2/1-Club System bids like 1NT - 2NT, 1NT-4NT are never used since they ignore the opportunity to find secondary suit 8-card fits. This is also the case for the Grand Slam Force convention. We do not need these conventions.

Slam 8 Dealer East N-S Vulnerable

	North	
	♠ J9	
	♥ A984	
	♦ J109	
	♣ Q1087	

West		East
♠ K10642	N	♠ AQ875
♥ 10762	W E	♥ 3
♦ AQ	S	♦ K765
♣ A3		♣ K42

	South	
	♠ 3	
	♥ KQJ5	
	♦ 6432	
	♣ J965	

Suggested Bidding:

West	North	East	South
		1♠	Pass
2NT*	Pass	3♥*	Pass
4♥*	Pass	4♠*	Pass
4NT	Pass	5♣	Pass
6♠	Pass	Pass	Pass

*Alerts

91

West with 19.5**HLDF** points bids 2NT* showing a game-forcing raise with at least four spades. The bid of 3♥* shows a singleton or void. Hearing shortness, and with four hearts, east bids 4♥* to ask whether west if it is a singleton or a void. The first level bid of 4♠* shows a singleton. Now, west bids 4NT (1430 Blackwood) to ask about keycards. The response 5♣ shows one or four; with an ace missing, west signs off in 6♠.

Slam 9

Dealer North N-S Vulnerable

	♠ KJ832	
	♥ A92	
	♦ Void	
	♣ AK1084	
♠ Q9	N	♠ 5
♥ 10764	W E	♥ J83
♦ A965	S	♦ KQJ103
♣ 97		♣ Q653
	♠ A10764	
	♥ KQ5	
	♦ 872	
	♣ Q2	

For this example, the bidding goes:

North	East	South	West
1♣*	Pass	1♥*	Pass
1♠	Pass	3♦*	Pass
5♦	Pass	5♥	Pass
6♣	Pass	6♥	Pass
7♣	Pass	7♥	Pass
7♠	Pass	Pass	Pass

*Alerts

North 22**HLD** points and South has 11.5**HL** points. 1♥* is a transfer to spades and after the accept bid to show the fit, the bid of 3♦ shows 3 controls (AK or KKK). The bid of 5♦* is ERKCB. And 5♥ shows 1/4 excluding diamonds. Cue bidding gets the North-South to the Grand Slam.

Slam 10

East-West Vulnerable South Deals

		♠	K1064		
		♥	A2		
		♦	854		
		♣	A865		
♠	2			♠	975
♥	KQJ973		N	♥	1065
♦	KJ7		W E	♦	962
♣	1032		S	♣	J974
		♠	AQJ83		
		♥	84		
		♦	AQ103		
		♣	KQ		

Playing traditional 2/1 the bidding at one table the bidding went:

South	West	North	East
1♠	2♥	3♥	Pass
3♠	Pass	4♣	Pass
4♦	Pass	4♠	Pass
4NT	Pass	5♦	Pass
5♠	Pass	6♠	All pass

At other tables instead of making the cue bid of 4♣ some bid 4♠ with 12HL points and the South passed missing the slam and playing in a spade game.

Using the Modified Optimal 2/1-Club approach, south has 22.5**HLD** [7.5H+1Q+1L+7H+5H+1D) points and would open 1♣*, and west would over call 1♥. North has 12.5**HL** points, and bids 2NT*=12/13+ (see Chapter 8). East passes and south bids 3♠ natural. With spade support south bids 4♠*= 5 controls. North bids 6♠.

1430 Baby Blackwood in Serious 3NT*

The bid of 3NT* may be used in a variety of artificial ways in possible slam auctions when playing the Modified Optimal 2/1-Club System. Consider auctions of the following type:

West	East	West	East
1♠	2♥	1♠	2♣
3♥	3NT*	2♥	3♠
		3NT*	

What does the bid of 3NT* mean?

Clearly, not to play! The problem is that neither player has limited his hand. At this point, both east and west could have near maximum hands with reasonable controls or could have substantial extra values. In both bidding sequences, we have agreed upon a major, hearts and spades, respectively.

At this point, I suggest that the bid of 3NT* be used as1430 Baby Blackwood which must be alerted since it is a keycard ask below the 4-level. It begins the keycard sequence at a low level and allows one to bail out at the five-level of the major.

It can also be used as "Serious" 3NT* convention proposed by Eric Rodwell which merely proposes slam interest as an artificial bid not as keycard asks. See for example Rodwell (2017), "Eric Rodwell's Bidding Topics" Book 1, page 133. If one does not bid 3NT*, one begins a cue bidding sequence! It is a courtesy cue bid in case partner has substantial extra values. The cue bidder usually has a near minimum. If he has substantial extras, he bids 3NT*, saying that he is "serious" – with slam interest. Hence with a minimum, the bidding might be:

West	East	West	East
1♠	2♥	1♠	2♣
3♥	3♠/4♣/4♦	2♥	3♠
		4♣/4♦	

This sometimes is referred to as non-serious no-trump or frivolous no-trump.

With no interest in slam, one would sign off in four of the major and not bid 3NT or cue bid. If you cue bid, there are some important rules:

(1) A cue bid in partner's bid suit shows one of the top three honors (A/K/Q). (2.) A cue bid in your own bid suit shows two of the top three honors. (3.) A cue bid in an unbid suit shows any first or second round control (A/K/singleton/ void). Cue bidding is always done up-the-line. By skipping a step, you deny an appropriate "control" in the step you skipped. 4NT is always RKCB (1430/3014).

Slam bidding is the most rewarding and possibly one of the toughest aspects of the game. You must make one-trick decisions, and if you're wrong (either way), the penalties are severe. The bid of 3NT* (as 1430) is a tool that may help you improve your decision-making.

When using this convention or others, it's important to remember the three aspects that make slams:

1. Power. Playing tricks and total points define the joint power of the hands.
2. Controls. If the opponents can take the first (in seven) or first two (in six) tricks in any suit, you will go down. So, you need to assure you have the necessary first and second round controls.
3. Trumps. Obviously, not important for NT slams, but in a suit, the trump suit must be both long enough to generate tricks and solid enough to not lose two.

Examples of serious 3NT*

Case 1:

Opener	Responder
♠KJ765	♠AQ2
♥A98	♥7
♦Q2	♦AKJ1098
♣Q56	♣A54

Opener	Responder
1♠	2♦
2♠	3♠
4♦	4NT
5♥	7NT

Opener's 4♦ denies serious slam interest (else 3NT*) and denies first or second round club control (else 4♣) but shows one of the top three honors in diamonds. Responder can count thirteen tricks.

Case 2:

Opener	Responder
♠AQJ98	♠K432
♥J7	♥KQ
♦K987	♦AQJ43
♣Q7	♣J9

Opener	Responder
1♠	2♦
3♦	3♠
3NT*	4♥
4♠	Pass

Opener's 3NT* shows serious slam interest. Responder's 4♥ bid shows two keycards. Opener's 4♠ bid is an absolute sign-off. Responder, despite holding extra values, must pass. Note: If you did not use "Baby 3NT," you may have over bid!

Case 3:

Opener	Responder
♠K98	♠Q7
♥AJ10765	♥K32
♦97	♦AQ10654
♣K7	♣AQ

Opener	Responder
1♥	2♦
2♥	3♥
3♠	3NT*
4♥	Pass

When hearts are agreed at the three-level, opener must bid 3♠ if he has a control in spades. Any other bid would deny a spade control (3NT* would be Baby Blackwood - Serious 3NT). Responder has extra values and shows this by bidding 3NT*. 4♥ shows two keycards, and responder passes.

If there is one lesson to be learned from this discussion, it is that there is significantly more too effective bidding than merely writing down the name of a convention or a system on your convention card. Good partnership agreements are considerably more important than the system you play. If you and your partner decide to play a complex non-standard system, put in the time and do it right. Discuss your auctions and make sure you understand why you make bids and what they mean! When you truly understand your system, you will start to see the benefits in your results.

Cue bidding for Slam

Cue bidding sequences are critical to reaching a slam in game force auctions. In addition, we have been warned: (1) don't use Blackwood with a worthless doubleton; (2) if you use Keycard Blackwood (without kickback) and want to investigate slam in a minor, the use of 4NT can be disastrous. So, how do you investigate slam? The answer is by using cue bidding,

To stimulate how you might use cue bidding, we look at two examples from the 2005 Bermuda Bowl round-robin event. How would you bid the following hand?

West	East (dealer)
♠ Q10832	♠ K754
♥ K2	♥ A84
♦ AK1085	♦ Q74
♣ 5	♣ A92

East with 12.5**HLD** (-1 for 4333) opens 1♦*; west with 14.5**HL** points bids 1♠. East now bids 2♠ to establish the suit fit.

Having determined a fit in spades, East must reevaluate the hand: +1 for 8-card fit +1 for K in spade suit or 14.**5HLDF** points. West has a strong hand but with singleton and a doubleton in a suit cannot bid 4NT He next bids 3♣ since 2NT would show a weak balanced hand. The bidding goes:

East	West
1♦	1♠
2♠	3♣ Control Cue bid
3♥ Cue Bid	3NT*
4♣ 1 Keycard	4♦ Queen ask
5♦ yes and ♦K	5♥ (Control Cue Bid)
5♠	6♠

Did you reach the spade slam? If you did not, do not feel bad, the contract by both teams in the Bermuda Bowl was four spades making six.

One final comment on cue bidding, while a cue bid at the 4-level may show an Ace or a King, first or second round control in a suit. Any control bid at the 5 level must show an Ace.

Dealer North N-S Vulnerable

	♠	KJ832	
	♥	A92	
	♦	Void	
	♣	AK1084	

♠	Q9		♠	5
♥	10764	N	♥	J83
♦	A965	W E	♦	KQJ103
♣	97	S	♣	Q653

	♠	A10764
	♥	KQ5
	♦	872
	♣	Q2

For this example, the bidding goes:

North	East	South	West
1♣*	Pass	1♥*	Pass
1♠	Pass	3♦*	Pass

5♦	Pass	5♥	Pass
6♣	Pass	6♥	Pass
7♣	Pass	7♥	Pass
7♠	Pass	Pass	Pass

North has 22**HLD** points and South has 11.5**HL** points. 1♥* is a transfer to spades and after the accept bid to show the fit, the bid of 3♦ shows 3 controls (AK or KKK). The bid of 5♦* is ERKCB. And 5♥ shows 1/4 excluding diamonds. Cue bidding gets the North-South to the Grand Slam.

Roman Keycard Gerber (RKCG)

After one agrees on a major, the bid of 4♣ is played as 1430 Keycard Gerber. Partnerships that do not play kickback also use 1430 Keycard Gerber to keep the bidding at a low level, in place of 4NT.

Responses to 4♣ RKCG

4♦	1 or 4 keycards
4♥	0 or 3 keycards
4♠	2/5 keycards without the queen
4NT	2/5 keycards with the queen

To show a void with two or four keycards, bid 5NT; with and odd number of keycards, bid the void at the six-level. After a void bid, next step is SKA.

4♥/4♠ over 4♦/4♥ is queen asks

4♠	SSA

4NT	To play

Suppose you have the following hand: ♠AJ7 ♥AK105 ♦KJ76 ♣98. Your partner opens 1NT. Do not ever make a quantitative bid! Why? If you make a Quantitative Raise, you will not be able to bid Stayman. If you and your partner can find an 8-card major fit, you can often make slam with only 31-32 points, so it behooves you to always try Stayman first.

To deal with this type of hand, **you need two bids: one to ask for Key Cards when partner bids the right major—the one you also have—and a different bid to make a Quantitative Raise when partner bids the wrong major—the one you don't have.**

The solution is simple, **after a Stayman inquiry and a major answer, a jump to 4NT is Quantitative**: "You bid the wrong major, partner. Pass or bid 6NT." **A jump to 4♣ is Roman Key Card Gerber, agreeing to the major that was bid.**

Roman Keycard Blackwood over Preempts

When your partner preempts, there are many ways to investigate the hand further. For two-level preempts, one may bid 2NT to ask your partner for a feature or you may use the Ogust Convention, Modified Ogust, Two-step Ogust, Roudinesco rebids, Romex rebids, the McCabe Adjunct Convention, etc.

Need better information regarding the trump suit. We may at times use the Kantar **Four Club Convention** or the **Weak Roman Keycard Blackwood (WRKCB) Convention** over the weak 3-level bids 3♣/3♦/3♥/3♠ and the bid of 2NT.

The responses are to 4♣ are:

4♦	first step 0 keycards in the agreed suit
4♥	second step, 1 keycard without the Queen
4♠	third step, 1 keycard with the Queen
4NT	fourth step, 2 keycards without the Queen
5♣	fifth step, 2 keycards with the Queen

The only step in which the queen is not known is the first step. The next bid of 4♥ is the Queen ask --- 4♠ = no and 4NT = yes. A jump over the four hearts bid (5♣/5♦/5♥/5♠) is the Specific Suit Ask (SSA).

After the preemptive bid of 3♣, the bid of 4♣ is natural, it advances the preempt; a jump to 4♦ is WRKCB ask for clubs. The responses follow.

4♥	first step 0 keycards in the agreed suit
4♠	second step, 1 keycard without the Queen
4NT	third step, 1 keycard with the Queen
5♣	fourth step, 2 keycards without the Queen
5♦	fifth step, 2 keycards with the Queen

Over 4♥, 4♠ is the Queen ask --- 4NT = no and 5♣ = yes. Over the four spades bid, (5♦/5♥/5♠) is the Specific Suit Ask (SSA).

Let's look at an example.

Opener	Responder
♠ A 7	♠ K 2
♥ K 10 9 8 7 6 5	♥ A Q 2
♦ 7	♦ A Q 6 5 4 2
♣ K 4 5	♣ A 7

Opener Bids	Responder Bids
3♥	4♣ (1430 WRKCB for hearts)
4NT (2 w/o)	5♦ (SSA for diamonds)
6♥ (singleton ♦)	7♥
Pass	Pass

CHAPTER 5

MORE ON PREEMPTS WITH REBIDS

In chapter 1 we reviewed opening 2-level major suit preempts and 3-level preempts for the majors and the minors, the bids of 2NT* and Gambling 3NT*. An overview of the bids for the Modified Optimal 2/1- Club System discussed so far are as follows.

1♣*	Artificial 18+**HLD** points any distribution
1♦*	12-17**HLD** artificial with 0-2 diamonds
1♥/1♠	12-17**HLD** and 5+ Majors
1NT	15-17**HLD** All Seats with Crawling Stayman
2♣*	15-17**HLD** 5/6+ Clubs (may have a 4-card major)
2♦*	15-17**HLD** 7-diamonds
2♥*/2♠*	12-14**HLD** 6-cards
2NT*	12-14**HLD** 5-5 in the Minors
3♣*	12-14**HLD** 7+clubs
3♦*	12-14**HLD** 6-diamonds
3♥*/3♠*	12-14**HLD** 7-card Suit
3NT*	GAMBLING solid 7+ minor suit (AKQxxxx)

In this Chapter we review higher level opening preempts, responding to 2-level minor suit preempts and 3-level preempts, responding to 2NT*=21-23**HLD** after the bid of 1♣*, and defense against the opponent's preemptive bid.

Preemptive 4-level Major Suit Bids

A 4-level bid of 4♥/4♠ in the 1ˢᵗ and 2ⁿᵈ seats show a good, but not necessarily a solid, 8+card suit with 7-8 playing tricks (non-vulnerable)/8-9 playing tricks (vulnerable), without a 4-card side suit, and 12-14**HLD** points.

♠52 ♥ AK987654 ♦3 ♣J9 non – vulnerable 7.5H +4L+2D=13.5**HLD**

♠QJ765432 ♥ 74 ♦K5 ♣6 vulnerable 12**HLD** = 3.0H +4L+3H+2D

NAMYATS

NAMYATS was created by Sam Stayman who, after creating the Stayman 2♣ response to partner's no-trump opener, coined the NAMYATS Convention using his name in reverse order. The NAMYATS Convention, allows one to differentiate between a strong distributional hand, which may provide a slam opportunity with less opponent interference, and a preemptive bid that has no slam opportunity.

It shows a strong 8+ card major card suit that is too good to open a preemptive bid of 4♥/4♠ but often good enough to open 1♣*. The suit has 8 ½ - 9 playing tricks (with no help from partner).

The major suit has two of the top three honors non-vulnerable and three of the top five honors vulnerable, and both require an outside ace or protected king. Thus, you almost have game in hand; partner must only cover one loser in a major game contract. The bids use the minor preemptive four-level bids:

4♣*   transfer to hearts
4♦*   transfer to spades

If responder bids the transfer suit, this usually denotes no interest in slam. However, if one bids the next step (the gap), it indicates slam interest in the major.

4♣*   4♦ slam interest
4♦*   4♥ slam interest

Since we are using the preemptive 4-level minor suit bids for the majors, we defined 3NT* as showing along strong minor.

General

In first and second position, 4♣* and 4♦* openings show "good" four-level preempts in hearts and spades respectively. The requirements for such an opening are:

1. exactly two key cards (five aces and trump king), and
2. no more than one uncontrolled suit, and
3. a losing trick count of at most five, and
4. at most three of the nine side-suit aces, king, and queens, with no side suit containing all three of these honors, and
5. a main suit at least as good as
   1. KQT9xxx or KQJxxxx or a side void, when holding a seven-card main suit, or
   2. KQxxxxx when holding at least an eight-card main suit, and
6. if holding a void, opener must also hold
   1. An uncontrolled suit and a main suit of at least AKQxxxx or AKxxxxx
   2. A suit lacking first- or second-round control but holding third-round control (doubleton or queen) and a weaker main suit.

A controlled suit is one in which the ace or king is held, or one in which at most one card is held.

Responding to NAMYATS

After 4♣* opening

Responder may inquire with 4♦ when holding at least 2 key cards and some prospects of slam, or make other descriptive slam tries, or sign off in opener's suit at the four level. After the inquiry, in auctions where specific holdings are shown, "strong" holdings (void and honor combinations) are shown naturally, and uncontrolled suits are shown in the order other-major, clubs, diamonds.

4♦				Inquiry, showing at least two key cards
	4♥			Minimum requirements
	4♠			Better than minimum, unspecified void
		4NT		Inquiry
			5♣/5♦/5♥	Club/diamond/spade void
	4NT			Better than minimum, no void, all suits controlled
	5♣/5♦/5♥			Better than minimum, no void, no control in spade/club/diamond suit
	5♠			AKQxxxxx with two singletons and a KQx suit, or AKQxxxxx with one singleton and two Kx suits, or KQJxxxxx with two singletons and a AKx suit
		5NT		Inquiry
			6♣/6♦/6♥	Club/diamond/spade suit with KQx, Kx or AKx respectively according to the hand type held for the 5S response
	5NT/6♣/6♦			AKQxxxxx and a spade/club/diamond suit of KQJx with two singletons, or AKQxxxxx and a spade/club/diamond suit of KQx with a singleton and a Kx suit
	6♥			AKxxxxxx, two singletons and a Kx suit
4♥				To play
4♠/4NT/5♣				Spade/diamond/club void, slam interest and at least one key card
5♦				Small doubleton trump, three side aces and possibly nothing else
5♥				Small singleton trump, three side aces and nothing else

After a 4♦* opening

Responder may inquire with 4H when holding at least 2 key cards and some prospects of slam, or make other descriptive slam tries, or sign off in opener's suit at the four level. After the inquiry, in auctions where specific holdings are shown, "strong" holdings (void and honor combinations) are shown naturally, and uncontrolled suits are shown in the order other-major, clubs, diamonds.

4♥			Inquiry, showing at least two key cards
	4♠		Minimum requirements
	4NT		Better than minimum, unspecified void
		5♣	Inquiry
		5♦/5♥/5♠	Diamond/heart/club void
	5♣		Better than minimum, no void, all suits controlled
	5♦/5♥/5♠		Better than minimum, no void, no control in heart/club/diamond suit
	5NT		AKQxxxxx with two singletons and a KQx suit, or AKQxxxxx with one singleton and two Kx suits, or KQJxxxxx with two singletons and a AKx suit
		6♣	Inquiry
		6♦/6♥/6♠	Diamond/heart/club suit with KQx, Kx or AKx respectively according to the hand type held for the 5NT response
	6♣/6♦/6♥		AKQxxxx and a club/diamond/heart suit of KQJx with two singletons, or AKQxxxx and a club/diamond/heart suit of KQx with a singleton and a Kx suit
	6♠		AKxxxxxx, two singletons and a Kx suit
4♠			To play
4NT/5♣/5♦			Heart/club/diamond void, slam interest and at least one key card
5♥			Small doubleton trump, three side aces and possibly nothing else
5♠			Small singleton trump, three side aces and nothing else

Holding the following hand, what do you open?

♠KQJ76543 ♥ 74 ♦A5 ♣6

The hand is too strong to open 4♠ with 21.5**HLD**. Playing NAMYATS one would open the bidding 4♦*.

2♣* Openings (5/6 clubs)

Responder's responses

Pass	0-6**HLD**
2♦*	7+**HLD** conventional asking for 4-card major, forcing for one round

Opener	Rebids
2♥	4-card ♥ suit
2♠	4-card ♠ suit
2NT	15-17**HLD**, 5/6-card club suit

3♦*	requests opener to clarify stoppers

Opener	Bids
3♥*	♥ stopper
3♠*	♠ stopper
3NT	♥ and ♠ stoppers
4♣	no stoppers

3♣	12-14**HLD** with 5/6- club suit
3♦	12-14**HLD** with 4+diamonds
3NT	Solid club suit

2♥/2♠	Natural with 4-cards, 7-9**HLD**

3♣	12-14**HLD** with clubs
3M/4M	15-16**HLD** 4-card support/17**HLD**
3NT	To Play

2NT*	**Lebensohl (for two-suited hands – 10+HLD)**

Opener Bids   3♣* (may be passed)
Responder next bids

3♦*	=	5-5 diamonds and hearts
3♥*	=	5-5 hearts and spades

3♠*	=	5-5 spades and diamonds

3♣	10+**HLD** with 3- clubs
3♦/3♥/3♠	5+ card suit, 10+**HLD**
4♣	Minorwood for clubs
4♥/4♠	Natural and to play

With interference

Redouble	10+**HLD**
Cue bid	12+**HLD**
2X bid	7-9**HLD** and NF and denies 2 clubs

(1)

What do you bid? Partner opens 2♣* and you hold ♠K986 ♥QJ87 ♦ Q98 ♣K5.
Clearly 2♦*= Do you have a 4-card major?

(2)

Opener:	♠Q2 ♥432 ♦KJ6 ♣KQJ1097
Responder:	♠A102 ♥KQ9865 ♦954 ♣9

Opener has 16.0**HLD** [1(Qx) +4+7.0 +3Q+2L-1 no A] and opens 2♣*. Responder has 13.5**HL** (4.5+7+2D) and bids 3♥. Opener next bids 3NT and responder bids 4♥.

(3)

Opener:	♠76 ♥AQ7 ♦105 ♣AQ10952
Responder:	♠KJ543 ♥98 ♦AJ542 ♣K7

Opener has 17.0**HLD** (6.5 +1D+7.5+2L) and opens 2♣*. Responder has 14.5**HL** (4+5.5+1L+3+1D) and bids 2NT*. Opener next bids 3♣* and responder bids 3♦*; opener next bids 3♥ and responder bids 3NT.

2♦* Openings (6-card)

Responder's responses

Pass	0-6**HLD**
2♥/2♠	Natural with 4-cards, 7-9**HLD**
2NT*	**Lebensohl (for two-suited hands -10+HLD)**

        Opener Bids   3♦* (may be passed)
        Responder next bids

3♥*	=	5-5 hearts and clubs
3♠*	=	5-5 spades and hearts
4♣*	=	5-5 clubs and spades
3♣*		10+**HLD** with 4+clubs
3♦		10+**HLD** with 2+diamonds
3♥/3♠		10+**HLD** with 5+ major
4♦		Minorwood for diamonds
4♥/4♠		Natural and to play

With interference

Redouble	10+**HLD**
Cue bid	12+**HLD**
2X bid	7-9**HLD** and NF denies 2 diamonds

Example:

Opener:	♠KQ ♥32 ♦KJ109876 ♣Q2
Responder:	♠A102 ♥KQ9865 ♦95 ♣J10

Opener has 15.0**HLD** [5 +5+4L+1(Qx)+1**D**-1 no A] and opens 2♦*. Responder has 13.5**HL** [4.5+5+2L+1**D**+1(J10)] and bids 3♥. Opener next bids 3NT.

3♥*/3♠* Openings (7-cards)

How many times has your partner opened 3-level major and you find yourself with a very good hand? Suppose you pick up the hand: ♠AQ ♥AKQ6542 ♦ A10 ♣ 84

And your partner opens three spades. What do you bid? The problem revolves around what your partner has in the club suit.

Or consider the following two hands and partner opens 3♥=12-14**HLD**

(1) ♠KJ109765 ♥32 ♦K76 ♣A   17.5**HL** (5+3Q+4L+3+3.5-1 no Q)

(2) ♠KJ109763 ♥32 ♦K9 ♣AQ   21.5**HL** (5+3Q+4L+3+6.5)

To find the best contract one may use ASKING BIDS over a natural three/four-level bid.

For a three-level bid, any JUMP response in a suit is an asking bid in that suit.

Thus, after 3♠ followed by 5♣* asks, what do you have in clubs?

After 3♦ followed by 4♥* asks, what do you have in hearts?

Following a FOUR-level bid, any five-level bid becomes an asking bid.
After 3/4♥ the bid of 4/5♦* asks, what do you have in diamonds?
After 4♠, the bid of 5♣* asks about clubs.

These bids do not interfere with normal bidding procedures because a new suit in response to a preemptive bid is usually forcing so that responder need not jump to game. Thus, the jump bid may be used more profitably. When opening at the four-level, opener should have a good suit and responder is not likely to have a better suit. Hence, responder is more likely to make an asking bid.

Asking Bids

Let's consider an example with the sequence: 3♠ followed by 5♣*. What do you have in clubs?

Responses to asking bids ALWAYS start with the next suit.

First Step - two or more quick losers' xx, xxx, xxxx - skipping NT
Second Step - singleton
Nearest NT bid regardless of step = king
Fourth Step - ace
Fifth Step -A-K/A-Q
Sixth Step - Void

Example 1:

Opener: ♠43 ♥654 ♦AK10943 ♣43	13**HLD** (1D+8+3Q +2L -1 no Q)
Responder: ♠87 ♥AKQJ1098 ♦J4 ♣AK	26.0**HLDF** [10.5+3Q+2L+1F+1SF +7.5]

The bidding goes, 3♦ followed by 4♠*. What do you have in spades? The bid of 5♣ (first step shows two quick losers and responder bids 5♦. The bit of 4NT would have shown a ♠K, closest NT, and responder would bid 6NT to protect the king.

Warning: THERE IS NO DISASTER WORSE THAN A MISUNDERSTOOD ASKING BID! The asking bids discussed here are based upon: Edwin B. Kantar (1974), "Bridge Conventions," Wilshire Book Company.

Partner opens 3♥* and you hold the following hand: ♠A84 ♥KJ2♦A93 ♣10862.

You have 15**HLDF** [4.5+4+3F + 4.5 -1(4333)] and you know partner has between 12-14 points with a 7-card heart suit. Your total points are between 27-29 total points. Do you bid 3NT or 4♥? You must think tricks and not points given your weak club suit. Which is easier 9 or 10 tricks? Unless partner has at least Jx, in clubs you may not be unprotected in clubs with the balanced hand (losing 4-clubs). So bid 3NT and not 4♥, a safer contract with a higher percentage of success.

3♣* Openings (7-clubs)

Responder's responses

Pass	0-7**HLD**
3♥/3♠	Natural with 5-cards, 8-10**HLD**
3NT	13+**HLD** with stoppers
4♣	11+**HLD** with 2+clubs
4♦	11+**HLD** with 6+diamonds

With interference

Redouble	10+**HLD**
Cue bid	12+**HLD**
2X bid	**8-9HLD**

3♦* Openings (6-diamonds)

Responder's responses

Pass	0-7**HLD**
3♥/3♠	Natural with 5-cards, 8-12**HLD**
3NT	13+**HLD** with stoppers
4♣	11+**HLD** with 2+diamonds
4♦	11+**HLD** with 6+clubs

With interference

Redouble	10+**HLD**
Cue bid	12+**HLD**
2X bid	**8-9HLD**

Partner opens 3♦*=12/14 with 6-diamonds, and you hold ♠82 ♥A74 ♦K10732 ♣A96 and your RHO passes, what do you bid where all are non-vulnerable?

You have 16.5**HLDF** (4.5+3.0+0.5+1L+3F+1 for♦K+4.5-1 no Q) points or 28.5-30.5 total points. Passing is out of the question as is 4♦ since it does not prevent the opponents from bidding 4♠ (with a diamond void) or making a takeout double. Bid 3NT. On a club or heart lead you make 7 diamonds + 2 aces and will survive if spades are 4-4. If they run 5-spades you are down 1 for -50 which is better than 5♦'s doubled for down 1 or for -100, and the opponents may be intimidated from entering the auction.

Stayman after 2NT*

After a 1♣* opening bid, at some point opener may make a re-bid of 1NT*=18-20**HLD**, or 2NT*=21-23**HLD** points. Again, the Stayman Convention may be used to locate a 4-4 major suit fit. Over 2NT* the asking bid becomes 3♣; an artificial bid to inquire whether partner has a four-card major. The convention is so engrained in bridge that it need not be alerted. Opener's responses are:

3♦	no 4-card major
3♥	denotes a 4-card heart suit, but may have 4 spades
3♠	denotes a 4-card spade suit

To initiate the convention over 1NT* requires 5+**HLD** points since opener now has 18+ points not 15-17. However, over 2NT*=21-23, it requires 3+**HLD** points.

Responder's rebid, with game going values, will be either 3NT or a raise of opener's major to game with a fit. With more than an opening hand, cue bids or jump bids are used to investigate slam.

What happens if partner bids 3♦* (no four-card major)? Then the bid of 3♥/3♠ shows a hand that is 5-4 in the majors where the suit bid has four cards. If you are 6-4 in the majors, once again uses, as with the one no-trump opening, extended transfer bids.

Is there a Garbage Stayman Convention over 2NT? Yes, it works as follows. After the bid of 3♣, if partner responds 3♦, your next bid is 4♣ "pick a major".

With the magic 4=4=4=1 distribution, you may still use Drop Dead Stayman and pass any suit bid by the opener after bidding three clubs.

Jacoby Transfers Four-Way

Over the bid of 2NT*, transfers to the majors when responder has 5+ cards are called Jacoby Transfers. After the bid of 2NT*, responder makes the following bids, promising at least 5+ cards in the transfer suit (the bids are announced, not alerted).

3♦	transfers to hearts (announce)
3♥	transfers to spades (announce)
3♠*	transfer to clubs (alert)
3NT*	transfer to diamonds (alert)

Opener's responses for **majors' suit transfers**

3♥	shows only 2 hearts
4♣/4♦	shows 5 hearts and at least 4 cards in the bid minor with slam interest
4♥	shows 4 hearts and mild slam interest
4♠	Roman Keycard Blackwood with kickback for hearts (Chapter 3)
3♠	shows only 2 spades
4♣/4♦	shows 5 spades and at least 4 cards in the bid minor with slam interest
4♠	shows 4 spades and mild slam interest
4NT	Roman Keycard Blackwood for spades (Chapter 3)

When responder is 5-4 in the majors, the other major is bid showing the distribution.

Opener's responses for **minor suit transfers**

3NT	shows good clubs, 3 pieces with 2 of top 3 honors (e.g., AQx, AKx, KQx, etc. - super accept)
4♣	poor clubs or doubleton
Pass	shows good diamonds, 3 pieces with 2 of top 3 honors (e.g., AQx, AKx, KQx, etc. - super accept)
4♣	poor diamond support
4♦	diamonds no honors or doubleton

After a club transfer, responder can next bid, after 3NT, 4♣ to play with 6+ clubs. Any other suit bid (4♦ /4♥/4♠) shows slam interest with perhaps four cards in the bid suit.

After a diamond transfer, you can correct the bid of four clubs to five diamonds with 6+ diamonds and a weak hand (you cannot pass). If you have interest in a diamond slam, bid 5♣ as super Gerber over four clubs. After the bid of 4♦, bid 4♥ as Roman Keycard Blackwood with kickback.

Texas Transfers (4♦ and 4♥)

After opener bids 2NT*, suppose you have a six-card major with game going values and no interest in slam. Using the principle of fast arrival, one employs the four-level bids of which are announced.

4♦	transfers to hearts (announced)
4♥	transfers to spades (announced)

Bidding after an Opponent's Preempt

Most of the bridge literature has been written about defending against weak three-level bids. Examples include the optimal double, 3NT for takeout, Fishbein, Lower Minor, Smith, Weiss, FILM, Reese, and Two-Suiter takeout, etc. Many of these approaches involve numerous artificial bids that most players FORGET. Our goal is to keep it simple because there is no optimal system. The underlying principle that you must use is to devise a system that enables you to reach your own BEST contract and do not worry too much about penalizing the opponents.

5-level Bids

To play straight penalty doubles at this level does not make sense. Opener will always have a long and strong single suit and the opponents are trying to steal the contract! DOUBLE should always be for takeout, not penalty, and the bid of 5NT shows the two lowest unbid suits. This can be played in both the second and fourth positions.

4-level Bids

When the preemptive bid is made at the four-level, one has more options. We consider each in turn.

(1)   Over 4♣ or 4♦

Again, a double is for takeout suggesting a good hand with no clear-cut bid and all four-level bids are natural. A cue bid usually indicates a two-suiter (both majors) and perhaps a three-suited rock crusher.

(2)   Over 4♥

Here, 4NT is not natural but a takeout bid for the minors. Double is for PENALTY, but I have tolerance for the other suits, particularly for spades. Partner, please decide. (3) Over 4♠.

Here, 4NT is generally takeout and again double is primarily for penalty. Partner will again pull the double on a very shapely hand. Alternatively, a double may be used for takeout; then, 4NT is used to show the minors. Discuss this with your partner.

For more information, see Brian Senior's (1984) "Defending against Pre-empts," by Apsbridge Services Ltd.

Mc Cabe Adjunct

When your partner opens a weak two bid and they double, what are your options?

With a weak hand, the contract usually belongs to the opponents; hence your partners bid should help you with the lead since it may be the opponent's contract. A convention developed by Mr. J. I. McCabe of Columbia, South Carolina, United States does just that. His article was published in January 1994 issue of *The Bridge World*.

The Mc Cabe bids are:

A simple raise of partner's weak two bids show an Ace or a King in the bid suit. With this information the weak two-bidder may lead the suit. A bid in a lower ranking suit is also lead directing. It also shows an Ace or a King. And it suggests to the weak two- bidder to bid again without interference.

Without a fit, partner bids 2NT* as a relay to three clubs. Responder then corrects or bids a new suit at the three level. The opening bidder must pass. However, if responder next bids partners weak two bid suit at the three level, after the relay bid of three clubs, he denies a good lead and it again shows an Ace or King in the weak two-bidder's suit and a good hand.

Some partnerships reverse the meaning of Mc Cabe's Adjunct.

Mc Cabe Adjunct (reversed)

In this method, raising partner bid suit **denies** an Ace or a King and merely advances the preempt. A new suit at the two level is to play. A three-level bid over a major suit bid shows an Ace or King in the major bid. 2NT* is again a relay to three clubs and is as in the Mc Cabe Adjunct. A redouble of the bid suit shows a strong hand, it is designed to punish the opponents.

To be more specific with reverse Mc Cabe, we have the following structure.

2♥* - X then	Redouble shows a strong hand
2♠	=Spades
2NT*	=Clubs (partner bids clubs)
3♦*	=transfer into suit bid suit shows A/K of Hearts
3♥*	=No A/K of Hearts
2♠*- X then	Redouble shows a strong hand
2NT*	=Clubs (partner bids clubs)
3♥*	=transfer into suit bid suit show A/K of Spades
3♠*	=No A/K of Spades

Over 2♣* all two-level bids are natural and 3♦* shows A/K of diamonds; the bid of 3♣* shows the A/K of clubs.

CHAPTER 6

OVERCALLS AND TAKE OUT DOUBLES

Suit Overcalls

Overcalls are complicated and countless books have been written about them. However, there are basically only four common types of overcalls: simple overcalls, no-trump overcalls, jump overcalls, and two-suited overcalls.

We briefly discussed a simple 1-level overcall in Chapter 3.

To open 1M requires 12-17**HLD** points; however, for a suit overcall in a competitive auction one needs 12-17**AOC** points for a 1-level bid and for a 2-level overcall bid one needs 15-17**AOC** points. Evaluation of **AOC** is a 3-step process:

(1) Starting Points HLD
(2) Adjustments for Opponent's suit length and Honors Held in their suit
(3) Adjustments for Honors in 3 or 4 suits Outside the Opponents' suit

Do not let vulnerability influence your decision or use the commonly used Culbertson's rule of "2 or 3" (i.e., do not go down more than 2 -tricks vulnerable or more than 3-tricks non-vulnerable). Use the Adjusted Optimal Count. Recall that the adjustments are:

Overcall Suit Adjustments

Deduct -1 point for 3-cards in the opponent's suit
Deduct -2 point for 4-cards in the opponent's suit
Deduct -3 point for 5-cards in the opponent's suit

Add +1 for a singleton in the opponent's suit (i.e., 2**D** becomes 3**D**)
Add +1 for a void in the opponent's suit (i.e., 4**D** becomes 5**D**)

The opponents open 1♥ open and you hold:

♥xx	No adjustment
♥xxx	-1L point
♥Axx	-1L point = 3.5 points (4.5-1L)
♥Axxx	-2L point = 2.5 points (4.5-2L)
♥Kxxx	-2L point = 1.0 points (3.0-2L)
♥x	+1D so total =3D
♥ -	+1D so total =5D

A second factor that effects an over call bid are **honors in and outside the opponent's suit**. The honors in 3 and 4 card suits and lone honors help to determine whether your hand is more defensive than offensive orientated.

Overcall Honor Adjustments

(1) Honors in Opponent's Suit

Kxx/Kxxx (K alone) deduct -1 point (regardless of position) with KJx or Kx no adjustment
K with Q -1 when before opponents' suit
+1 when after opponents' suit
Qxx/QJx no adjustment

J **without** a 10 -0.5 (e.g., Jxx/Jxxx J alone); otherwise, no adjustment

(2) Honors in 3/4 card side suits

Kxx/Kxxx alone -1 point with Q/J no adjustment
Jxx/Jxxx alone -0.5 with 10 no adjustment

(3) No other honor adjustments

A simple overcall at the one-level requires 12-17**AOC** points and includes 2 zones 12/14 and 15/17; for a 2-level bid one needs 15-17**AOC** points.

Playing "traditional" 2/1, many use the rule that a simple, non-jump, 1-level overcall bid requires only 7-17H points and a 5-card suit and with 18+, one must X and bid.

For example, on BBO recently after the bid of 1♣, 12 of 20 pairs over called 1♥ with the following hand: ♠J98 ♥ KJ965♦ 7 ♣ QJ75. A hand with only 8H (9.5**HLD**=9.5**AOC**) points. Partner with ♠KQ ♥ 1087♦ AKJ987 ♣ Q10 bids 3♦ and they ended in 4♥ doubled for down 3! Yes, a poor decision. Why? Few points and only a 5-card suit.

A one-level overcall often shows a 6+ card suit with an A/K. Why is it useful to have an A or a K? The over call bid always suggests an opening lead if you do not win the contract. If you do not satisfy the over call criteria, it is often better to best to pass and wait for partner to bid. **Do not overcall with a jack high six-card suit.**

With 18+**HLD** one doubles and bids (over a 1♣ bid, one makes a power X). If you are in the lower range 12/14**AOC** **DO NOT X and PASS** it forces partner to the 2/3 level; however, in the in the middle range 15/17**AOC**, you may double and then perhaps invite.

Many duplicate bridge players are afraid with a strong 4-card major (e.g., AKQx) at the 1-level. This may be because they are afraid, they will be penalized, or they are an afraid partner will raise with only three cards, or if after passing they may be afraid partner will return to the major suit and bid. All these fears are unfounded. The advantages of the major overcall are that it is lead directing, it allows one to compete aggressively for a part score, it allows one to get a bid in early, and it often disturbs the bidding of the opponents.

When overcalling with a four-card major one may use the following guidelines.

1. The four-card major overcall should only be made at the one level.
2. Overcall at the one level with 12/14**AOC**.
3. Overcall at the two level with 15/17**AOC**.

(1) The opponents open 1♣ and you hold ♠65 ♥KQJ98 ♦AJ3 ♣Q32 what is you bid? You have (6H+1L +1Q +4.5+1+1.5) = 15**HLD** = **15AOC** no adjustments, bid 2♥.

(2) The opponents open 1♥ and you hold ♠QJ9 ♥K65 ♦KQ9832 ♣7 what is you bid? You have 14**HLD** (-1 for no Ace -1 for 3 hearts -1 for ♥K) = 12**AOC**. Don not over call 2♦.

(3) Let's change the hand in (2): ♠QJ9 ♥5 ♦KQ9832 ♣765. Now we have 14.5**HLD** + 1 for singleton in the opponent's suit=15.5**AOC,** so now overcall 2♦.

(4) The opponent's open 1♦ and you hold: ♠A984 ♥5 ♦K32 ♣KQ765. You have 4.5+2+3+5+1L=15.5**HLD** (-3 for 3 diamonds -1 for ♦K) = 11.5**AOC**. Do not overcall 2♣.

(5) The opponent's open 1♦ and you hold: ♠AQ987 ♥56 ♦K3 ♣KJ43. You have [6.5+1L+1D+3+4 -1 no Q] = 13.5**HLD** = 14.5**AOC**. **Do not X you need 15AOC.** While you would prefer a 6-card suit when making an overcall, the boss spade allows one to overcall 1♠ with only 5 spades.

Responding to a Suit Overcalls

With 3+card support, provided the opponents pass, you should:

Raise one level	with 7/9**HL**
Jump-raise	with 10/12**HL**
Bid game	with 13+**HL**

With no major suit fit, bid no-trump provided you have a stopper in the opponent's bid suit.

1NT   with 7/9**HL**

2NT   with 10/12**HL**

3NT   with 13+**HL**

If you do not have a stopper, or three-card support for partner's overcall suit, bid your own five-card suit with13+**HLD**/13+**AOC**. How do you play the bid of a new suit? You may play it Forcing for one round, non-forcing constructive, or non-forcing (see the back of your convention card). What is the meaning of a cue bid of the opponent's suit?

In general, a cue bid of the opponent's suit is always forcing. All good hands start with a cue bid! However, the responses to a major overcall and a minor overcall are different.

Let's look at the major overcall, the bidding goes:

1♣ - 1♠ - pass – (?)

1NT	7/9**HL**, non-forcing
2♣	asking bid, how good is your overcall (10/12**HL**)
2♦/2♥/2♠	non-forcing
2NT	10/12**HL**, with club stopper and non-forcing
3♣	**Fit Bid forcing with 4-card support**
3♦/3♥	Very good suit, non-forcing constructive
3♠	Preemptive non-forcing
3NT	13+**HL**, to play with stopper

If partner overcalls 1♦/1♥, you may follow the same general rules as above. However, if you have stoppers in the opponent's suit and 11/12**HL**, you should consider not raising partner's suit but instead bid 1NT. No-trump will often be the easiest game to make, especially if you have at least a partial fit with partner's suit (at least doubleton honor).

Example 1:

The bidding goes 1♦ and you hold ♠KQJ43 ♥QJ65 ♦7 ♣K102. You have (6+1Q+1L+3+2D+3.5-1 for no Ace) = 15.5**HLD** (+1 for singleton in opponents' suit) =16.5**AOC**.

Your partner (the advancer) has: ♠98 ♥K943 ♦986 ♣AQ97 has 9**HL** and bids 1NT.The bidding has gone:

North	East	South	West
1♦	1♠	Pass	1NT
Pass	2♥	Pass	4♥

West may now add 2 points for your 8-card heart fit with the King honor and 2**D** points for the spade doubleton with 4 trumps for 13**HLDF** points and bid 4♥.

Not playing the Optimal Modified 2/1-Club System, many traditional 2/1 pairs may pass 1NT with only 12H points and a 5-card suit.

Example 2, playing 2/1 at a recent regional tournament, East and West had the following hands:

West:♠7 ♥Q654 ♦K75 ♣AK984   East: ♠K543 ♥982 ♦76 ♣QJ82.

North	East	South	West
1♦	2♣	Pass	3♣
Pass		3♦	4♣
X	Pass	Pass	Pass

X – Down 2! What went wrong?

After West's over call of 2♣, East has 11**HLDF** points, enough for a raise. However, West has a 5-card club suit with 15**HLD** points – (+1point for 3 diamonds and -1 for the ♦K) = 13**AOC**; not enough for his 2-level overcall bid and should not have bid 2♣.

Jump Overcalls

J-R Vernes found that weak jump overcalls were effective only when your hand was short in the over called suit, a suit with a singleton or void. He called the difference between your own long suit and the opponents short suit Delta (D). He also observed that for a bid to be effective, a jump over call at the 2-level should have a D=5: a 6+card suit (or its equivalent, a 5-5 two suited hand) with a **singleton** in the suit opened and 16**HD** points.

A jump over call at the 3-level needs a D =6: a 6+card suit (or its equivalent, a 5-5 two suited hand) with a **void**, and for a 7-card suit and a **singleton** you needed 18+**HD** points. **These jump overcalls must be altered they are not weak!** Playing 2/1 most make weak jump over call bids.

Example 1: The opponent's open 1♥ and you hold: ♠ AK10987 ♥ KJ76 ♦54 ♣ 7

Do you bid 1♠/2♠? You have a 6-card suit with a singleton (D=5) with 14**HD** (4.5+3.0+0.5+4.0+2D). **So do not bid 2♠.**

What about **AOC?** 16**HLD** with 4-cards in hearts = (-2 no honor adjustment for KJ in opponents heart suit, no adjustment for honors in other 3/4 card suits) =14**AOC**; so, bid 1♠.

When making jump overcall bids you should consider both D and AOC/

Example 2

Dealer West N-S All Non-Vulnerable

	♠	
	♥	AQ9876
	♦	K7
	♣	QJ1087

♠	KJ10732
♥	64
♦	AQ7
♣	K9

and

♠	9865
♥	7
♦	J1032
♣	A653

	♠	AQ8
	♥	KJ52
	♦	9432
	♣	654

West has 16.5**HLD** (3+1+1+2L+4.5+2+3) and opens 1♠.

As North do you bid 2♥ or 3♥?

You have 6-hearts with a void with D=6, but only 17.5**HD** not 18**HD** so bid 2♥* not 3.

South with 4-hearts and 15.5**HLDF** bids 4♥ since a 2-level bid requires 15.5**AOC**.

Note that North has 20.5**HLD** [4+4.5+2+2L+3+2+1+1+1L].

East next bids 4♠. Now what? North with the spade void has no defense against 4♠ and bids 5♥ which is doubled for a good N-S result since E-W can make 4♠.

Observe if North has a D=5 and south has a D=1 (4hearts - 3 spades), that the total D=7 added to 13 cards in a suit suggests 19 probable tricks. This means East/West can make 10 tricks in spades and North/South only 9 tricks in hearts. So, bid to the 5-level (5♥) for down 1.

Example 3

The opponents open 1♦ What is your overcall with each of the following hands?

(a) ♠AK10987 ♥765 ♦7 ♣KQ7   D=5 14.5**HD** bid 2♠; 16.5**HLD**; 17.5**AOC**

(b) ♠K107 ♥ AQ107654 ♦5 ♣87   D=6 13**HD** bid 2♥; 17**HLD**; 18**AOC**

(c) ♠AQ109876 ♥K105 ♦- ♣543   D=7 15**HD** bid 3♠; 19**HLD**; 20**AOC**

Example 4

Both Vulnerable and the opponents open 1♥

And you hold ♠987 ♥A4 ♦AQ105432 ♣7 should you compete?

You have 7 diamonds with a D=5 and 14**HD** and 18**HLD**, and 18**AOC**. Yes!

Bid 3♦*. However, bidding 5♦ doubled over 4♥ would be very expensive!

Example 5

The opponents open 1♥, and you hold ♠KQ1065 ♥654 ♦A109 ♣76; should you bid 1♠? No! You have 11.5**HLD** points and 10.5**AOC** points (-1 for 3 hearts).

Example 6

The opponents open 1♥ and you hold ♠7 ♥654 ♦AQ9876 ♣KJ4; should you bid 2♦*? You have 13.5**AOC** points, not enough for a 2-level bid.

But suppose you held: ♠AQ10654 ♥7 ♦1098 ♣KJ4. You have 16.5**HLD**=16.5**AOC** points. Now D=5 with, but only 13.5**HD** points, bid 2♠.

Jump overcalls at the 2-level show a 6-card suit, so you need a fit and quick trick (aces and kings) to consider a game. If you're weak or if you lack support for partner's suit, you should generally pass. If you do have a fit (3+card support) and a few tricks, you may make a simple raise usually below game. A raise is not invitational; it is only furthering the jump bid. You need about 10+**HLDF** points to bid game.

1NT Overcall

When considering a 1NT overcall bid, holding 4+ cards in the opponent's suit is neither a liability or an asset since it may not generate an additional trick or add any additional protection. However, if the opponent's card were in another suit, it would add offensive value to the hand by having 5-cards in a side suit. Hence, one must deduct -1 point for having 4-cards in the opponent's suit; but not 2. And holding 5-cards, while rare, is a greater liability so one must make a -2-point adjustment.

NT Overcall Suit Length Adjustments

Deduct -1 point for 4-cards in the opponent's suit
Deduct -2 point for 5-cards in the opponent's suit

NT Overcall Honor Card Adjustments

Deduct -1 point for a King alone (Kxx/Kxxxx) in any 3/4-card suit
Deduct -0.5 points for a lone Jack in any suit

The ACBL regulations state that a direct overcall of 1NT shows 15-17/18 Points with a stopper (most often) in the opponent's bid suit. This is considered "standard" and need not be alerted. For now, let's assume you are playing the standard approach. Then the bids for NT overcalls are as follows.

15-17/18AOC	Overcall 1NT
19-21AOC	Double and then bid 1NT
22-24AOC	Double and then jump to 2NT
25-27AOC	Double and bid 3NT (or double and cue bid)

(1) The opponents bid 1♠ and you hold: ♠A98 ♥ K654 ♦A5 ♣QJ107. You have 16**HLD** [(4.5 + 3 +4.5+4) – 1 alone K] = 15**AOC,** overcall 1NT.

(2) Change the hand to ♠K98 ♥ KJ4 ♦AJ5 ♣QJ67. You have 14.5**HLD** points (-1 for 4333 -1 for a lone K) = 13.5**AOC** points. You are in the lower range do not X, but Pass.

(3) Change the hand to ♠AJ8 ♥ KQ54 ♦A5 ♣QJ107. This hand has 19**HLD**=19**AOC**. It is too strong, X and then bid 2NT.

(4) In a recent team tournament event, west and east had the following hands:

West: ♠AQ8 ♥ AQ54 ♦K53 ♣1075 and East: ♠K74 ♥ 102 ♦9862 ♣KJ82

And in one of the rooms, the bidding went:

South	West	North	East
1♥	1NT	X	All Pass

Down two for -500. Why? West has 13**AOC** (6.5+6.5 +3 -1 4333 -1 for 4 hearts -1 for lone ♦K) not 15H points. An incorrect over call bid using the Work/Goren 4-3-2-1point count method. West must not bid but pass as would be the case using the OPC method.

When you overcall 1NT, many play that their bidding systems are on over a X or 2♣ or you may play systems off.

Systems On

Most partnerships play that all systems are on which means you do not differentiate between a 1NT openings from the overcall bid of 1NT. Thus, Stayman, Jacoby Transfer, etc. are all in effect over a X or 2♣.

Systems Off

Alternatively, you may play those systems are off. If you do, one does not use transfer bids.

Keeping systems off allow you to bid at the 2-level. All 2-level bids are "drop" dead bids and 3NT is to play. All 3-level bids show a 5card suit. If you overcall 1NT and partner cue bid's the opponents bid suit, it is Stayman.

Consider this: If your LHO opens 1♠ and your partner overcalls 1NT, you can only play one of the remaining three suits at the two-level, and that's hearts. What if you want to play two diamonds or two clubs? You can't if you play systems are on.

If your LHO has about 12 points and your partner has 16, then there are only about 12 points left for your RHO and you. Sometimes you don't get your fair share, right?

Look at your partner's hand and yours.

Opener ♠ KJ9 ♥ AJ107 ♦QJ8 ♣ K87   Responder ♠ 876 ♥ 7 ♦109762 ♣ 5643

Where do you think it plays best? Not 1NT. Responder's hand has no values for partner, but if you play it in two diamonds, the hand may take several tricks. If the A/Q of spades and the ♣A are on your left, you will make two diamonds.

If you don't play natural bids at the two-level, you will either pass and apologize for such a poor hand or play at the three-level. Good luck.

Suppose you have a good hand? When you hold points there are several ways to show them.

You can cue bid the opponent's suit and partner should respond as though it were Stayman. You can discover a 4-4 fit by using a cue bid, the convention is called Cue bid Stayman.

You can also jump to the three levels with an unbalanced hand and a good suit. Let your partner decide what to do.

Summary

When you have some points, you don't have a problem playing Systems On. It's when you don't have them, which is more likely, that you need a way to find the best contract using Systems Off. Rather than playing in a hopeless NT contract, you might consider not playing Systems On, then if your partner overcalls 1NT bid naturally and if you have <7**HLD** and a balanced hand, you should pass.

1x – 1NT – Pass -?
2y = to play 7-9**AOC**
2x= Stayman at least 8/9**AOC** and a 4-card major
3y= invitational values and unbalanced hand 10+**AOC**

Over a 1NT overcall bid, most play that the bid of 2NT shows a 1NT hand (15-17). If it does not show a NT hand but is unusual for the minors, then the 1NT overcall bid must be alerted.

1NT Overcalls in the Balancing Seat (Range/Inquiry Stayman)

The bid of 1NT in the balancing seat usually shows 12-14**AOC**. However, if partner doubles and then bids 1NT, he should have 15-17**AOC** when playing a strong NT system. This usually works well when the opponents open with a minor; however, when opening with a major there is less room to bid since partner must now bid at the two level.

To solve this problem, over a major suit opening bid the balancing no-trump bidder usually has more values, 15-17**AOC**. To avoid getting too high, one uses the Range/Inquiry Stayman convention. Now a bid of 2♣ is not only Stayman, but also an asking bid. With 12-14**AOC**, you make the normal response of 2♦ with no 4-card major or respond two of a major if you have one.

If, however you are in the 15-17**AOC** range you next bid 2NT, delaying your normal Stayman response. Partner next continues with the re-Stayman bid of 3♣ if he wants to know if you have a four-card major.

Reuben Advances

How many times have the opponents opened a club and your partner overcalls a major and you have the other major or a good minor suit and no support for your partner's major. What should you do? If you bid a new suit, is it Forcing or NF constructive? There is no accepted standard; however, most partnerships play it as NF constructive.

However, you play it, you in general need a good suit to prefer it to partner's overcall. What is needed is a method of showing a good suit, even if you have a bad hand. Jeff Rubens, editor of "Bridge World" recommends the use of transfers.

Here is how it works, with a few modifications, after the bid of 1♣ - 1♠ - pass - ?

1NT	natural
2♣*	transfer to diamonds
2♦*	transfer to hearts
2♥	cue bids (takes the place of the bid of 2♣, a strong bid)
2♠	natural with support for spade

With interference 1♣ - 1♠ - 2♣ - ?

X*	transfer to diamonds
2♦*	transfer to hearts
2♥	cue bids (a support bid too strong for a natural raise)
2♠	natural supports

Similarly, after the sequence 1♣ - 1♥ - pass - ?

1♠	natural
1NT	natural
2♣*	transfer to diamonds
2♦	cue bids (a support bid too strong for a natural raise)
2♥	natural support bids

With interference 1♣ - 1♥ - 2♣ - ?

2♦*   transfer to spades
2♥   natural with support
2♠   cue bids (support bid too strong for a natural raise)

If the overcall is a touching suit 1♥ - 1♠ - ?

2♣   natural, forcing one round
2♦   natural, forcing one round
2♥   support bid too strong for a natural raise
2♠   natural with support

Let's investigate a few examples to see how the transfer works, your partner bids 1♠ natural and you hold the following hand:

♠5 ♥987 ♦ KQJ865 ♣J43 what do you bid?

You have a very weak hand 12.5**AOC**; hence you must bid 2♣* transferring partner to diamonds and pass. Alternatively, suppose you have the hand:

♠5 ♥K87 ♦ AQJ865 ♣QJ6 with 18.5**AOC**

You again bid 2♣*, however, after hearing 2♦ by partner you bid 2NT. If partner has no interest in notrump because of weak clubs, he may return to 3♦ and you would bid 5♦.

In the above example, we had only a single spade. With at least two spades and one honor, you can transfer and then support spades. This sequence shows good diamonds and some support for the major.

Continuing, suppose you have a hand that has shortness in spades with great hearts.
For example, you hold the hand:

♠5 ♥AQJ843 ♦J107 ♣543 what do you bid?

Now you bid 2♦* to transfer to hearts. Because you have a weak hand, you then pass.

With a stronger hand you may raise hearts. For example, if your hand was:

♠5 ♥AQJ843 ♦AJ7 ♣543 or even better with ♠Q5 ♥AQJ843 ♦QJ10 ♣A43

You would again bid 2♦* as a transfer to hearts, but instead cue bid 3♣ to invite notrump.

What if the opponents bid at the two level? Can we still employ a transfer system? Yes!

For example, suppose we have the sequence:

If the overcall is a touching suit 1♠ - 2♥ - pass

X*	transfer to diamonds
2♠*	transfer to clubs
2NT	natural
3♣*	transfer to diamonds
3♦	cue bids (support bid too strong for a natural raise)

The "Under-call" ♣ Convention

In a competitive auction, after the opponent's open 1♣ and you overcall a major, the responder will make a negative X to show the other major. Or you make an overcall and win the contract and the weak hand is on lead? Is there a convention you can use that can prevent the often-used negative double or ensure that the strong hand leads?

The answer is YES; let us look at an example.

In the second seat, after the bid of 1♣, you pick up at favorable vulnerability the following hand.

♠AQ9873 ♥432 ♦ J8 ♣A7 what do you bid?

Not playing the under-call club, most with 14**AOC** would bid 1♠ to show a good suit and lead directing! However, if you win the contract, the weak hand is on lead. In many situations it is better to get the strong hand on lead. Thus, you want your partner to play the contract. To accomplish this goal, you may use the "Under-call" ♣ Convention that is based upon transfers.

The convention applies ONLY over the opening bid of 1♣. In the direct seat, the overcall bids are:

1♦* = transfer to hearts (5+ hearts) (12/14**AOC**)

1♥* = transfer to spades (5+ spades) (12/14**AOC**)

1♠* = transfer to diamonds (12/14**AOC**)

1NT* = shortness in clubs = Take Out X (12+**AOC**)

X= 18+**HLD=power X**

2♣* =both majors -15/17**AOC**
2♦* = transfer to hearts -15/17**AOC**
2♥* = transfer to spades - 15/17**AOC**
2♠* = 5-5 in the majors -15/17**AOC**
2NT* = 5+diamonds and 5+hearts (two lowest unbid suits) -15/17**AOC**

What do you gain by using the transfer bids?

1) You get partner to declare the hand in your long suit, putting the strong hand opening bidder on lead.

2) With diamonds, you preempt their one-level overcall by bidding 1♠.

3) You escape a penalty double if partner happens to hold length in the suit you bid and shortness in the suit you have shown.

4) You get to make two bids (usually) for the price of one, since most of the time partner will bid your suit or something else and you get to make another bid (standard transfer advantage).

5) By transferring into your major suit, it may take away their negative double.

Now, let's look at the complete deal and employ our new "Under call" club convention

♠ AQJ873		
♥ 432		
♦ J87		
♣ A		

♠ 2		♠ 64
♥ AQ75	N W E S	♥ J108
♦ KQ10		♦ 654
♣ K10973		♣ Q8642

♠ K1095		
♥ K96		
♦ A632		
♣ J5		

Not playing the Under-call Club Convention, north would overcall a spade and N-S would reach a part score or game in spades and make eight or nine tricks with east leading the jack of hearts.

Playing the Under-call Club Convention, the bidding would proceed as follows.

West	North	East	South
1♣	1♥*	Pass	1♠
Pass	3♥**	Pass	4♠
All Pass			

*Alert
**Help suit game try – alert

With south playing the contract, west leads the king of diamonds. South wins the ace, cashes the ace of clubs, leads a trump to hand and ruffs a club, draws a second trump, and leads a diamond toward dummy, ending in hand. A heart is discarded on the thirteenth diamond. If west started with two diamonds, he is end-played. If west started with four diamonds, he gets out with a diamond and declarer wins the jack, leads a third trump to hand and plays a diamond, throwing a heart. Now, west is end-played. Four spades bid and made - but only from the south side.

It is true that even if south plays the hand, a club or spade lead with defeat 4♠, but only if west defends perfectly. After winning the first round of diamonds, he must shift to a heart, leading away from AQxx. It is not that easy!

What do you lose by playing the Under-call Club Convention?

You lose the ability to hear partner bid 1♥ or 1♠ to show a 4-card suit as he would after a 1♦ overcall. Also, if you bid 1♠ with diamonds, committing your side to the two level, you will need a better diamond suit than for a 1♦ overcall.

Can you refuse the transfer? Yes, bid 1NT without a fit (a void or only one card in the transfer suit, with three cards – accept the transfer). Or you can bid your own 5+ suit. And, if they interfere, you can pass without support. Finally, you can bid 2♣* to ask over caller to bid his second suit.

Let's look at few more examples: The opponents open 1♣ and you hold the following hands:

(1) ♠ 975 ♥ A75 ♦ AK1096 ♣ 75

(2) ♠ K75 ♥ A75 ♦ AK1096 ♣ 75

(3) ♠ A75 ♥ A75 ♦ AK1096 ♣ 75

For hand (1), you would bid 1♥ as a transfer to diamonds (lead directing); however, with hand (2), you would bid 1NT as takeout (tells partner you have 12+**AOC** and can support all suits), and with hand (3), you would double 18+**HLD**.

Finally, with the following hand: ♠ AKQJ7 ♥ 7 ♦ 987652 ♣A, you would bid 1♥ (transfer to spades) and (if necessary) perhaps bid diamonds later (e.g., if partner bids 2♣).

This is the basic Under-call Club "Transfer" Convention; it is best played only over a 1♣ bid (provided the club bid is not the strong Precision Club).

However, you may also play transfers over other one-level opening bids as follows. Discuss these additional transfers with your partner if you want to include them with the system (optional).

WHAT HAPPENS IF THEY OPEN 1♦? Can we extend the transfer bids? Yes!
One can again use transfer bids:

Opener	You
1♦	1♥* = transfer to spades (12/15**AOC**)
	1♠* = transfer to hearts (12/15**AOC**)
	1NT* = shortness in diamonds – take out (13+**AOC**)
	X= **18HLD** with shortness
	2♣*= 4-4 in the majors (15/17**AOC**)
	2♦*= transfer to hearts (15/17**AOC**)
	2♥* = transfer to spades (15/17**AOC**)
	2♠* = 5-5 in the majors (15/17**AOC**)
	2NT* = 5+clubs and 5+hearts (15/17**AOC**)

WHAT HAPPENS IF THEY OPEN 1♥?

Opener	You
1♥	1♠* = transfer to clubs (12/15**AOC**
	1NT* = shortness in hearts – take out (12+**AOC**)
	X= 18+**HLD** with stopper in hearts
	2♣*=transfer to diamonds (15/17 **AOC**)
	2♥*=transfer to spades (15/17**AOC**)
	2NT* = 5+clubs and 5+diamonds (15/17**AOC**)
	3♥* = transfer to spades (15/17**AOC**)

AND FINALLY, if they open 1♠

Opener	You
1♠	1NT* = shortness in hearts – take out (12+**AOC**)
	X= 18+**HLD** with shortness in diamonds
	2♣* = transfer to diamonds, may have a 4-card major (15/17**AOC**)
	2♦* = transfer to hearts (15/17**AOC**)
	2♠* = transfer to clubs (15/17**AOC**)
	2NT* = 5+clubs and 5+diamonds (15/17**AOC**)

The convention proposed here is an extension of the Under-call Club Convention discussed in "Bridge Conventions in Depth" (2003) by Matthew & Pamela Granovetter by Master Point Press.

Offensive versus Defensive Power

In a competitive auction one must decide when your hand is offensive or defensive. With offensive power a person is more likely to overcall with a direct bid or a transfer depending on your agreement. While if the hand is not offensive but defensive, has more defensive than offensive power, then you should not bid but defend or double the opponent's contact penalty.

Let's look at two hands

(A) ♠KQJ108 ♥A5 ♦K10 ♣54   (B) ♠Q10987 ♥K10 ♦AKJ3 ♣54

Hand (A) has 18**HLD** and may generate 5 to 5.5 tricks, but against a club contact maybe only 3. However, it is clearly an offensive hand.
Hand (B) has only 15**HLD** even though the honors in each hand are identical: an Ace, 2 Kings, a Queen, a Jack and two 10's. Clearly a defensively orientated hand.

The OPC method in general tends to decrease the point count in a hand that is more defensive than offensive.

In a competitive auction one compares **AOC** points. Let's return to example 2 above. North has 19.5**AOC** (-1 for lone ♦K) and West has 15.5**AOC** (-1 for lone ♣K). Thus, N is more offensive than W.

Offense to Defense Ratio (ODR)

For a given hand, the Offense to Defense Ratio is defined as:

ODR=**HL** in 4 or 5+ suits/**HD** in the 3 or less card suits

Returning to Example 2 above: For North ODR=(4.5+2+2L+5)/3=13.5/3=4.5 and for West ODR=(5+2L)/(4.5+2+3+1D) = 7/10.5=0.66.

Takeout Doubles

A double of a suit bid normally shows 12+**AOC** points. However, if the opponents bid 1♣, unless it is a strong club, a X is a power X which signifies a hand with 18+**HLD** points. Responds as if X (partner had bid 1♣*).

Example - Dealer West All Non-Vulnerable

♠	AQ82	
♥	AK764	
♦	AQJ	
♣	9	

♠ 6	N	♠	10753
♥ Q983	W E	♥	J52
♦ K62	S	♦	54
♣ AK1052		♣	Q643

♠	KJ94
♥	10
♦	109873
♣	J87

The Bidding

West	North	East	South
1♣	X	Pass	1♦*
Pass	1♥	Pass	1♠
Pass	4♣*	Pass	4♥
Pass	6♠	Pass	Pass

The X by north is a power X (north has 23.5**HLD** points). The 1♦* response by south shows 0-6**HLD** or 13+**HLD** points; then north bids his 5-card heart suit. With no heart support, South bids his 4-card major. The bid of 4♣* by north is a splinter in support of spades. South next showed his heart shortness and north bids 6♠. West led his spade singleton.

Except for the double of 1♣, a takeout double is a competitive auction is used to show an opening hand with at least 12+**AOC** points in the direct seat. The purpose of the bid is to get into the auction. The ideal hand for the doubler is 4-4-4-1 or 5-4-4-0 where the singleton or void is in the opponent's bid suit. It tends to deny a five-card major.

Over a 1-level suit bid the X shows12-17**AOC** points for and includes 2 zones 12/14 and 15/17. Over a 2-level it shows 15-17**AOC** points. Or the X may show 18+**AOC** points, when followed by a jump raise in partner's suit, a new suit is bid, or one makes suit a cue bid.

If you double and then bid a new suit, how do you know whether the bid is forcing? Does it make a difference if you partner made a free bid? Let's look at an example.

Suppose the bidding goes:

West	North	East	South
		1♦	X
Pass	1♥	Pass	?

If South next bids 1♠ or 2♣ he is showing a good hand, but since partner (North) can have nothing, the bids are NOT forcing. Partner (North) may pass. Even if you jump to the three level for these bids, partner may pass. If South has a good hand, he must cue bid 2♦.

However, suppose partner made a free bid:

West	North	East	South
		1♣	X
1♦	1♥	Pass	?

Now a new suit by South is forcing for one round. However, it is not forcing to game.

Returning to our example, suppose partner bids 1NT:

West	North	East	South
		1♦	X
Pass	1NT	Pass	?

West	North	East	South
		1♦	X
1♥	1NT	Pass	?

Now if you bid at the two level (2♣) a lower ranking suit, you are not showing a good hand – you are running from no-trump. However, if you bid at the two level, a higher-ranking suit (2♠), you are showing a very good hand, 18+**AOC**.

How big a hand does one need to double and then bid NT? You again should have a 15/17**HLD** points hand with a stopper in their suit.

Finally, suppose you double and double again without hearing from partner? The second double is again for takeout, not penalty.

The doubler will normally have no more than three cards in the opponent's opening suit (do not double with a stack in the opponent's suit, make a trap pass, if partner balances with a double, use the delta rule (to be discussed shorty) to see whether you pull the double or leave it in for penalty). When the doubler doubles a major suit opening, he will usually have four cards in the other major or have a strong hand and will bid his own suit or cue bid.

The takeout double is not restricted to the direct seat. It occurs when partner has not yet bid, passes do not count but redoubles are considered bids, and the double is of a suit bid (not NT) at the 1, 2, or 3 bidding levels. Thus, one may also use a takeout double in the fourth seat when the bidding has gone 1x – pass – pass – double. The double is for takeout since partner has not yet bid; it is virtually never used for penalty in this situation.

Let's look at some simple auctions:

South	West	North	East
	1♦	1♥	3♦
Pass	pass	double	

Because partner south has not bid, the double is for takeout. Some authors refer to this double as a Responsive Double. It shows support for the other three suits. However, some play the double as a Rosenkranz double showing three card supports for hearts with the Ace, King, or both (see Chapter 10).

South	West	North	East
1♥	pass	1NT	X

In this example, the double by east is equivalent to a direct takeout double of the heart opening bid. If opener had bid a minor, the double is more than likely asking for a major suit. Additionally, the double by east is equivalent to a direct takeout double of the heart opening bid.

Getting more complicated, E-W vulnerable and N-S non-vulnerable

West	North	East	South
	1♦	1♠	pass
Pass	X	pass	pass
2♥	X		

What is the second double by north? South's pass of the first double is a "penalty pass," equivalent to bidding spades since the first double of the spade bid should have showed hearts (at least three and maybe four) with a shortage in spades. Even though partner has passed in the auction, it is not for takeout but for penalty. When three different suits have been bid, the second double is usually for penalty.

Responding to a Takeout Double

Takeout doubles are very common in competitive auctions. But many of today's players tend to use them with any opening hand. This is incorrect.

Yes, they promise values of an opening hand; at least 12**AOC** points, **but they also guarantee at least 3-card support in all the unbid suits and 4-cards in any unbid major.**

In addition, they are not often used with a strong one or two-suited hand; instead, an overcall is most appropriate.

When partner makes a takeout double and the opponents do not bid, you must respond; the double is forcing. Your options are (**not playing transfers or Marionette responses**):

Suit bid	7/9**AOC** and 4+ cards in the suit bid
Jump Longest Suit	10/12**AOC** Starting Points 4+ cards, forcing one round
Double Jump	13/15**AOC** Starting Points 5+ cards, forcing, may bid game
1NT	7/9 **AOC** balanced with a stopper, no 4-card major
2NT	10/12**AOC** balanced with a stopper, no 4-card major
3NT	13/15 **AOC** balanced with a stopper, no 4-card major
Cue bid	12+ **AOC** over natural bids, artificial and forcing
Pass	Converts take-out double into a penalty.

Cue bids in response to takeout doubles

A cue bid is the only forcing bid an advancer may make to a takeout double. All other bids, including jumps, are non-forcing.

With a good four-card suit or 5+ card suit and an opening hand, it may be easy to get to game after a double; however, suppose you have good values and two suits, what do you do? For example, with equal length and perhaps even equal strength in two suits when the bidding proceeds:

1♦ - X - pass and the advancer holds one of the following hands.

1) ♠K986 ♥K986 ♦8 ♣AK64

2) ♠A975 ♥A975 ♦98 ♣AJ9

3) ♠KQ9 ♥KJ10 ♦AQ43 ♣765.

With two four-card majors (hands 1 and 2), you must cue bid 2♦. It asks partner to bid his best major.

With hand 3, if the takeout doubler bids spades, advancer may repeat the cue (3♦) that suggests less than four-card support for the doubler's major suit but with game going values. The doubler would often bid 3NT with stoppers in the opponent's suit.

When partner makes a takeout double and the opponents do not bid, you must respond; the double is forcing.

Responding to a Takeout Double with Interference

How high to play takeout doubles is a matter of partnership agreement. Many partnerships play takeout doubles through the 3♠. A double above the bid of three spades is then often taken as penalty. However, some may play it to the level of 5♦ or no limit. You should discuss the level with your partner.

In the preceding three examples there was no interference; suppose the bidding now goes:

1♣ - X – 1NT – (?). Now what do you bid?

You again invoke the Michaels cue bid of 2♣ in the balancing seat for the first two hands; however, with hand (3), a double is used to show the two lower ranking suits (hearts and diamonds). Note you must be at least 4-4 to use the cue bid or the double.

If the opponents open a diamond and the bidding goes 1♦ - X – 1NT – (?), again 2♦ shows the majors and a double shows clubs and hearts.

The bids may also be used with a major suit opening where now a cue bid of the major shows the other major and a minor and again a double is used to show the lower ranking suits. Be careful here since if partner does not have the major, you are at the three levels in a minor. You should have 10-12 points to cue bid the major.

Follow-up Bids

When making a takeout double, remember, partner may have nothing. You have forced partner to bid; on average he usually has 7/9**HL** points.

After a minimal response, you will need at least 18+ points for game in partner's bid suit. You can invite with 15-17. With 18-20 or 21-23 jump, bid at the three- or four-level, respectively.

Summary:

With a Minimum Hand (12-14**AOC**)

- Responder made the cheapest possible response – pass
- Responder jump, pass, raise to invite or bid game, you must decide

With a Medium Hand (15-17**AOC**)

- Responder made the cheapest possible response – raise one level to invite, game is still possible.
- Responder has jumped, raise to game

THE OPTIMAL MODIFIED 2/1-CLUB SYSTEM

With a Maximum Hand (18+**AOC**)

- Responder has made a cheapest possible response – jump raise
- Responder has jumped, raise to game

Takeout Double over Weak Two Bids

Over a weak 2-level bid by the opponents, a X is for take-out, NOT PENALTY (unless you play Fishbein). While in most cases you would bid your best suit, suppose you have zero points; partner doubles their bid of 2♠ and you have a weak hand with four hearts:

♠ 872 ♥ 7654 ♦ 983 ♣ 876

What do you do? You cannot bid 3♥. You bid 2NT* as a relay bid which is part of the Lebensohl or Transfer Lebensohl systems played over interference to 1NT (Chapter 10). It asks partner to bid 3♣* so you may sign off at the three-level in a suit with no interest in game. If the doubler does not accept the relay and bids any other suit, it shows 18+**AOC**. If you do not bid 2NT* but bid a suit at the three-level, you are showing about 12+**AOC**.

2NT followed by 3NT denies four of the other majors and shows a stopper in the weak suit bid. A direct cue bid of the weak suit shows a very strong hand; it is game forcing.

Doubling 1NT (penalty or takeout)

The double of a 1NT opening may be for takeout or penalty. Whether the double is for penalty or takeout usually depends on the convention you play as defense over NT. Several approaches will be discussed in Chapter 10. However, before we get there, let me explain what you need to double a strong 1NT bid for penalty with a balanced hand.

If the opponents are playing 15-17, you need 18+**AOC** to double for penalty. If the opponents are playing 12-14 or 10-12, you need 15+**AOC** to double for penalty.

The experts do not agree on whether a double should be for penalty or takeout; however, all have opinions. You may read about it at: www.clairebridge.com/defensevsnt.htm.

Some partnerships use the simple rule that all doubles when partner has not bid are for takeout. Your agreements must be discussed.

Overcall or Double

When you overcall, partner does not know whether you have 12 or 17**AOC** while a double usually shows at least 12+**AOC**. Is their "best" strategy?

Advantages of Overcalling

1) It is usually lead directing.

You should have an ace or a king in the bid suit! Do not overcall with junk. However, if you have two bids and an opening hand, it is usually better to double provided you have support for the other three suits.

For example, with the hand: ♠K75 ♥AK1096 ♦K75 ♣ 75, you would overcall 1♥ after the opponents bid 1♦.

But, with the hand: ♠K75 ♥AK1096 ♦75 ♣ K75, it would be better to double. Telling partner, you have at least an opening hand and support for the other three suits is much better than telling him to lead a heart.

Suppose partner has the hand: ♠64 ♥KQ9864 ♦ 4 ♣ A842 and you overcall a spade. The bidding went: 1♦ - 1♠ - 3♦ - (?), partner would probably pass fearing a misfit and only moderate values. However, if instead you double so the auction is: 1♦ - X - 3♦ - (?), partner would confidently bid 3♥.

What do you do in the fourth seat? The bidding goes 1♥ - P - 1♠ - (?). And you hold the following hand: ♠87 ♥K ♦ KQJ932 ♣ K764. Your partner has passed, and you are not going to outbid the opponents. Clearly, a lead directing bid of 2♦ is better than a takeout double. In addition, your bid will certainly not be doubled for penalty.

2) An overcall does not give the opponents (or your partner) information about your distribution.

This may be important for declarers when deciding to finesse a queen in a suit that you have doubled for takeout. This is the price you pay for describing your hand accurately with a double. You must weigh what information you need to give partner versus the opponents.

3) You can sometimes bid a second suit, clarifying your distribution.

Suppose you hold the following hand: ♠AK875 ♥7 ♦ AJ10652 ♣ A and the RHO opens 1♥. What do you bid?

You must overcall a diamond and then bid spades (reverse by over caller). You have two very good suits, always bid the longer. However, if instead you had the hand: ♠AK875 ♥7 ♦ 987652 ♣ A, bid 1♠, you do not have the strength to reverse.

Disadvantages of Overcalling

1) The bidding may die before you can show support for the other suits.

This may happen if you have a strong hand on which you have decided to overcall instead of double. Sometimes it is better to describe your two-suited hand which may only happen if the bidding continues.

2) A fit in another suit may be missed. It happens.

3) Defensive values are undervalued or overvalued.

Partner does not know whether you have 12 or 17 points, this is a significant drawback when you have support for all unbid suits. Even though you are very distributional, it is sometimes better to double and take a change since partner knows you have at least an opening bid.

4) You may get doubled and go down when you have a fit elsewhere.

Advantages of Doubling

1) Shows high card strength.

A double show at least 12+**AOC** and hence defensive values; partner better able to place the contract with this information.

2) Allows partner to double the opponents.

Even though you have 13 points, you should not always double. For example, suppose you have the following hand: ♠ 42 ♥KQ109 ♦ KQJ75 ♣ Q5. With this hand you should bid 1♦ over 1♠. You do not have defensive values to double.

3) Allows partner to bid a suit confidently, knowing you will have at least three-card support.

4) A new suit bid by you later shows a hand too strong for a simple overcall.

For example, the opponents open 1♠ and you have five hearts and 18+**AOC** points. Do not overcall, double, and bid hearts. If your partner now bids 4♥ and the opponents go to four spades, you can then double for penalty.

5) Avoids being doubled when you have a better fit.

If you overcall and are doubled, usually you just must sit and take your medicine. It is often too dangerous to scramble around trying to find the right spot. Starting off with a double, you have a better chance of finding a fit. A double behind a bidder is usually for penalty. In front of a bidder, it is usually for takeout.

Disadvantages of Doubling

1) Partner may miss the best lead.

This is especially true against a no-trump contract. However, unless you have a very top-heavy suit, doubling may in fact be your best chance of getting the defense off to the right start.

2) You might misjudge your fit.

It is easy to make the wrong decision as to how high to bid, or what defensive values you have, as you may have a nine- or ten-card fit which you think is only an eight- or nine-card fit. This issue is often overlooked.

For example, over a heart opening, you have a choice of bidding 2♦ or to double with the following hand: ♠Q86 ♥98 ♦ AKJ107 ♣ J64 (14.5**AOC**). Again, any bid may work; however, if you overcall and partner is all diamonds, he will know either to preempt or keep quiet hoping the opponents misgauge their fit.

Let's look at an example

	♠ J752	
	♥ J75	
	♦ Q1984	
	♣ 9	
♠ K1043	N	♠ A9
♥ Q6	W E	♥ AK1043
♦ 632	S	♦ Void
♣ AK73		♣ Q10852
	♠ Q86	
	♥ 98	
	♦ AKJ107	
	♣ J64	

With east-west vulnerable, if south doubles east's 1♥ opening, the bidding might go:

West	North	East	South
		1♥	X
Redouble	1♠	2♣	Pass
3♣	Pass	5♦*	Pass
5NT	Pass	7♣	All Pass

* Exclusion Keycard Blackwood, asking partner not to count keycard in the diamonds.

However, if instead you bid 2♦, things may go:

West	North	East	South
		1♥	2♦
X	6♦	X	

Down four for =800 for east-west, instead of +2140

Some of the material in this section is based upon information in the book by Neil Kimelman (2008) "Improve your Bidding Judgment" by Master Point Press. There are many more topics in the book to help bridge players know when to be passive or aggressive. Neil Kimelman is a Canadian expert bridge player.

Cue Bidding Principles

Cue bids have become an integral part of contract bridge and you do not have to be an expert or an advanced player to use them. They allow one to reach the appropriate level for a part-score, game, or slam. They are used to show support for partner's overcall, responses to takeout doubles, looking for no-trump contracts, getting to slams, as conventions and more. There are more than fifty conventional cue bids listed in the Official Encyclopedia of Bridge. We review a few common uses that may help to improve your partnership agreements.

How good is your overcall?

Overcalls in an unbid suit are natural and usually include a five-card or longer suit with 12/14**AOC** for an overcall at the one-level and 15/17**AOC** for an overcall at the two-level. Given these one often needs to know how good the overcall bid is. To find out, one may make an asking cue bid! For example, suppose the bidding goes 1♦-1♠-pass -**2♦**.

The cue bid of 2♦ to the over caller is the only forcing bid partner may make and is asking partner how good your overcall is. It usually promises 10/12**HLD** points with a fit (3+ cards) since a simple raise shows 7/9**HLD**. A jump cue bid shows 13+**HLD** with four-card support where again **D=flatness.**

A rebid of the suit (by the over caller) at the lowest level conveys a "minimum range overcall (12/14**AOC**)." Any other bid (a new suit, no-trump, or a jump) shows a sound overcall with an opening hand (15/17**AOC**).

With more points (18+**AOC**), the over caller would double and bid! If the opener doubles the advancer's cue bid (showing a good suit), a pass by the over caller shows the lightest overcall (12/14), a rebid of the suit shows a respectable overcall (15/17), and a new suit or jump shows a very good hand (18+).

Cue bids by responder (after Opponent's Overcall)

A cue bid by responder shows a limit raise or better in opener's suit, with at least three-card support for opener's major suit or at least four-card (and preferable five-card) support for opener's minor suit.

1♥ - 1♠ - 2♠ promises a limit raise or better in hearts 10+**HLDF** points. Responder may hold:

(1) ♠842 ♥A876 ♦AK65 ♣54

(2) ♠7 ♥Q875 ♦Q86 ♣AKQ64

(3) ♠A54 ♥987 ♦AQ109 ♣Q87

A cue bid is a one round force. With the second hand, some responders would prefer to bid 2♣ since that bid is forcing (any new suit by an unpassed responder is forcing) and hearts could be supported later. And, with the third hand, some would perhaps bid 2♦ for the same reason. However, it is best to show your fit as soon as possible.

If the cue bid forces your partner to the four-level, it shows an opening bid or better.

1♥-1♠-3♠ shows a game forcing heart raise with at least three-card supports. Hands could be:

(A) ♠92 ♥QJ76 ♦9874 ♣AKQ

(B) ♠K5 ♥A632 ♦A543 ♣K75

(C) ♠876 ♥AK7 ♦A8432 ♣K6

What if the bidding went 1♥-1♠-pass-4♥*? A double jump cue bid is a splinter in support of spades and is game forcing.

Sandwich 1NT*/2NT* and Skew Cue bids (Hess Bids)

Sandwich 1NT*/2NT*

The bid of 1NT* is usually made in the fourth seat after your partner has passed and the opponents have bid two suits at the one-level. It must be alerted and shows five-five in the unbid suits and **less than a full opener** (12**AOC**). You are usually willing to play at the two-level.

With the same distribution and 18+**AOC**, you make a Sandwich 2NT* bid (also called a Roman Jump Overcall). Now, you are willing to play at the three-level. And a X shows 5-5 and 12-17**AOC**.

Example 1: 1♦/pass/1♥/1NT* with ♠KJ987 ♥7 ♦109 ♣QJ543, bid 1NT*.

Suppose instead of the hand in the Example 1, you have the hand:

Example 2: ♠KQ987 ♥K7 ♦A ♣AKJ87. Now, one would bid 2NT*.

When one is four-four in the two unbid suits or five-four in the unbid suits, the Sandwich NT bids are replaced by a Takeout Double or Skew Cue bids, respectively.

Skew/Hess Cue Bids

When the opponents have bid two different suits, then a cue bid of the higher-ranking suit shows five cards in the higher unbid suit and four cards in the lower unbid suit. A cue bid of the lower bid suit shows five cards in the lower bid suit and four cards in the higher unbid suit.

Takeout Double

The takeout double may be 4-4: ♠AKJ7 ♥96 ♦456 ♣AQ92, but more than an opening hand if partner is forced to bid at the three-level. If partner is forced to bid at only the two-level, the doubler needs only 12-17**AOC**.

Overcall

The previous bids are used to represent shape and values. In general, the shapelier the hand, the lighter the values may be. An overcall of an unbid suit at the two-level will show length in the suit with little value. As in the case of the sandwich NT bid, if the bid is made at the two-level, one must again have about eight losers non-vulnerable and seven losers vulnerable. A three-level bid requires extra values.

Some Examples

1♦/pass/1♥/1NT*	shows clubs and spades with 5-5 shape 12/17**AOC.**
1♦/pass/1♥/double	shows clubs and spades with 4-4 shape 12/17**AOC.**
Pass/1♣/pass/1♠/1NT*	shows diamonds and hearts with 5-5 shape 12/17**AOC.**
1♠/pass/2♣/2NT*	shows diamonds and hearts with 5-5 shape and 18+**AOC.**
1♠/pass/2♣/2♠	shows hearts and diamonds with 5-4 shape and 15/17**AOC.**
1♠/pass/2♣/3♣	shows diamonds and hearts with 5-4 shape and 15/17**AOC.**

Final Note: In the sequence 1♣, pass, 1♠, pass / pass/1NT, the 1NT bid is not Sandwich 1NT; it shows some values (12/14) and you do not want the opponents to play at the one-level.

Unusual 2NT* Overcall

The Unusual 2NT* overcall is used after one has made a major's suit bid. A 2NT* overcall shows at least five cards in each of the lowest unbid suits with 15/17**AOC**; partner is expected to bid the one he likes best. Some examples:

1♣ - 2NT*= shows the lowest two unbid suits, diamonds, and hearts.
1♦ - 2NT* = shows clubs and hearts.
1♥ - 2NT* = shows clubs and diamonds.
1♠ - 2NT* = shows clubs and diamonds.

In each of these cases, the partner of the 2NT* bidder normally corrects to the suit for which he has the most tolerance. With equal length in both suits, especially with two doubletons, he bids the cheapest suit. If he has a weak hand with at least four-card support, he can consider making a preemptive jump bid to the four-level in one of the known suits.

When the opponents interfere using the 2NT overcall bid, you may use the convention known as **Unusual over unusual 2NT** which is a series of cue bids to show support for your partner's bid suit.

Because we know the two suits when the opponents use employing the unusual 2NT bid, we can use this information to your advantage. One uses the suits of the opponents (the cheapest suit and their second suit, as cue bids) and the two natural available bids to describe the hand of the responder:

Cheapest Cue bid: A limit raise or better in the bid suit.

Second Cue bid: Game forcing hand in the fourth unbid suit.

Raise in the fourth suit: Natural and non-forcing.

Raise in the bid suit: Competitive raise (weak).

An example follows.

1♥ - 2NT* (clubs & diamonds) – (?)
   3♣   the Cheapest Cue bid is a Limit raise or better in hearts (the bid major).
   3♦   the Second Cue bid, is a game forcing bid in spades.
   3♥   is a competitive raise and weak.
   3♠   is natural and non-forcing

NOTE: Some play the second cue bid as invitational only, not forcing; it depends on your partnership agreement. Check with your partner!

If the bidding goes:

1♠ - 2NT* (clubs & diamonds) – (?)

3♣	the Cheapest Cue bid, is a Limit raise or better in spades (the bid major).
3♦	the Second Cue bid, is a game forcing bid in hearts.
3♥	is a competitive raise and weak.
3♠	is natural and non-forcing

NOTE: Some play that three clubs over the major bid still shows support for hearts. Discuss these bids with your partner.

What about bids above the three-level? Discuss these with your partner.

3NT is usually natural with stoppers in the two suits.
4♣*4♦* is splinter raise in hearts (for our example).
4♠ is natural.

When should the double be used? It usually shows 10 + Starting Points (with or without a fit) and is primarily used as if the bid of two no-trump was a double (for our example, 1♥-X).

Thus, a double after the bid of 2NT is like a redouble. Because the opponent's bid of 2NT is forcing, the opener can now double the opponent's bid with good trumps, make a descriptive bid with an offensive hand, or make a forcing pass.

Example: South opens 1♥ and West holds ♠105 ♥7 ♦ AJ975 ♣ QJ1032 and partner holds:

East: ♠AQ ♥A106♦ KQ10 ♣ K9765

West has 13.5**HLD** [0+2D for singleton +4.5+1+1L+4+1L+1Q-1 no K] +1 Sig Heart =14.5**AOC** and bids 2NT as unusual.

East has 20.0**HL** [6.5-1 for doubleton+4.5+6+3+1L] and bids 3♥ asking for a heart stopper (Western cue – Chapter 8). Adding 20 to 12 = 32 points and East next bids 5♣. West with 14.5**AOC** points bids 6♣.

Playing 2/1 most West hands passed with 8H points, bidding at several tables went:

South	West	North	East
1♥	Pass	Pass	2NT
Pass	3NT	Pass	Pass

South	West	North	East
1♥	Pass	Pass	X

Pass	2♦	Pass	2NT
Pass	3NT	Pass	Pass

South	West	North	East
1♥	Pass	Pass	X
Pass	2♦	Pass	2NT
Pass	3♥	Pass	4♣
Pass	5♣	Pass	Pass

Not one pair playing 2/1 found the club slam!

Some partnerships also play unusual 2NT in the balancing seat: 1♥-pass-pass-2NT, showing the minors; however, in the Direct seat over weak two bids, the bid of **2NT IS NOT UNUSUAL**. The bid shows strong no trump bid with 15-17 and at least two stoppers in the overcall bid suit.

Michaels Cue bid

This is a direct cue bid of the opponent's opened suit (one club by RHO, two clubs by you) to show 5+card length in the two other suits. One of your suits is always a major, but the exact two you promise to depend upon the opening bid.

- Over a **minor-suit opening**, a Michaels Cue bid (1♣-2♣* or 1♦-2♦*) shows **both majors**.
- Over a **major-suit opening**, a Michaels Cue bid (1♥-2♥* or 1♠-2♠*) shows **the OTHER major and an unspecified minor**.

When using Michaels and the two suits of the opponents are known, the bids by responder are identical to those used in Unusual over Unusual 2NT. To illustrate, after the bids of 1♣-2♣* (the majors, hearts, and spades), we have that where 2-level bids are 12/14**AOC** and 3-level bids are 15/17**AOC**.

2♦	is natural and non-forcing.
2♥	the Cheapest cue bid, is a limit raise or better in clubs.
2♠	the Second cue bid, is a game forcing bid in diamonds.
2NT	is natural and invitational.
3♣	is a competitive club raise and weak.
3♦	is natural and forcing.
3♥/*3♠*	is splinter raises in clubs.
3NT	is natural with stoppers in the two suits.
4♥*/4♠*	is splinter raise in clubs.
5♣	is natural.

A double is again takeout.

What about when the second suit of the Michaels bid is ambiguous? (See footnote (**) below.) Then only **one** suit is known: for example, with the bids 1♥-2♥*, and 1♠-2♠*. Now, we can no longer do everything since we have only one known cue bid. For example, for the bid 1♠-2♠* (shows hearts and a minor), we have the following bids.

2NT	is natural and invitational.
3♣	is a non-forcing club raise.
3♦	is a not forcing diamond raise.
3♥	the only cue bid, shows a limit raise in spades.
3♠	is competitive and weak.
4♥*	is splinter raise for spades.

If the opener doubles the opponent's three-level bid after Michaels or Unusual 2NT, it is generally for penalty, not takeout.

(**) Some play that the opponents' cue bids show the upper two unbid suits; then one heart followed by two hearts would show spades and diamonds; and one spade followed by two spades would show hearts and diamonds! It is called Modified Michaels and all suits are known. Hence, the responses may be patterned after the one club-two club bid discussed above.

Some partnerships also play Michaels if the bidding goes, for example, 1♣ - pass – pass - 2♣*; or if the bidding goes 1♣ - pass – 1NT - 2♣*, a balancing seat Michaels.

Michaels bids need to be alerted. YOU MUST AND SHOULD ALWAYS ASK WHAT THE CUE BID MEANS. If the club bid is a Precision club bid or announced as short, some play that a club bid as natural and then it is no longer Michaels.

If you adopt the under-call club convention only over 1♣, you cannot also play Michaels over the club bid.

Responding to Michael Cue bids or Unusual 2NT

We introduced Michaels Cue bid and Unusual 2NT as overcalls and showed how the opponents (opener and responder) may use cue bids when it is used. The two bids are used with either very strong 5-5 hands or with weak hands in a competitive auction. With between with 12/17**HLD** points, one may either overcall or a double. Unusual 2NT shows the two lowest unbid suits, either both minors or a major and a minor.

Let's first look at Michaels:

1)   Without a good fit for either of the known suits, give simple preference for the one you like best (or dislike least).

2)   With a good fit for a known suit, make a single raise or double jump in a known suit with 12+**HLD** Starting Points.

3) With an even better hand (18+**HLD** Starting Points), cue bid the opponent's suit as a game force bid. The suit will be revealed later.

4) With a strong balanced hand (15+**HLD** Starting Points), and stoppers in opener's suit and the "other" suit, one may bid 3NT

5) After 1♠ - 2♠* or 1♥ - 2♥* over caller's second suit is not known. A reply of 2NT* is forcing and asks which minor is held.

6) A bid in a suit not promised by the over caller is natural and non-forcing, based on a very long suit. Over caller will not bid again unless he is extra strong.

When the opponents interfere above the level of 2NT, a bid of 4♣ is a request to play in the minor at the four levels and the bid of 4NT is forcing to game in the minor.

Without interference, a bid of 3NT is to play and the bid of 4NT is Blackwood, no agreed upon suit. A direct cue bid of the opponent's suit shows a strong hand and is game forcing. If your partner bids a suit not bid by the opponents or shown by the cue bid, it is natural and wants to play in the suit bid.

If after a Michaels Cue bid or Unusual 2NT and partner responds with a weak bid and partner bids again with 18+**HLD** Starting Points, like a double and bidding a suit. The responses to the 2NT overcall are similar.

Example: You hold the following hand: ♠7 ♥AQ986 ♦42 ♣KQ1042 and the opponents bid 1♦. What is your overcall bid?

You only have 16.5**AOC**, enough to bid 2NT*=15/17**AOC**. A 1-level overcall requires only 12-14**AOC** points.

Leaping Michaels

Leaping Michaels utilizes the 4♣* and 4♦* bids. Like the Michaels cue bid in case this minor suit overcall is in the opposing suit, both major suits are implied. In case the overcall is not a Cue bid, the suit bid plus a major suit is indicated. So, on preempts of the opponents (indicated between brackets), the following applies when playing Leaping Michaels (also called Roman Jump Overcalls).

(2/3♥)	4♣*:	Clubs and spades
(2/3♥)	4♦*:	Diamonds and spades
(2/3♠)	4♣*:	Clubs and hearts
(2/3♠)	4♦:*	Diamonds and hearts
(3♣)	4♣*:	Majors
(3♣)	4♦*:	Diamonds and an undisclosed major
(3♦)	4♣*:	Clubs and an undisclosed major
(3♦)	4♦*:	Majors

All bids show at least 5-5 shape or a 6/7 card suit with 15/17**AOC** points since these are 4-level bids.

After 3♦ or 4♣*, the bid of 4♦ asks for a major. The bids 4♥ and 4♠ are to play. Following 3♣ or 4♦*, the bid of 4♥ is played as pass-or-correct.

Some partnerships prefer to interchange the meanings of the 4♣* and 4♦* bids following a 3♣ preempt so that 4♣* denotes diamonds and an undisclosed major. This has the advantage that the 4♦* becomes available to ask for the major suit. The 4♥/4♠ responses may then be played as natural (to play). Discuss this with your partner!

Leaping Michaels can be utilized after natural 2/3-level preempts and after conventional preempts using **Muiderberg Convention,** also called the Dutch Two opening. It is a preemptive opening based on a two-suiter with precisely a five-card major and a minor suit (four-cards or longer). In Muiderberg, the 2♥ opening denotes five hearts and an unknown minor suit, while 2♠ denotes five spades and an unknown minor suit.

It can also be played against a weak 2♦ bid; here, Leaping Michaels may be utilized to good effect:

> (2♦) - 4♣*: Clubs and an undisclosed major (4♦ asks for the major)
> (2♦) - 4♦*: Diamonds and an undisclosed major (4♥ is pass-or-correct).

And for example, over the majors: 2♥/2♠ - Pass – Pass - 4♣*/4♦* shows clubs/diamonds and major. These bids are forcing to game bids and may not be passed.

If you are currently play using Michaels Cue bids, you may want to consider adding the Leaping Michaels Convention.

Example:

You hold as East ♠AQJ76 ♥7♦43 ♣AKJ64 and North opens 3♥. You are 5-5 in spades and clubs with

16**HLD** [4.5+2.0+1+1L+2D+4.5+3+1+1L+1Q] + 1 sig Heart =17**AOC** and bid 4♣* to show Clubs + Spades.

Example:

You hold as East ♠K42 ♥43♦A2 ♣AKQJ64 and north opens 2♥. Now you would bid X. You have 24**AOC** [3+ 4.5+1D+10.5+3Q+2L] points. If partner bids 3♥ (western cue see Chapter 8) or 3♠, you will bid 5♣. If the opponents bid 3♥, you would X for penalty.

Scrambling 2NT*

Another use of the 2NT bid is in the auction 1M - pass -2M - 2NT*. The bid of 2NT* is for takeout and only played over major suit bids (it is not Sandwich). You usually have no more than two cards in the major bid, and it asks partner to bid his four-card suits up-the-line. It allows you to perhaps find a partial contract in a minor or the other major. It may also force the opponents to an un-makeable three-level contract. Playing duplicate bridge, you never allow the opponents to play in a one-level contract, and you normally do not want them to play in a two-level partial.

Equal Level Conversion Double

When partner doubles and bids his own suit, we have said that he usually has a "big" hand, at least 18+ points. However, there is an exception called the Equal Level Conversion (ELC) double. It is used when partner has a two suited hand with diamonds and hearts, diamonds and spades, and the opponents open one club or with hearts and spades (5-4 in each case) and the opponents open one club or one diamond. Eric Rodwell and Jeff Meckstroth called the convention **Minimum Equal Level Conversion Double.**

The ELC double was developed by Robert B. Ewen and published his book "Doubles for Takeout, Penalties, and Profit in Contract Bridge" (1973); however, he did not name it as such. The double is illustrated by him on Page 25 of his book.

South
♠KJ97
♥64
♦AQJ982
♣8

East	South	West	North
1♥	?		

With this type of hand what is south to do? He has values for a takeout double but not the distribution. He doubles and when partner bids 2♣, he corrects to 2♦. This does not show a big hand with diamonds. It corrects partner's bid at the two level to show diamonds and spades or after the bid of bids 3♣ by partner he bids 3♦ if the opponents enter the auction at the two level by bidding 2♥. The ELC double is useful since partner can now show two suits, five diamonds and four spades.

The ELC double can also be employed when the opponents open 1♦ and you have five hearts and four spades. To show the 5-4 hand you double and bid hearts to show your off-shape distribution after partner bids 2♣. If you were 5-5, you would use the Michaels cue bid. With five spades and four hearts there is no problem, you can overcall one spade and bid hearts.

CHAPTER 7

THIRD AND FOURTH SEAT OPENINGS

Overview

Playing traditional 2/1 many say you may open with a hand light in either the 3rd or 4th positions since it may increase the probability of a part score. Other rules like having at least 4 spades when in the fourth seat or at least 3-cards in each major have been suggested. None of these guidelines work very well. Playing the Optimal Modified 2/1-Club System, all hands are opened with 12-17**HLD** points in **all seats.** There are NO GADGETS, like the Rule if 15 or the Rule of 20, etc.

Why this position? Using the 4-3-2-1, one expects a deck to have 40 points and if two have passed, there remains 20 points. Wrong. While the value of aces and kings are fixed, queens and jacks have variable values, and their combinations (of AKQJ) add up to between 9.5 and 10.5 points not 10! Hence, a deck has between 38 and 42 points and not 40!

The 4-3-2-1 system also ignores the values of 10's and we know that a 10 accompanied with a Q or J is worth 1 full point. Hence, a deck has between 38 and 46 points. And because the negative value of 4333 hands is also ignored, it brings the point total to between 36-46 points.

Lastly, considering 5-card suits with at least 3**H** points with length points, **a full deck contains between 34 and 50 points. It is not a fixed number like 40!** Each hand has between 8.5 and 12.5 points not 10!

Looking at two hands: (A) ♠A854 ♥K52 ♦Q92 ♣J95 (B) ♠AJ104 ♥652 ♦KQ32 ♦92

Each has 10**H** points. Wrong! (A) has 8.5**HLD** points and (B) has 11.5**HLD** or changing (B) to hand (C) ♠AJ10 ♥652♦KQ432 ♦92 it would have 12.5**HLD and** you would open 1♦*.

Conventions like Drury, Reverse Drury, and Two-Day Drury are not needed playing the Optimal Modified 2/1-Club System.

The next question that one may ask is why the average value of an Ace is=4.5 which equates to approximately 3 tricks since 26/3 for 3NT =2.9 tricks. But an Ace may only take 1 trick!

This obviously means that the value of 4.5 pts given an Ace account for more than just its trick-taking ability. On must also consider its trick-generating potential when combined with other honors (e.g., A J 10 x) and/or its trick-stopping ability, or its "control feature", when it prevents the opponents from exploiting a suit (i.e., hold up play with Axx in a suit lead in a NT contract). Therefore, strictly equating the value of an Ace with the number of tricks is misguided.

As stated by Patrick Darricades "The value of Aces represents the number of tricks they take **plus** the tricks they generate and/or prevent the opponents from making".

Four aces although valued as 18**H** points cannot take 6 tricks. To illustrate, Darricades considers several examples.

Hand A ♠K Q J x x x x x x x ♥x ♦x ♣x

Without a single Ace, this hand will only make 9 tricks; the OPC count gives this hand 23**HLD** pts (6H+2 pts for 3 honors in a 6 + card suit, -1 point for no Ace+ 10L+6D). The points for 9 tricks.

Let's now add one Ace to the above hand:

Hand B ♠K Q J x x x x x x x ♥A ♦x ♣x

This hand will now make 10 tricks; the OPC count gives this hand 27.5**HLD** pts (3.5 pts for the singleton Ace). The points for 10 tricks.

Let's now give the above hand two Aces.

Hand C ♠K Q J x x x x x x x ♥A ♦A ♣x

This hand will now make 11 tricks; the OPC count gives this hand 31**HLD** pts. The points for 11 tricks.

Giving the above hand three Aces.

Hand D ♠K Q J x x x x x x x ♥A ♦A ♣A

This hand will now make 12 tricks: the OPC count gives this hand 34.5**HLD** pts. The points for 12 tricks.

Finally, let's now give the above hand all four Aces.

Hand E ♠AK Q J x x x x x x ♥A ♦A ♣A

This hand will now make 13 tricks; the OPC count gives this hand 40**HLD** pts (3 pts for 4 honors in a 6 + card suit). The points for 13 tricks.

The last hand should be played in 7 NT, the singletons should not be counted since all four Aces can be given their full value of 4.5 pts each. And the OPC count then gives this hand 37**HL** pts, the points for 13 tricks.

Two-level Major Suit Bids in the Third and Fourth Seats

In the first two seats, preemptive major suit bids at the two-level show 12/14**HLD** points. In the third/fourth seat this is also the case.

Three- and Four-level Preempts

These bids are also unchanged in the 3rd and 4th seats.

CHAPTER 8

BIDDING WITH INTERFERENCE

We have assumed up to this point in our bidding that the opponents have not interfered. If there is direct interference with, for example, a suit bid or a double, **the 2/1 game force bid is off**.

2/1 Bids with Interference

1) You open one heart and your LHO doubles, partner bids two diamonds. Is it forcing to game? No --- it is not even forcing for one round.

2) You open one heart and your LHO bids one spade. Partner again bid two diamonds. Is the bid forcing to game? NO --- However, since the overcall was at the one level, it is forcing for ONE ROUND! Opener must bid again.

3) You open one heart and your LHO bids two spades. Partner next bids three clubs, is it forcing to game or for one round? When responder bids a new suit at the three level, it is not only forcing for one round, but also to game!

4) You open one heart and your LHO bids three diamonds. Partner bids three spades. Is the bid forcing? Over the preemptive bid, the bid is only forcing for one round, but not necessarily to game. Alternatively, you can double and bid a new suit. This sequence is forcing to game. Note, some partnerships play that all three level bids are forcing to game over any preempt.

When a partnership is committed to game and the opponents choose to interfere, opener may double the contract of the opponents instead of proceeding to game, if he believed the double would result in a better score. Doubles (penalty, responsive, cooperative, etc.) will be discussed in more detail in Chapter 9. For now, if the bidder is on the opener's right (he is sitting behind the bidder), a double is usually for penalty. When the bidder is on the opener's left, it is called a cooperative double and partner may leave the double in or choose to bid.

Finally, opener may make a cue bid (western of the opponent's suit usually at the three-level) used to investigate whether partner has a stopper for no-trump. Cue bids of suits not bid are used for slam investigation as discussed in Chapter 3 or they may show exceptional hands with voids and significant strength.

Cue bids by opener (Western Cue)

The term "Eastern Cue bid" refers to a style of low-level cue bidding of the opponent's suit showing stoppers in the bid suit. It has been replaced by the more popular "Western Cue bid" that asks for a full stopper in the opponent's suit. One is a telling bid while the other is an asking bid. The repeat "Western" cue bid (sometimes called a Directional Asking Bid) is usually asking for more information at low levels below 3NT and the cue bidder is asking for a partial stopper (Qx or Jxx). The Western, Eastern, and repeat cue bids are used to help the partnership reach a no-trump contract. An example follows.

West	North	East	South
	1♠	pass	2♦
2♥	3♥#	pass	3NT

The 3♥-cue bid is asking if south for a heart stopper. If he does, he should bid 3NT. If not, he would either rebid diamonds or with spade support bid four spades. Cue bids are not alerted or announced.

An example of a repeat cue bid asking for a partial stopper which sometimes combines Eastern and Western cue bids follows.

West	North	East	South
		1♠	2♥
Pass	2♠#	pass	3♦
Pass	3♠##	pass	3NT

How good is your overcall and I have a spade stopper (Eastern Cue)?
Do you also have a partial stopper in spades, if yes bid 3NT?

When the opponents interfere, they may or may not take up bidding space. When the overcall allows you to bid at the one-level, your response is natural, limited, and non-forcing. If the opponents bid a suit, you may have room to bid your own suit or no-trump. For example, if you open one club and the opponents overcall one diamond, the bid of a major show 5+ Starting Points. However, the bid of 1NT shows a stopper in the overcalled suit. If you are allowed to make a bid at the one-level, it is the same as if the overcall did not occur. This is also the case when the opponents make a takeout double.

Responder Bids after a takeout double

When the opponents make a takeout double over partner's one-level bid suit, it usually shows support for the other suits (at least three cards) with an opening hand of 12+**HLD** Starting Points. The takeout double asks your partner to bid a suit and implies shortness in the suit doubled.

Most players ignore the double and make their normal responses, assuming the double did not occur. The following guidelines apply.

1. A new suit is forcing at the one-level.

2. A bid suit at the two-level is weak (a weak jump shift) and is non-forcing.

3. 1NT is semi-forcing, shows a stopper in the over caller's suit with lack of fit.

One may also redouble the double. It shows 10+**HLD** points with or without a fit (some play that it always implies no fit).

Truscott Jordan 2NT*/Redouble

If used, it is not the same as the "Jacoby" 2NT bid. The bid is typically used to show a limit raise with three- or four-card support for the bid of a major over a double (it must be alerted). To keep the bidding at a lower level a redouble that shows 10+**HLD** points with or without a fit. After a redouble, if one next supports the major (it shows 15+**HLD** with three- or four-card support for the major). If you redouble and bid your own suit, you are denying a fit and again showing 15+**HLD** points.

Responder Bids when opponent (advancer) interferes after 2NT

To illustrate suppose the bidding goes: 1♥-P-2NT*-3♦

4♥	- is signoff, no shortness
Pass	- forcing pass, shows shortness in opponent's bid suit
New Suit	-shows shortness in bid suit
3NT	-medium or maximum hand, no shortness

After a forcing pass bid by opener, rebids by responder are:

Double	-Penalty
3M	-new Major, Ace in suit and 0-1 losers in opponent's bid suit
3NT	-King in Opponent's bid suit
4m	-Ace in suit bid and 0-1 losers in opponent's bid suit

Opener's Rebids after a redouble

If the opponents make a runout bid to compete and the opener cannot double the bid for penalty, it is always best to pass and allow responder to bid. Partner will show his suit or support for the opening bid suit. In most situations as opener, **you should pass a redouble.** This allows your partner to show his hand; do not be quick to bid.

However, if opener has a long suit or a strong two-suited hand that is not suited to a penalty double, opener must bid. For example, a reverse would show a strong hand.

When the opponents bid over a redouble, a rebid of the suit shows a long suit with a weak hand, a double usually shows 4+ cards in the opponent's bid suit. A bid (or jump bid) of a new suit shows 5-5 distribution and a weak hand. A pass is forcing. If responder passes first and then bids, it shows a stronger hand, usually 5-5 in the two suits and 15+**HLD** points.

Negative Doubles by Responder

The **negative double** is like a takeout double. It is made by the responder after his right-hand opponent overcalled at the first round of bidding. A negative double guarantee that responder has at least **ONE** of the unbid suits (there is one exception, if partner bids a minor and the opponents overcall the other minor a double always implies both majors; however, some may do it with only one). In addition, if partner bids a major, the negative double usually shows support for the other major.

The starting point requirements for a negative double provided the overcall bid is no higher than 3♠, the most popular option (this is marked on the back of the convention card, some may play that they are in effect with higher level bids, e.g., 4♥, 5♠ or higher because they do not want the opponents to steal the bid), is:

You need 7+ HLD to double at the 1-level

You need 10+HLD to double at the 2-level

You need 13+HLD to double at the 3-level or higher

Note that all the Point Ranges are Unlimited.

Negative doubles never apply after a NT bid or a two-level cue bid such as Michaels.

After one Minor – (one or two of Major), a negative double promise only the single unbid major. It says nothing about the unbid minor.

After one Major – (one or two of Other Major), a negative double promise only **one minor,** not both. It does not deny both.

After one Minor – (two of Other Minor), a negative double promise two **four**-card majors. After responder's negative double, opener must make a rebid that describes both his strength and his support for the suit partner may have shown with the double.

Opener Rebids - one/two-level overcalls with negative doubles

When responder makes a negative double, the only way to create a forcing auction on the next round is to cue bid the opponent's suit. If partner opens a minor and you double for a major and next bid, it usually shows a weak hand. Rebidding a major after bidding it the first time shows more values. Neither of these bids is forcing. The only way to make a forcing bid is to cue bid the opponent's suit on your next turn to bid. It is often used to reach a no-trump contract and called a Western Cue bid. If partner does not bid no-trump, returning to opener's first bid suit shows a strong hand. An overview of bids by Opener follows.

A cue bid is forcing to game.
All jumps below game are invitational.

1NT for one-level overcalls and 2NT for two-level overcalls usually promise a stopper in over caller's suit.

Opener may be forced to rebid a five-card suit or introduce a three-card suit.

A double jump to 3NT shows length and strength in the suit opened and a bid hand. It does not require a balanced hand.

Double and triple jump to game in a major show great shape and is weaker than a cue bid followed by a jump to game.

A reverse bid by opener is forcing to game.

We consider two examples of cue bidding.

A cue bid is the only forcing bid a negative doubler may make. The cue bid often shows a good hand with no other clear course of action.

1♣ - 1♥ - X - pass
2♣ - pass - 2♥ =cue bid

The two-heart bidder may hold ♠AQ94 ♥763 ♦AK75 ♣J5.

Responder is hoping the opening bidder has a heart stopper and can bid 3NT. For example, opener may have the following hand: ♠K5 ♥KJ6 ♦63 ♣AQ10987.

Jumps by a negative doubler are non-forcing, but highly invitational. For example:

1♦ - 1♠ - X —pass
2♦ - pass - 3♥ which shows less than 10 Starting Points, and 6+ hearts – an invitational bid.
The 3♥ bids may be based upon: ♠7 ♥KQJ965 ♦Q87 ♣987.

With 10+ Starting Points and 5+ hearts, for example, with a hand as:
 ♠7 ♥KQ965 ♦A87 ♣954   or   ♠A6 ♥AQJ107 ♦876 ♣954,

responder would not double but bid 2♥. The negative double at the two-level shows a hand with only four hearts and unlimited point count or five or more hearts and not enough points to bid at the two-level.

Opener Rebids - three-level overcalls with negative doubles

A cue bid is forcing to game.
3NT guarantees a stopper in clubs.
Opener may be forced to rebid a five-card suit and rarely introduce a three-card suit.

After (one Level and 3♦ or one Level and 3♥ or one Level and 3♠), the negative double is called a trump double by Marty Bergen. It asks partner to bid 3NT with a stopper in the opponent's overcall suit (with a stopper do not use a negative double, bid 3NT directly).

Opener in general has three types of hands when responding to a negative double.

Minimum (12/14**HLD**)	with support for suit - partner's implied suit with the double, you should bid it.
Invitational (15/17**HLD**)	Jump one level to show support
Game values (18+**HLD**)	Jump to game or Cue bid the opponent's suit; this allows partner to show his suit

Instead of a negative double, one may bid a new suit at the two-level with 10+ Starting Points. These are called a "standard" free bid. However, some play Negative Free Bids.

Responder Bids used with interference over 1♣* Openings

Direct Seat Interference

1X – (natural 1-lv bids)

Pass	0-6**HLD**
X*	7+**HLD**

Over 1♦ 1♥ shows 7+ points, 5+ hearts
 1♠ shows 7+ points, 5+ spades
 2♣ 12+ points, 5+ clubs
 2♦ 12+ points, 5+ diamonds

Over 1♥ 1♠ shows 7+ points, 5+ spades
 2♣ 12+ points, 5+ clubs
 2♦ 12+ points, 5+ diamonds

Over 1♠ 2♣ 12+ points, 5+ clubs
 2♦ 12+ points, 5+ diamonds
 2♥ 7+ points, 5+ hearts

With a stopper in their suit and 7+ without one of the above bids, bid 1NT*; with 12/13+, bid 2NT*, without a stopper and no other suitable bid with 7+, cue bid their suit.

Interference at the 2-level, is similar - just sometimes a level higher in the next bid. 3-level interference is less common, and any action requires 13+**HLD** points

X -	Pass	0-6**HLD**
	1♦	7+**HLD**
	1NT	All transfer bids apply – systems on
	1♠	7-12**HLD** and artificial
	Redouble	10+**HLD**

1NT* - the Minors

	Pass	0-6**HLD**
	X	7+**HLD**
	2♣	Stayman
	2♦	7-12**HLD** transfer to Hearts 5+
	2♥	7-12**HLD** transfer to Spades 5+
	3♣/3♦	Western Q

At 3/4 level – (natural)

	Pass	0-6**HLD**
	X*	7+**HLD**
	Suit bid	7-12**HLD** and 5+card suit

Balance Seat Interference

After 1♣* - (Pass) - 1♦ - (1♥/♠)

	Pass	balance minimum no 5-card suit
	X	support for the other three suits
	Suit Bid	Natural, non-forcing
	1NT	shows stopper with (18-20**HLD**)
	2NT	shows stopper with (21-23**HLD**)
	Cuebid	18+ HCP no stopper

After 1♣* - (Pass) - 1♦ - (1NT for Minors)

	Pass	balanced minimum no 5-card suit
	X	support for both majors
	2♣/2♦	unusual extra values shows ♥/♠

2♥/2♠	Natural non-forcing
2NT	shows stopper with (21-23**HLD**)

After 1♣* - (Pass) - 1♦ - (Double = Majors)

Pass	balanced minimum no 5-card suit
X	support for both minors
2♣/2♦	natural 5+ card suit
2♥/2♠	unusual extra values shows ♣/♦

Responder Bids used with interference over 1♦* Openings

While we have stressed major suit openings, there are also several bids that may be used when the opponents interfere over a minor suit opening. Let's suppose you open 1♦* (12-17**HLD**) and the opponents bid a major. A summary of responses follows.

1♦* - 1M

X	Negative double shows other major
1NT	7-9**HLD**, 4-diamonds and a stopper in the major
2♦	Less than 10 Starting Points, 6-diamonds
2♣/2♥	Natural with 7/9**HLD**
2M	Cue bid, 13+**HLD** and asking for a major stopper
2NT	10/12**HLD** with a major stopper and 6-diamonds
3♣	Splinter (singleton/void) in support of diamonds
3♦	Weak raise 7-9**HLD** 6-diamonds
3M*	Splinter in major with 5+ card support in diamonds

Balancing Double by Opener

Often, your partner bids and your right-hand opponent (RHO) interferes at the 2-level, and you have their bid suit. You make what is called a trap pass. When the opponents bid to 3/4-level, your partner often makes a **balancing double** when holding at most two cards in their overcall suit, he is asking you to bid. Do you bid or pass the double? To decide, one uses the delta rule. It works as follows:

Rule of Delta: If the Σ trumps $- 11 \leq \Sigma$ bids then Bid; Otherwise Pass

Example: North Deals

		♠	QJ10987		
		♥	7		
		♦	A5		
		♣	KJ103		
♠	A6			♠	K7
♥	K87		N	♥	AQJ6543
♦	KQ1075	W	E	♦	98
♣	43		S	♣	76
		♠	543		
		♥	106		
		♦	J987		
		♣	AQ53		

North	East	South	West
1♠	3♥	3♠	4♥
X	Pass	?	

Do you bid 4♠ or leave the X in for penalty? Thus

From the bidding you know the opponents have 10 hearts from the 3-level bid and the 4-level bid by west. Since you have 2-hearts, partner must have but one and likely 6-spades.

Hence 10+9=19-11=8 and since 4+4=8, bid 4♠ and do not pass the X for penalty!

You also know partner has 12-17**HLD** and that you have 9**HDF** points; enough for 3♠ so bid 4♠ vulnerable or not.

Or South can infer that North has a D=5, adding his own D=1 (3♠-2♥), the total of D=6 +13 = 19 possible total tricks (the sum of the trumps in both hands).

The above example illustrated a competitive auction, what is one to do when the opponent's make a preemptive game bid

East- West Vulnerable and South Deals

		♠	Q1042		
		♥	-		
		♦	A765		
		♣	AJ652		
♠	AK875			♠	J963
♥	K2	**N**		♥	A1097
♦	Q9	**W** **E**		♦	43
♣	KQ93	**S**		♣	874
		♠	-		
		♥	QJ86543		
		♦	KJ1082		
		♣	10		

The bidding goes:

South	West	North	East
4♥	X	Pass	?

Do you bid 4♠ or Pass? Let's apply the delta rule: 9/10♠+8♥ = 17/18-11 =6/7 £ 8 so bid 4♠. If you would not bid, N-S makes 4♥X from the Daily Sun February 1, 2022, played by the Norwegian expert Tolle Stabell. The lead was ♠A by west.

Responder Bids after a 1NT overcall

When the opponents interfere by bidding 1NT, they usually have the suit bid stopped, a balanced hand showing a no-trump opener with 15-17/18 points. If this is not the case, the bid must be alerted. Some partnerships play that the bid of 1NT for takeout with shortness in the bid suit to interfere with the opponents' agreements.

When the opponents bid 1NT, responder's options are limited. The bid has taken away the negative double. Responder may pass, raise his partner's suit, or **double for penalty**. Observe that if partner has 12-17**HLD** points and the over caller has 15; the remaining points shared between the remaining hands is about 13.

With 7-9**HLD** points and at least three-card support, raise your partner's major suit to the 2-level. A jump bid in partner's major shows 10-12**HLD** points with support with three or four-card support. With 4-card support and 13-15**HLD** bid game.

Unless you have 10+**HLD** points and a good 5+ card suit, do not bid it.

With 13+**HLD** and good suit consider doubling 1NT for penalty.

Bidding Over Weak Jump Overcalls

After a preemptive jump overcall, for example 3♦, after partner has bid a major you have several options: pass, support, bid your own suit, etc. If you have support for partner's major and 10/12**HLD**, show support immediately. With a stronger hand, make a cue bid or bid your own suit freely and the support partner's major. The advantage of bidding your own suit is that if the opponents compete in the auction, opener (your partner) will be a better position to decide whether to double the opponents for penalty or bid on.

Fishbein Convention

The **Fishbein Convention** is a bidding convention developed by Harry Fishbein. It is in the direct seat when the opponents preempt at the two or three levels. Instead of doubling for takeout (negative), one bids the next higher suit (excluding 2NT) for takeout. Then double is for penalty. The bid of 3NT is usually to play.

An example of the Fishbein Conventions (from the World Championships in Sao Paolo, Brazil

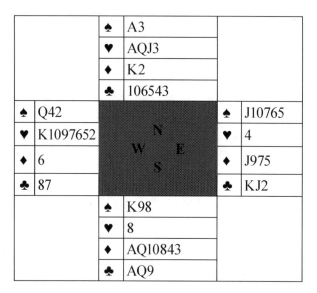

In this example, the bidding goes

South	West	North	East
1♦	3♥	(?)	

You have a heart stack against the opponents; you cannot make a negative double since you do not have spades. Playing the Fishbein Convention, one would double for penalty. Not playing the convention, you must pass, and hope partner reopens with a double. Do not bid 4♦.

Interference over NT

In the October 2007 issue of the ACBL "Bridge Bulletin," several experts recommended and discussed systems they play over the bid of a strong 1NT (14/15-17 HCP). Even if you have read the article (also available at www.clairebridge.com/defensevsnt.htm), you still may not have a clear picture regarding which system is "best."

A well-known British tournament director David Stevenson has posted 55 no-trump defenses at: http://blakjak.org.def_1nt01.htm.

What system should you play over a weak 1NT (12-14 or 10-12, say), should your approach change when playing Match Points vs IMPS, and should the system change be depending upon whether you are in the direct or balancing (pass-out) seat? There is no clear or best system for all situations: weak vs strong no-trump, Match Points vs IMPS, direct vs balancing seat. We consider each in turn, and then recommend an approach. When considering a system to play over the bid of 1NT (weak or strong), the first question you should ask yourself is whether a double should be value-showing and penalty-oriented.

Clearly, over a weak NT bid, a double must show values (15+) and be for penalty. Over weak no-trumps, if you do not double, and defeat the 1NT contract by one or two tricks, you will get an inferior score at Match Points or IMPS. Furthermore, over a weak

NT, you may easily compete at the two levels. Thus, over weak no-trumps (Match Points or IMPS) you need a system where a double is for penalty and that can show the majors (80 percent of all game bids are played in a major). Finally, over the weak NT bid, it does not matter whether the declarer is in the direct or pass-out seat. Hence, it is best to bid your suit, as soon as possible, especially if it is spades! A system designed with these requirements is Mohan. Like most systems designed to interfere over weak no-trumps, it is based upon transfers (e.g., Weber). This allows the over caller a second opportunity to bid, especially with a moderate to good holding.

The John Mohan system over weak NT follows:

Mohan

Double	Penalty
2♣*	Shows both majors (either 4-4 or 5-5)
2♦*	Transfer to hearts
2♥*	Transfer to spades
2♠*	Spades and a minor
2NT*	Hearts and a minor

All three-level bids are natural, usually a six-card suit and preemptive.

What if the bid is a strong NT (14/15-17 HCP)? Again, most would agree that a double is value showing and penalty oriented. NOT ALL AGREE ON THIS. Cappelletti is unwavering in his view: "It must be penalty-oriented. On a particular hand it might not work, but in the long run it's best. Remember that you're 'over' the 1NT opener and that you get to make the opening lead." If you agree, do not adopt any system (IN THE DIRECT SEAT) where a double is not for penalty. Hence you would not use, for example, DONT, Meckwell, or Brozel.

Even though Larry Cohen likes DONT because it allows you to show all one- and two-suit hands without having to bid at the three-level, the double is NOT for penalty. Furthermore, the system must be able to show the majors at the two-level either directly or indirectly and one usually wants the strong hand on LEAD. If you agree with the above comments and want a system that may be played over either weak or strong no-trumps (Match Points or IMPS) it is, in my opinion, a better system is Modified Cappelletti.

Modified Cappelletti

Double: Any double over weak no-trump is for penalty. However, over strong no-trump bids it may be used for takeout/penalty.

2♣*: Shows a single-suited minor suited hand OR a two-suited holding in an unspecified major suit and minor suit. After a pass by the partner of the no-trump bidder, the advancer bids 2♦*, this is forcing for one round. Then the over caller will either pass or raise with diamonds if holding stronger values or bid clubs at the three level.

If the over caller shows the two-suited holding after the 2♦* bid, then the advancer can bid 2NT to return to the actual minor suit (clubs or diamonds) or pass if the major suit is preferred.

2♦*: Shows both major suits (as in Cappelletti).

2♥*: Shows a single-suited holding in hearts. Partner should pass after a no-trump opening by an opponent.

2♠*: Shows a single-suited holding in spades. Partner should pass after a no-trump opening by an opponent.

2NT*: Shows both minor suits (5+ in each).

WHAT SYSTEM SHOULD YOU ADOPT IN THE PASS-OUT SEAT? Clearly, in the pass-out seat, a double for penalty is not as valuable since the doubler is not on lead against 1NT. In the pass-out seat you should perhaps use Modified DONT also called Meckwell.

Modified DONT (Meckwell)

Double*: Shows a one-suited hand (6+ cards) or both majors.
2♣*: Shows clubs and a major suit (5-4 or 4-5 or longer).
2♦*: Shows diamonds and a major suit (5-4 or 4-5 or longer).
2♥: Shows hearts (5+)

2♠: Shows spades (5+)
2NT*: Shows both minor suits (5+in each).

Modified Cappelletti and Modified DON'T (Meckwell) are good selections for interference over no-trump. There have been many methods proposed. These methods both show the majors immediately and may be used with two-suited or single suited hands.

In both above conventions, 2NT* is used to show the minors. This is sometimes modified to show an equivalent no-trump hand. Discuss this option with your partner - *=alert.

Hello

A convention that is very similar to the Modified Cappelletti convention is the Helms-Lohman "Hello" convention. Here are their bids.

Double: Any double over weak no-trump is for penalty. However, over strong no-trump bids it may be used for takeout/penalty.

2♣*: Shows a single-suited holding in diamonds OR a two-suited holding in an unspecified major suit and an unspecified minor suit. After a pass by the partner of the no-trump bidder, the advancer can bid 2♦*, which is forcing for one round. Then the over caller will either pass or raise with a single-suiter in diamonds if holding stronger values OR bid the major suit if the holding is a two-suiter.

If the over caller shows the two-suited holding after the 2♦* bid, then the advancer can bid 2NT to return to the actual minor suit (clubs or diamonds) or pass if the major suit is preferred.

2♦*: Shows show 5+ hearts.
2♥*: Shows both majors 5-5.
2♠: Shows a single-suited holding in spades. Partner should pass after a no-trump opening by an opponent.
2NT*: Shows 5+ clubs.
3♣*: Shows both minors 5-5.
3♦*: Shows both majors with a very good hand.
Double* by a passed hand shows either clubs or diamonds and hearts.

Multi Landy

While the number of conventions used to interfere over no-trump is many, I came across a new system developed by Martin Johnson on the Web site:

www.freewebs.com/bobbybridge/conventions/conventions.htm.

While it is similar Modified Cappelletti and Meckwell, the clear advantage is that it may be played in both the direct and balancing seats. One convention for both the direct and balancing seat is attractive. The system Martin Johnson suggested follows; also included are his comment and analysis regarding systems one should use over no-trump openings.

1NT (opponent)   ?

2 ♣* - Landy (at least 5-4 or 4-5 in majors). Advancer bids 2♦ to ask opener to show longer major (over weak no-trump, may be 4-4).

2♦*- Multi (one-suiter in a major). Advancer bids 2♠ with good spades, else 2♥.

2♥*/2♠*- 5 card suit with a minor suit (usually 5-5). Advancer bids 2NT to ask for minor suit.

2NT* - minors

3m - 6+ suit, sounds vulnerable, may be pure preempt not vulnerable

Double* - 4-card major and 5-card minor, typically opening hand or better. Advancer may pass with a decent hand, otherwise bids 2♣ to ask opener to show his minor (passing with clubs, else 2♦) or 2♦ to ask for the major (will usually be 4-4 at least in majors), or 2M to play (own decent six-card suit).

Double* - Versus a weak no-trump, double is played as for penalty.

Modified Blooman

While many players of the 2/1 Game Force System play either DON'T or Cappelletti or their modifications, a major disadvantage is that they are both geared toward two-suited hands and if the contract is played in a suit the NT bidder is often NOT on lead.

Looking at Hand and Suit patterns, two-suited 5-5 hands occur far less frequently than one-suited hands and cards with SIX cards are 3.5 times more frequent. The 5-5 patterns occur about 4% of the time, while a 6-card pattern occurs more that 15% of the time. Thus, we need a convention that shows SIX cards and has the no-trump bidder (opener) on lead. One such convention is what I have called Modified Blooman. It is a modification of BLOOMAN devised by Robert (*Bob*) Hoffman of Boynton Beach, Florida, United States, and Irv Bloom of West Palm Beach Florida. And published in the "Bridge Bulletin", March 2006, page 28.

The very best convention when interfering over strong 1NT bids. It puts the strong hand on lead!

Modified Blooman (Direct Seat)

Bid	Meaning
X*	Relay to 2♣ then bid Cappelletti to show two-suited 5-5 hand
2♣*	Transfer to 6-card diamond suit
2♦*	Transfer to 6-card heart suit
2♥*	Transfer to 6-card spade suit

2♠*   Transfer to 6-card club suit

2NT*   Shows the minors (usually 5-5)

If you win the contract, NT bidder is on lead.

Modified Blooman (Balance Seat)

Bid your 6-card suit 3♣/3♦/3♥/3♠ Natural
If 5-5 X* and Partner makes the relay bid of 2♣* then follow this Cappelletti bids:

2♦*   5-5 in the majors
2♥*   Hearts + a minor
2♠*   Spades and a minor
2NT*   5-5 in the minors

If partner does not like the major bid, he bids 2NT which asks one to bid the minor.

Interference over Weak/Mini NT Bids

Many play the same convention over strong or weak no-trump bids by partnership agreement. However, a commonly used convention is **Landy** (played in both seats). Then Double*=penalty; 2♣ is Stayman, 2-level bids are natural, and 2NT*=minors.

Consistent with Modified Blooman – I recommend a convention I have called Modified Meckwell, following Blooman. With the weak range it does not matter who is on lead.

Modified Meckwell (Direct Seat/Balancing Seat)

Bid	Meaning
X*	Shows equal values – if the opponents bid 2♣ make a jump bid over their bid where 3♥/3♠ show a 6- card suit and 2NT shows the minors (5-5)
2♣*	Spades or a rounded suit (hearts or clubs); advancer bids 2♦*
2♦*	Unspecified Major
2♥	6-card heart suit
2♠	6-card spade suit
2NT*	Long minor, advancer bids 2♣; partner passes or corrects

When the Opponents Interfere Over 1NT Opening

Lebensohl is a common convention used over weak two bids, reverses, and interference over no-trump. It is explained in the book by Ron Anderson (1987), "The Lebensohl Convention

Complete in Contract Bridge, Devyn Press. An updated reference on Lebensohl is in a recent book by John Lute (2021), Lebensohl for Intermediate-Advanced Partnerships.

However, a less common convention is the Rubinsohl convention, which uses transfer bids and Lebensohl bids in a competitive auction aimed at allowing a player to show his distribution with both weak and strong hands. It is like the "stolen bid" convention played by many of club players. The method was introduced by Bruce Neill of Australia in an article in "The Bridge World" in 1983. The concept was based upon the article published in the same magazine by Jeff Rubens, who used the term Rubensohl. However, the method had been previously used in the United States by Ira Rubin, and therefore named Rubinsohl and not Rubensohl. Both names (Rubinsohl and Rubensohl) appear in the Bridge Literature. A convention like the Rubensohl, used in the United States, is the Transfer Lebensohl convention.

Lebensohl

Lebensohl is used after one opens no-trump when the opponents interfere to show game forcing hands immediately. However, the downside of Lebensohl is that you must go through relay bids to find out partner's real suit and if RHO competes you might never know that you have a good fit. In today's game, the opponents always seem to use their "toy" to disturb your no-trump and the RHO is getting into the action more and more to re-preempt the auction. Ira Rubin and Jeff Rubens thought it was better for partner to announce his suit directly and to show strength later.

The structure of Lebensohl is, briefly:

Double is for penalty (I play it as take-out to show cards)
Two-level bid is to play.
Three-level bid is forcing to game.
Two no-trump is artificial, forcing opener to bid three clubs.
An immediate cue bid by responder is Stayman (except after two clubs, double is Stayman).
A direct jump to 3NT denies a stopper.
Two NT followed by a cue bid of the enemy suit after opener's forced club relay bid is Stayman.
Two NT followed by 3NT, after a relay to three clubs, shows a stopper, and asks opener to pass and to play in three NT.

For example, consider the hand where opener has (♣, ♥, ♦, ♠) xxx AQxx AKxx Kx and the bidding goes: 1NT-2♠-2NT-4♠ and your partner has the hand: x Kxxxxx xx QTxx. You are forced to pass and miss the huge heart fit. Or you hold xxx Ax Axxx AKxx and the bidding goes 1NT-2♠-2NT-3♠ and partner holds x xxx QJTxxx Qxx and you guess that he was competing in hearts so you pass. You missed the five-diamond contract. In the first hand, it would be better to transfer to hearts, and in the second, one would want to transfer to diamonds.

To avoid these disasters, one may play Rubinsohl or Rumpelsohl that is part of the Kaplan Sheinwold bidding system.

I do not recommend either; instead, my system of choice is Transfer Lebensohl.

The Major disadvantage of Lebensohl is that it results in the play of a hand from the WRONG side since it is a relay-based system instead of a transfer-based system. This is not the case for Basic Rubinsohl and Transfer Lebensohl.

Transfer Lebensohl**

A close cousin to Basic Rubinsohl, and often confused with it, is Transfer Lebensohl. The conventional bids follow. The primary difference in the two systems is in the meaning of the bid of three spades. First off, all two-level bids are to play, identical to Lebensohl.

The primary difference between Lebensohl and Transfer Lebensohl is that 3-level bids are transfers to right-side the contract.

Transfer Lebensohl over no-trump and weak two bids.

After (1) 1NT (2X)?
(2) (2X) Dbl (P)?

(a) X = Diamonds/Hearts/Spades.

Double = Penalty/negative (over 2♠ or higher)
2Y to play where Y is not equal to X.
2NT*: Puppet to 3♣
-> Pass /Lower Suit: To play.
3X cue bid Stayman with stopper GF
Over X=H, 3♠=both minors
3NT with a stopper
3♣*: Transfer to diamonds, INV or better.
3♦*: Transfer to hearts, INV or better.
3♥*: Transfer to spades, INV or better.
If transfer to opponents -> Stayman w/o stopper
3♠*: Transfer to clubs no stopper
3NT*: To play, w/o a stopper
4m: Leaping Michaels. 5-5 up
(X=M: 4♣=C+oM. 4♦=D+oM.
X=D: 4♣=C+One major. 4♦=H+S.)
4M: Unbid: NAT. with stopper.
Jump Cue: Minors. Strong.
4NT: Minors. (Weak if X=M.)

(b) X = Clubs.

Double = Cue bid Stayman w/o stopper

2Y where Y is not equal to X: To play.
2NT transfer to diamonds no stopper (weak).
-> 3♦=Accept. 3♣=Decline.
3♣: Stayman with a stopper GF
3♦*: Transfer to hearts, INV or better.
3♥*: Transfer to spades, INV or better.
3♠*: Transfer to diamonds no stopper (INV)
3NT: To play but no stopper
4m: Leaping Michaels.
4M: NAT. with stopper.

It may also be played in the sequence 1x - X – 2x?

**Modern Lebensohl (Modified Transfer Lebensohl) is like Transfer Lebensohl except that 3NT* shows a stopper and 3-level bids ask for stoppers (like Western Que bids) and are not transfers!

The best system to play after an overcall of partner's 1NT bid has a long history in "The Bridge World." For an informative discussion, one may consult the May/June 1989 Issue of "Bridge Today" and the article by Alvin Roth (one of America's foremost bidding theorists) "Doctor Roth's What Do You Bid and Why?" pages 39 – 41. He recommends that one NOT play Lebensohl but use a transfer-based system like either Transfer Lebensohl or Basic Rubinsohl.

The Basic Rubinsohl bids follow (fast no longer denies).

Over a natural 2♠ overcall

2NT*	transfer to clubs
3 ♣*	transfer to diamonds
3 ♦*	transfer to hearts
3 ♥*	(transfer into their suit) is Stayman without a stopper
3 ♠*	transfer to 3NT with a stopper
3NT*	natural with a stopper in the bid suit.

Over a natural 2♥ overcall

2 ♠ *	natural and non-forcing
2NT*	transfer to clubs
3 ♣*	transfer to diamonds
3 ♦*	(transfer into their suit) is Stayman without a stopper
3 ♥*	shows spades with a heart stopper
3 ♠*	shows spades without a stopper in hearts
3NT*	natural with a stopper in the bid suit.

If the opponents overcall a natural minor, the treatment is as follows. Two-level bids are natural and non-forcing. With the overcall 2♦, 2NT* shows clubs as usual, but 3♣ is Stayman for both majors and asks if partner has a diamond stopper. If no major or stopper, one accepts the transfer. Jumps in the majors are natural and forcing. The bids of 3♦*/3♥* are transfers. But 3♠* is partnership defined most, use it to show a club bust (Minor Suit Stayman). A bid of 3NT* shows a stopper in diamonds.

With a 2♣ (natural or not) overcall, a double is Stayman without a club stopper and two-level bids are natural and competitive. 2NT is usually defined as Stayman with a club stopper. A jump to a three-level bid is a transfer and forcing.

What if their bid shows two suits, then transferring into their lower ranking suit shows the next higher suit which is not the opponents? So, if their bid shows hearts and a minor, transferring into hearts must show spades.

With so many "toys" being used over 1NT, Rubinsohl and Transfer Lebensohl have a distinct advantage over Lebensohl since you know your suit early and it ignores the RHO getting into the act. In both systems, a double is not for penalty but for takeout.

Defense over Transfer Bids after 1NT and NAMYATS

In duplicate bridge, transfer bids (e.g., Jacoby, Texas, and NAMYATS, etc.) are almost standard. How do you defend against these systems?

The following defenses against transfer bids will allow you to show two-suited hands with one call. They may be employed not only against transfers but against any bid that shows specific suits (e.g., 2NT to show the minors). A major disadvantage of transfer bids is that they give the opponent two opportunities for action: immediate or delayed. This aid to defensive bidding accuracy should be utilized.

When Your Side Has Been Silent

When the transfer bid occurs before your side has bid or doubled (e.g., vs Jacoby or Texas response to a 1NT opening, or vs an opening preemptive transfer bid), use the following defense:

- A no-trump bid asks for a preference between the lower two suits, excluding the one indicated by the transfer bid.
- A double of the transfer bid shows the higher two suits.
- A "cue bid" (in the suit indicated by the transfer bid) is top-and-bottom, asking for a preference between the top and bottom suits.

For instance, after a 2♦ Jacoby response to a 1NT opening

South	West	North	East
1NT	Pass	2♦	2NT* - both minors
			X* - spades/diamonds
			2♥* - spades/clubs
			2♠/3♣/3♦ - one-suited hand

The double may be made with less strength than any of the other two-suited calls. One of the suits indicated by the double is the suit bid by the opponent, so partner can pass with an unsuitable hand. This sequence has an easy mnemonic: Double for Diamonds and the other major, Cue bid for Clubs and the other major. Bids over a 2♥ transfer to spades have the same mnemonic.

When given a choice of suits in which you have equal length, prefer a major to a minor, hearts to spades, and clubs to diamonds. Partner can keep this in mind when deciding whether to overcall or pass with a marginal hand.

The immediate overcall with a one-suited hand should be quite sound. With a doubtful hand, simply pass and reopen the bidding if the transfer suit gets passed:

South	West	North	East
1NT	Pass	2♦	Pass
2♥*	Pass	Pass	2♠/3♣/3♦

These reopening bids can be made with moderate hands since partner is marked with some high cards when the opponents stop at the two-levels.

The soundness of immediate natural overcalls applies at higher levels, too:

South	West	North	East
1NT	Pass	4♦	4♠/5♣/5♦ - sound bids
			4NT* - for the minors

Remember that a direct bid of 4NT is for the minors and a balancing 4NT bid is natural. That is the general rule and for the sake of consistency it must be followed even at this level.

With a doubtful hand, perhaps taking a deliberate save with many playing tricks but little defense, east can pass on this round and bid next time. This policy may help partner when he must make a double/bid/pass decision.

You may sometimes have a three-suited hand with shortness in the suit indicated by the transfer bid. In that case, pass the transfer, then double for takeout on the next round. You can do this with a huge hand, since the transfer bid is forcing; there is no need to jump into the bidding immediately:

South	West	North	East
1NT	Pass	2♥	Pass
2♠	Pass	Pass	X* - takeout double strong 1NT

If 1NT was weak, this double is optional, just showing a strong balanced hand.

When the transfer is an opening bid that shows a preemptive bid in the next higher suit, the same principles apply. An immediate no-trump overcall still shows the lower two "unbid" suits. A reopening no-trump bid is therefore natural:

South	West	North	East
3♦	Pass	3♥	Pass
Pass	X= normal takeout double		
	3♠ competitive reopening bid		
	3NT natural		

South's 3♦ bid shows a preemptive type of hand. The double is not a reopening action since an immediate double would show a two-suited hand with spades and diamonds. It is true that passing 3♦ with a nine-trick no-trump hand gives north a chance to make a preemptive raise in hearts, but that must be changed. There are two advantages to this approach: (1) a two-suited hand in the minors can be easily shown by an immediate 3NT bid, and (2) the general principles of countering transfer bids remain the same, with no exceptions. We consider an example.

South	West	North	East
3♣	Pass	3♦	3♥/3♠/X

Believe it or not, east is making a reopening call. North has indicated that he would have passed a normal 3♦ opening bid, so east pretends that is just what has happened. He is no worse off than he would be with a normal preemptive 3♦ opening. This is especially true if he is short in diamonds. The hand short in the opposing suit must be quick to act since partner probably cannot.

Against Strong NAMYATS

The NAMYATS Convention uses a 4♣* opening to show hearts and a 4♦* opening to show spades. Even in the "strong" version a 4♥ or 4♠, the bids are usually weak in high cards (only 7- 7 ½ quick tricks), while a 4♣* or 4♦* opening shows a good hand (8-8 ½+ quick tricks) that would welcome a slam contract. The fact there is an intervening suit between the transfer bid and the indicated suit affects the usual defense against transfer bids:

- Passing and then doubling opener's major on the next round retains the same meaning: a strong three-suited hand short in opener's suit.

- Immediate overcalls in the ranking suit (i.e., the suit lying between opener the opening bid and opener's major) may be weaker than overcalls in the remaining two suits. If you don't bid now, you must bid higher next time.

- Immediate overcalls in the remaining two suits are very sound, because you can pass and bid on the next round with a sacrifice type hand, at the same level that an immediate bid would require.

- Jump overcalls are extra strong.

- The immediate double, "cue bid" of opener's suit, and no-trump bids all retain the same meaning: major/diamonds, major/clubs, and both minors, respectively:

South	West	
4♣*	X*	diamonds and hearts
	4♦	diamonds, may be a stretch
	5♣*	cubs and spades
	4♠/5♣	good hand
	4NT*	minors
	5♦/5♠	extra strong

With a sacrifice bid of 4♠ or 5♣, west could pass and bid on the next round. The immediate overcall shows a good hand both offensively and defensively. The difference may be important if partner must decide what to do when the opponents go to 5♥.

There are two ways to show spades and a minor: double/cue bid or bid 4♠ and then bid the minor (if you get the chance). Choose the natural bid when spades are strong and longer than the minor, the conventional call otherwise. You are not going to run if 4♠ gets doubled, so the spades had better be pretty good. When you show the suits conventionally, partner will not take a false preference to play the major suit.

There at least two ways of showing both minors: bid 4NT immediately or on the second round. Common sense says that an immediate 4NT bid is stronger than a delayed one. The immediate bid promises a good hand, both offensively and defensively, while a delayed bid implies poor defense.

When the opening is 4♣*, you can also show diamonds and clubs by bidding them instead of overcalling 4NT, which provides a third way of showing both minors. Show the minors this way when the clubs are not longer than the diamonds. Partner will then prefer diamonds with equal length. After a 4NT bid, he prefers clubs with equal length.

There are also three ways to get to 5♦ after a 4♣* opening: bid 5♦ immediately; bid 4♦, then 5♦, or pass and then bid 5♦. The jump is stronger; the delayed bid (passing first) is weaker. Bidding diamonds twice (a seemingly illogical action) allows room for partner to bid 4♠, so it could be based on a good hand with some spade support.

When the opening is 4♦* it is the immediate major suit bid that may be a stretch:

South	West	
4♦*	X*	diamonds and hearts
	4♥	may be a stretch
	4♠*	clubs and hearts
	4NT*	minors
	5♣/5♦	sound bids
	5♥	extra strong

West has three ways to get to 5♥: bid 5♥ immediately, obviously the strongest action; bid 5♥ on the next round (weakest); or bid 4♥, then 5♥, which is somewhere in-between.

There are two ways to show hearts and a minor: double/cue bid or bid both suits. With hearts longer than the minor, one bids 4♥ and then the minor. When the two suits are of equal length, or the minor is longer, double or cue bid.

There is no way left to double opener's eventual game bid for business unless you can overcall in the ranking suit and then double on the next round. That is not a big deal, because doubling a strong NAMYATS game bid is seldom profitable and often disastrous.

Against Weak NAMYATS

When the opening bid of 4♣ or 4♦ shows a weak major suit preempt, we must have a way of doubling the major for business. The delayed double therefore becomes a little more optional than takeout, not necessarily a three-suited hand. Otherwise, the defense is the same as against the strong version of NAMYATS.

NAMYATS NOTE: When playing strong NAMYATS, most people will open 4♥/4♠ directly with weak preemptive hands and long major suits. Warning, if **NAYMYATS is not played by the partnership, the "preemptive bid" may be strong!** Even if you play strong NAMYATS, you should discuss it with your partner. For example, some partnerships play the refusal of the transfer (4♦ over 4♣ and 4♥ over 4♦) to allow opener to play game (usually no tenace) while others use the intermediate bid to request partner to bid an ace if he has one or to sign off without an ace. For a review of bidding sequences, visit: members.shaw/ convention/Namyats.htm.

Action vs NAMYATS by Fourth Seat

When the opening has been passed by second seat, third seat will either bid four of partner's major or bid the next higher suit (as a query bid or as a "retransfer" to let opener play the hand).

- When third seat signs off in opener's suit, a double is for takeout and a 4NT bid shows both minors:

South	West	North	East
4♣*	Pass	4♥	X* - takeout
			4NT* - minors

Against the weak version of NAMYATS, the double of 4♠ is more optional than takeout, just as it would be over a normal preemptive 4♥ or 4♠ opening.

- When third seat bids the ranking suit so that opener can play the hand that is treated like a transfer bid:

South	West	North	East
4♣*	Pass	4♦	X* - spades and diamonds
			4♥* - spades and clubs
			4NT* - minors

South	West	North	East
4♣*	Pass	4♥	X* - hearts and diamonds
			4♠* - hearts and clubs
			4NT* – minors

Other defensive actions are similar in meaning to those used in the second seat.

Defense Against Forcing 1NT*

Using the 2/1 convention, after a major opening the opponents bid 1NT and announce the bid as forcing. How do you compete?

Suppose the bidding goes 1♥/1♠ - Pass - 1NT* -? And you want to compete. While some may play all bids as natural, sometimes you need a way to show hands that are widely varying in strength, without misleading partner, or a two-suiter. A clever way is to switch some bids around that allow one to compete in the fourth position. Using the Useful Space Principle (USP), one may employ the Vasilevsky Convention.

In the above forcing 1NT sequence, you bid as follows with 15/17**AOC** points since you are bidding at the 2-level.

X*	Transfer to clubs
2♣*	Transfer to diamonds
2♦*	Transfer to the unbid major
2 of the bid major	Good, distributional takeout "double"

2 of unbid major	Weaker takeout double, guaranteeing four of the major bids
2NT	Distributional takeout for the minors
3♣/3♦	Natural, but shows 6-4, the four being the unbid major

Let's see how it works. The bidding goes 1♥ - Pass - 1NT - ?
And you hold:

    a)   ♠K10654 ♥5 ♦A9 ♣KQ976

Double* to show clubs (*=alert). If opener passes and partner bids 2♣, you next bid 2♠*, showing a two-suited 5-5 hand. If you were 6-4 in clubs and spades, you would bid 3♣.

However, suppose you are 4-4 in clubs and spades. You have the hand:

    b)   ♠AJ54 ♥7 ♦AK93 ♣A874

You now bid 3♥*, showing a strong takeout double.

When you are a passed hand, Vasilevsky no longer applies. Since intervener's hand is limited, he doesn't need two bids.

The only disadvantage of the convention is that one may not penalize a 1NT bid; however, this does not occur that often. The advantage is that, using transfers, the calls are logical, hence easy to remember and show exactly the distribution and strength needed to compete.

The Useful Space Principle (USP)

The Vasilevsky Convention is based upon the Useful Space Principle developed by Jeff Rubens. The principle has formed the basis for the creation and development of many modern-day conventions, for example, Roman Keycard Blackwood with Kickback.

The definition of USP follows:

"When allocating bidding space under partnership agreements, assign it where most useful without deference to natural or traditional bridge meanings of calls."

Let's apply the principle in some situations.

Suppose the bidding goes: 1♣ - X - 1♥ -?

What do you bid if you are weak and have four spades? Bid 2♥ and with 10+ points and five spades, bid 2♠.

Recall that Leaping Michaels is a reasonable way to show a two-suited hand over weak level bids. Using the USP, suppose the bidding goes:

2♠ - Pass - 3♠ - (?)

How do you now compete? Consider the following bids.

4♣*	shows clubs and hearts
4♦*	shows diamonds and hearts
4♠*	shows game in a long minor and asks partner to bid 5♣ which may be corrected, if necessary, to 5♦
4♥	natural
4NT*	shows both minors

The previous are just two examples of exchanging the normal meaning of bids; you can invent many more if you are so inclined. For additional suggestions, consult "Competitive Bidding in the 21st Century" by Marshall Miles (2000) published by Master Point Press.

Instead of using the Vasilevsky Convention, **another option one may use when competing over the forcing 1NT* bid is to use the Modified Blooman convention. Then one transfers to 6-card suit and a X* is used to show a 5-5 two suited hand.**

Playing "traditional 2/1" an opening bid is between 11 and 21points and 1NT* forcing/semi-forcing shows 7-12 points counting only HCP. The minimal HCP for the opponents is between 18-23 points which makes game by the opponents unlikely. In addition, rebids at the 2-level rebid by the opener show 12-15H and 3-level suit bids or 2NT show between 16-18H points.

What does this mean? Complete over a forcing 1NT* bid with caution since even a 2-level bid may be doubled for penalty; so you should have at least a 6-card suit or two strong 5-5 suits with shortness in their bid suit and with 15-18+**AOC**.

CHAPTER 9

CONVENTIONAL DOUBLES

Support Double and Redouble

Support doubles, invented by Eric Rodwell in 1974, are used when the opponents overcall after they have bid a suit. For examples: the bidding goes 1♦ - Pass - 1♥ - 2♣ (overcall) – double. The double is not for penalty, it shows three-card supports (support double) for hearts and **no longer requires an alert**. A bid of 2♥ shows four-card support. The convention is usually played through 2♥ or 2♠. If instead of bidding two clubs, one doubles then the double is replaced by a redouble (no alert) to show three-card supports for hearts. Support doubles and redoubles must be alerted. The support double says nothing at all about the strength of you hand. It says "I have three card supports" for the bid major.

Support doubles are unusually only played for the majors; however, some play them for all suits. If you want to play support doubles over 3-level bids, they show three card support and extra values.

If the auction goes 1♣ - pass - 1♦ - 1♥ - and opener has a four-card spade suit, he should not use the support double with three hearts, but instead show the spade suit. If now the RHO bids 1NT instead of a suit, the double would be for penalty. Some examples follow.

1♦ - Pass - 1♥ - 1♠ (overcall) -X
The double shows three-card supports for hearts

1♣ - 1♦ - 1♥ - 2♦ (overcall) -2♥
Shows four-card supports for hearts.

1♥ - pass - 1♠ - 2♠ - 3♥
Shows 6+ hearts and denies spade support (less than three).

Some partnerships playing 2/1 do not like support doubles since it precludes making a penalty double of the overcall. Because penalty is not as likely at the two-level, this is not a problem for most players.

For more information on support doubles, read the article by Eric Rodwell on the web site: www. bridgetopics.com or Rodwell (2017), "Eric Rodwell's Bidding Topics", Book 1, page 3.

Responsive Doubles - Opponents Bid And Raise (OBAR)

A double used for takeout after partner has made a takeout double or a simple suit (not NT) overcall, and RHO has raised the suit bid by opener.

Example (1)   1♦/♣ - double (takeout) - 2♦/♣ - doubles (responsive

Example (2)   1♦/♣ - double (takeout) - 3♦/♣ - double (responsive)

In this auction, you should be 4-4 in the majors, and you are asking partner to pick a major. To use the responsive double, you should have 7-9 Starting Points at the two-level and 10+ at the three-level.

Example (3)   1♥ - double (takeout for spades) - 2♥ - double (responsive)

Example (4)   1♠- double (takeout for hearts) - 2♠ - double (responsive)

In (3) you must bid spades if you have four, if not you make the responsive double which denies four spades. Partner next bids his 5-card suit, if he has none; he bids 2NT asking you do bid your 4-card suits up the line. In (4) you must bid spades, if not double, and partner will bid his 5-card suit or bid 2NT again asking you to bid your 4-card suits up the line.

If the bidding were to go:

Example   1♣ - double - 1♥ - double

The second double is not responsive but shows hearts (4+ cards).

Responsive doubles are usually played through the same level as negative doubles, most partnerships use 3♠.

What if the bidding goes?

Example   1♦ - 1NT - 2♦ - double

You need an agreement for this double; it is either penalty or transfer. Playing systems on over the no-trump bid, it would be a transfer to hearts. If systems are off, it is probably for penalty. Few play the double for takeout (unlikely).

What if partner overcalls; the bidding goes:

Example   1♣ - 1♥ - 2♣ - double

This is also a **responsive double,** used by many to show the other two unbid suits. If this is your agreement, you may not play Snapdragon or Rosenkranz doubles.

Maximal Support Double

A double of a three-level bid that asks partner to bid game.

Example: 1♠ - 2♥ - 2♠ - 3♥ - double (maximal double). The double asks partner to bid 3♠ with a minimum and 4♠ with a maximum. If you merely compete by bidding 3♠, partner may take the bid as only competitive.

Snapdragon and Rosenkranz Doubles

If partner has overcalled a minor and all suits have been bid, the snapdragon double shows three-card support for the minor and a five-card major.

Example: 1♣ - 1♦ - 1♥ - double*

This is a snapdragon double (alert) that shows three-card support for diamonds and a five-card spade suit.

Alternatively, suppose partner overcalled a major:

Example: 1♣ - 1♠ - 2♣ - double*

This is a Rosenkranz double (alert) which a spade raise is promising an ace, king, or queen (some only use it to show and ace or king). The bid of two spades would deny a top honor. **Note: If you use this type of double, you must give up the responsive double.**

In the above, the bidding could also go:

Example: 1♣ - 1♠ - double – redouble*

This is also Rosenkranz (alert), showing three-card supports with an honor (A, K, or some promise a Q). Because the goal is to get to major suit contract, I recommend that Snapdragon Doubles be played over a minor overcall and that Rosenkranz Doubles/Redoubles be played over major suit overcalls.

Lead Directing Doubles

A lead directing double is used when the opponents make an artificial bid. For example, if the opponents Stayman after the bid of 1NT, a double of Stayman asks partner to lead a club. To make the double, you must hold either Ax or Kx. They may also be used over transfers, any artificial bid, and Splinter bids.

Fisher Double

Invented by Dr. John W. Fisher, the Fisher double is used when opening 1NT or 2NT. The double of the final no-trump contract at any level asks for a lead in a minor suit, CLUBS if the 2♣ Stayman Convention was NOT used and diamonds if Stayman was used but it was not doubled. A final note: some partnerships use the convention asking for a diamond lead, no matter if clubs were bid or not. Discuss this bid with your partner!

Lightner Slam Double

This convention was designed by Theodore Lightner and asks the partner of the opening leader to make a lead directing double of a slam contract.

If doubler has bid a suit, (1) partner MUST NOT lead the suit, (2) DO NOT LEAD a TRUMP, (3) assume that the double is based on a void or an unexpected AK (or AQ) in a suit bid by the opponents. (Very often dummies first bid suit.)

If doubler has NOT bid a suit, (1) partner MUST NOT lead the unbid suit, (2) DO NOT LEAD a TRUMP, (3) assume that the double is based on a void or an unexpected AK (or AQ) in a suit bid by the opponents or perhaps declarers side suit (second bid suit).

If both the doubler and the doubler's partner have bid a suit, (1) partner MUST NOT lead the suit bid by the doubler, (2) DO NOT LEAD a TRUMP, (3) partner is forbidden to lead his own suit, (4) lead the unbid suit.

Doubles of no-trump slams usually ask partner to lead dummy's first bid suit or an unusual lead.

Convention Card: Special Doubles

On the back of the ACBL convention card, there is the section called **SPECIAL DOUBLES.**

Special Doubles
After Overcall: Penalty ☐ _____
Negative   thru _____
Responsive ☐   thru _____Maximal ☐
Support: Dbl ☐   thru _____ Redbl ☐
Card-Showing ☐ Min. Offshape T/O ☐

We have discussed all Special Doubles on the Convention Card except for the card-showing doubles and off shape doubles, which we now define.

Card-Showing Doubles

If your low-level competitive doubles show values without being strictly penalty or negative in nature, check this box. For example, if partner opens 1♣, RHO bids 1♥, and you double simply to show a good hand regardless of the pattern, this would be a card-showing double.

Minimum Offshape Takeout Doubles

A takeout double of an opening bid usually shows a hand with at least opening values and shortness in the opener's suit. It also suggests support for the unbid suits. However, some players will make a takeout double on any hand with minimal opening values (twelve to fourteen HCP) even if the pattern isn't classic! For example, after RHO bid of 1♥ opening, and if you would double with the hand:

♠ A5 ♥ K873 ♦ KJ52 ♣ Q98.

CHECK THE BOX.

While the Box is not YET in Red on the Convention Card, it should be - just like Walsh Convention bidders should alert their bid (not required by ACBL if one holds 3 diamonds) in the sequence 1♣ Pass 1♦!

SOS Redouble

Many times, the opponents will double a part score suit contract at the two or three-level for penalty. When partner redoubles the penalty double, it is called an SOS Redouble. It asks partner for his best rescue bid.

CHAPTER 10

SOME USEFUL RULES

Rule of 7 (Hold Up)

When playing NT contracts and having only one stopper in the suit led headed by the ace, one may use the Rule of 7 to decide how many times to hold up. Rule: subtract the total number of cards you and dummy hold in the suit from seven. This is the number of times you should hold up when the suit is led by the opponents. The rule is also used with suit contracts.

Rule of 11

The Rule of 11 is used for placing the outstanding higher cards when partner makes a fourth best lead. One subtracts the spot of the card led from eleven (15-4=11) to determine the number of higher cards in the remaining three hands. Since the high cards in the dummy and your hand can be seen, the remaining cards are with declarer. This information is quite useful in deciding which card to play on the trick and how to play the suit if you take the trick. If the answer does not make sense, the card led may not be fourth best.

Rule of 10/12

When playing third and fifth best leads the concepts remain the same. Using fifteen as the base, subtract from fifteen the card led **(third or fifth best).** If partner's lead is third best, subtract spot card from twelve (15-3=12). If partner's lead is fifth best, subtract spot card from ten (15-5=10). If you are not sure, try both; one of the answers is likely to make more sense than the other, giving you an idea of partner's holdings.

8 Ever 9 Never

When finessing for the queen, with nine cards and no information, the odds for a drop are 52.18% vs 50% for finesse! This is a nominal difference. In general, if the finesse is into the safe hand, even with nine cards, one would finesse, with no information from the bidding, it is better to play for the drop of the queen.

Let me explain the percentage in more detail. With AJxxx (dummy) and Kxxx (hand), plan (1) is to cash the king, and if the queen does not drop, take the finesse and plan (2) is to cash the ace and king to drop the queen. Plan (1) wins if trumps are 3-1 with three on our left (24.87%), when they are 2-2 with the queen on the left (20.35%), and when they are 1-3 with the bare queen onside (6.22%), for a total of 51.22 percent. For plan (2), when the suit is 2-2 (40.70%) or 3-1 either way round with a bare queen (12.44%), for a total of 53.14 percent. I averaged these two approaches to obtain 52.18% or about 52%! It works! You say, if the queen does not drop with plan (1), each opponent follows low; do not finesse, but play for the drop. Now, the probability of queen to three on the left is 47.85% and queen doubleton on the right is 52.15%. Here the difference is 52.15-47.85=4.30%. This has a greater difference than playing for the drop, 53.14-51.22=1.92%. Thus, if no queen falls on first card, still play for the drop.

10 Ever 11 Never

A similar rule applies when finessing for the king; with eleven cards, it is again better to play for the drop; however, with ten cards, finesse. Again, the probability is small, about 52% vs 50%. I will not bore you with the details. However, let's look at an example.

If the king is missing and you have 11 cards, only two cards are outstanding in the suit. If they split evenly (1-1) which occurs 52% of the time, the king will drop. A 2-0 split occurs only about 48% of the time. Thus, play for the drop!

While simple rules may be used for the king and the queen, what happens missing the Jack? Suppose you have Q72 and AK106 in a suit. Do you finesse or play for the drop? You have seven hearts, and the opponents have six. If they split 3-3, the jack will drop. This is referred to as the Finesse Drop Test "FDT". Simply count the outstanding cards!

Rule of 210

How many times have you heard bridge players say that the 5-level belongs to the opponents?

THIS IS NOT THE CASE IN COMPETITIVE AUCTIONS!

If you are in a competitive auction and the opponents have bid to the 5-level, do you compete, double or pass. You may use the rule of 210.

With two (2) cards in the opponents bid suit you should DOUBLE for penalty.

With ONE (1) card in their suit pass, and with ZERO (0) cards in their suit, compete to the five level.

For example, you are bidding diamonds and they are bidding clubs. Use the rule to determine whether you should bid five diamonds over five clubs, double, or pass.

This is also the case for hearts over diamonds or spades over hearts. Remember the rule of 210; simple!

The rule comes from negative slam doubles, which are used to decide whether to sacrifice. Over a slam the secondhand doubles to show no defensive tricks but passes with one or more tricks.

Negative Slam Double - A Double of opponent's slam is used to indicate either a willingness to continue bidding or penalize the opponents

Example:

(1♥) - 2♠ - (4♥) - 4♠;
(6♥) – X

This Double indicates the player has no defensive tricks and, assuming partner's hand is limited to offensive values, suggests partner make a sacrifice slam bid (usually with favorable vulnerability).

Barry Crane Rules (commandments)

Finding the Queen is one of the most difficult tasks in the game of Bridge. If you have the following card combination:

	♠/♥AJxx				♦/♣AJxx	
West		East	or	West		**East**
	♠/♠K10xx				♦/♣K10xx	

You can finesse either way, West or East, you have a Two-Way finesse. Barry Crane one of the best American Match Play card players of all time recommends, with no information from the bidding, that you always do the same thing. Be consistent every time with no information.

In addition, he finds that for the MAJORS, the Queen lies UNDER the Jack and that for the MINORS, it is lies OVER the Jack.

Hence, he will always play WEST for the Queen for the Major suits and EAST for the Queen for the Minor suit. This rule is part of Barry Crane's 12 COMMANDMENTS; his commandments are as follows:

1. Never pull partner's penalty double.

2. Always take a sure profit.

3. Watch out for the three level.

4. The more you bid the more you got (no "fast arrival" here).

5. Sevens are singletons.

6. Don't bid grand slams at Swiss teams.

7. Don't put cards in partner's hand.

8. (Only) Jesus saves.

9. Don't east between sessions.

10. Never ask "How's your game?"

11. Never gloat.

12. The queen is over the jack in the minors and under the jack in the majors.

CHAPTER 11

CARDING

Standard Carding and MUD

On the convention card under defensive carding, one observes two boxes next to Standard: vs Suits vs NT. If these are marked, then standard carding means that on partner's lead, one is playing attitude and on the opponent's lead, one is playing count. Attitude is shown by playing a high card to encourage the suit lead and a low card discourages. The cutoff is the six, which means neither.

Count is given by playing high low for an even number of cards and low high for an odd number of cards. Count does not apply for the trump suit. If you do not play trump suit preference, then a high-low discard shows extra trumps (usually three). When the attitude signal is not needed (partner has led the ace and the king is in dummy) then one shows suit preference. A high trump card requests the higher of the remaining suits that are not trump and a low trump card requests the lower of the two suits that are not trump.

In no-trump, some use **BOSTON** leads which means BOS (**B**ottom **O**f **S**omething), an Honor, or **TON** (**T**op **O**f **N**othing). When partner has bid a suit, then one usually leads the highest card in partner's bid suit, if supported; otherwise, from three small one leads the lowest when the suit is not supported.

When leading a card most play fourth best leads for both suits and no-trump contracts; **but never from four small cards for no-trump leads.** However, using the Rule of 11, the fourth best lead helps the opponents whether playing in no-trump or suit contracts. Instead, one may use 3rd/5th best for **suit** contracts (the rule of 12/10, respectively) and attitude leads against NT (BOSTON); however, some use 4th best leads. When a low card is lead from 5-card suit and the 3-card is led from a 4-card suit. From 3 lead low from an honor.

Alternatively, some play MUD which is "Middle-Up-Down", or Roman MUD developed by Benito Garozzo of the famous Italian Blue Team. Versus suit and no-trump contracts, leading low promises a Jack or higher, hence leading low from three or fourth best when the suit is longer promises an honor. From three cards or longer in a suit with no honor one leads the second highest card; an exception; if you are holding 10-9-x or longer, lead the 10. The advantage of MUD is that you know whether partner has an honor, but do not know how many cards partner holds. Let's look at a few examples of MUD vs 3/5 leads for suit contracts

Cards led vs suit contracts

Holding	3/5	MUD
Q7542	2	4
Q742	4	2
Q72	2	2
872	2	7
9842	4	8
97642	2	7
72	7	7

Which is better for suit contracts, 3/5 or MUD?

Let's look at an example. Suppose we have the following situation:

DUMMY

Q754

PARTNER LEADS   **YOU**

2   AJ1063

Which card do you play?

Playing 3/5 leads, the 2 can be from K72 or K72 or K92. Should you play the Ace or the 10? You do not know. However, playing MUD you know partner has the king! MUD is better. To be fair, suppose the lead is not the 2 but the 7. Playing 3/5 leads, you know partner usually has a doubleton; however, playing MUD partner can have K72 or 972, you do not know. No scheme is foolproof. Partnerships must choose. The bridge expert Mel Colchamiro says for suit contracts including four spades or lower use MUD, but for five clubs or higher contracts use 3/5. For more, see his article in the September 2013 issue of the "Bridge Bulletin".

Against NT, if partner leads an ace, it usually requests partner to unblock, to play his highest honor. If the king is lead, partner is to play his second highest honor. If, however, the queen is lead, partner is requested to play the jack. Against suit contracts, the ace/queen requests attitude, and the king count from your partner.

When partner leads small and you take the trick as appropriate, then the standard return of a suit is the lowest card from three remaining cards or the highest from two remaining.

To show shortness in a suit, one plays high-low (playing standard). If you do get a ruff, the card returned should indicate whether you want the higher suit returned and a low card asks for the lower of the remaining suits.

Other Carding Agreements

While the "standard" carding system is played by many duplicate bridge players, some do not like the system since it tends to waste "high" cards. A popular option is upside down count and attitude which is the opposite of standard.

Upside-Down Count and Attitude

Playing upside-down count and attitude (UDCA), a low card is encouraging on a lead and a high card is discouraging. Now, a doubleton is denoted by low-high instead of high-low. However, on leads, one still uses the high-low single to show a doubleton. If you do not, it must be alerted because they are usually using 2/4 leads which is like MUD.

Count is also opposite of standard for UDCA, high-low is odd and low-high is even. When you cannot follow suit, a low card in a suit is encouraging and a high card is discouraging. Most partnerships playing 2/1 use this approach since high values are not wasted.

Playing UDCA many duplicate players also play 3/5 leads against suit contracts and BOSTON against NT. Never lead 4th best!

Odd-Even Discards

Odd-Even discards is also called Roman Discards. It is used when you cannot follow suit the first time, an odd card in a suit is encouraging and an even card is discouraging. A high even card says you like the higher of the suits not led, excluding the trump suit, and a low even card says you like the lower of the two suits do not lead, again excluding the trump suit. It is played against both suit contracts and no-trump. When played in no-trump contracts, a low even card says you want the lower of the two suits, excluding the suit lead.

Lavinthal Discards

Like odd even, except a low card (less than six) says you would like the lower of the suits that is not trump and a high card says you want the higher of the two suits that are not trump.

Suit Preference Discard

When you cannot follow suit the first time, a discard of any suit shows your suit preference.

Revolving Suit Discards

When unable to follow suit for the first time, you discard a card from a suit you do not want. A high card asks for the higher-ranking suit, and a low card asks for the lower-ranking suit.

What carding system should you adopt? Let's look at an example where both are vulnerable and north deals.

		♠ AKJ10			
		♥ 32			
		♦ 2			
		♣ AKJ1032			
♠ 9532				♠ 64	
♥ Q1094		N		♥ A765	
♦ K1095		W E		♦ AJ65	
♣ 6		S		♣ 987	
		♠ Q87			
		♥ KJ8			
		♦ Q876			
		♣ Q54			

The bidding goes:

North	East	South	West
1♣	Pass	1NT	Pass
2♠	Pass	2NT	Pass
3NT	Pass	Pass	Pass

Opening lead is the 4♥.

Playing upside-down signals, east wins with the ace. Now, to defeat the contract, the defense needs red suit tricks, so instead of making the routine return of a heart, east returns a low diamond. West now encourages with the five. East continues with the jack of diamonds and the defenders take the first five diamond tricks to defeat the contract. On a heart return, declarer makes eleven tricks.

If instead of playing upside-down signals, suppose you are playing standard signals and make the same switch. Now you must play the ten or the nine of diamonds, declarer covers the jack with the queen and the defenders get only three diamond tricks and a heart. The contract makes.

Of course, there is no "best" carding system. But why use a high card to encourage partner?

On average, the better carding system is upside-down count and attitude against both suit and no-trump contracts. Against no-trump contracts, some use 4th best or BOSTON; however, for suit contracts, it is usually better to use third and fifth leads.

Coded 9's and 10's

When leading against no-trump contracts, most people lead fourth best and when leading against suit contract leading third or fifth best in preferred. When leading fourth best, the rule of 11 is used by the defense and when leading 3rd or 5th best the rule of 15 and 10 are used.

These rules often help the opponents, a better strategy is to use coded 9 and 10 against both suit and no-trump contracts and to combine it with second highest from a worthless hold also called Roman Mud. Here Jack denies and ten or nine shows zero or two higher.

In principle, the lower the card you lead the more you like the suit. For example, if you lead the two it shows either a four or five card suited with an honor (AKQ or J). For example:

From K8752, lead the 2 and from Q872 lead the 7. From 10653 or perhaps 106543 lead the 6. If you hold J982 lead the 8 since the 9 would infer zero or two higher.

Most pairs only play coded 9's and 10' against no-trump contract, but it can also be used against suit contracts. For example, from 752 you would lead the 5 and on the second round paly the 7 so partners know it is not a doubleton. Some may lead the 2 here, but clearly you do not have an honor; however, from 532 you would lead the 5.

Trump suit Preference

The most "basic" trump echo signal is when declarer begins to draw trump. A high-low signal shows an odd number of trumps and a low-high shows an even number (upside-down count).

Instead of showing count, it is often better to tell partner where your strength is outside the trump suit (Trump Suit Preference). Now, going up-the-line shows strength in lower-ranking suit strength and high-low shows strength in a higher-ranking suit.

On the deal below, most wests would lead the ♥9 against the N-S 4♠ contract. East inserted the ten and allowed south to win the trick with the queen. South was reluctant to begin on diamonds before pulling trump. Playing Trump Suit Preference east played the 9-3 in spades to show hearts. When east wins the A♠, he knows to continue hearts, holding the contract to ten tricks.

		♠	A76	
		♥	K63	
		♦	QJ98	
		♣	Q75	
♠	42		N	♠	93
♥	9754	W E		♥	AJ10
♦	A7	S		♦	6542
♣	K10982			♣	J643
		♠	KQJ1085	
		♥	Q82	
		♦	K103	
		♣	A	

On the following layout, east again plays the ♥10; however, now he would play the 3-9 of trumps (low-high) showing suit preference for clubs. West must shift to clubs when he wins the trick.

		♠	A76	
		♥	K62	
		♦	QJ98	
		♣	Q76	
♠	42		N	♠	93
♥	9754	W E		♥	AJ10
♦	A7	S		♦	6542
♣	K10982			♣	J643
		♠	KQJ1085	
		♥	Q83	
		♦	K103	
		♣	A	

While Trump suit Preference is a commonly used carding convention when playing in a suit contract, the Smith Echo convention is used when one is playing against a no-trump contract.

Smith and Reverse Smith Echo

Devised and published in 1963 in the "British Bridge World" magazine by I.G. Smith of Great Britain, the Smith Echo is an attitude signal most often used against no-trump contracts to show partner either the desire to continue leading the opening suit or to switch to another suit. Unlike the usual suit signals, the Smith Echo is not made on the opening lead but when declarer is next on lead.

When declarer begins to run his own or dummy's long suit, a high-low signal in this suit by the defenders (opening leader and partner) has the following meaning:

If made by partner of the opening leader, it shows good support for the opening lead and asks partner to continue the suit led when regaining the lead. If made by the opening leader, it says that the suit led was weak and that partner should switch to another suit when gaining the lead.

When playing defense, we are all taught to return partner's suit! However, consider the following situation.

	♠ 832	
	♥ 94	
	♦ AQ3	
	♣ A10863	
♠ AQ104	N W E S	♠ J965
♥ Q1053		♥ J86
♦ 76		♦ J1092
♣ 942		♣ K7
	♠ K7	
	♥ AK74	
	♦ K854	
	♣ QJ3	

Against 3NT, west leads fourth best 3♥ which was covered by east's jack; declarer wins the king and returns the ♣Q and west sees that that declarer has four club tricks, possibly three diamonds and two hearts. The only hope in setting the contract is in spades. Playing Smith Echo, west follows with the 9♣ telling partner NOT TO RETURN HEARTS. Winning with the ♣K, east does not return a heart, his partner's lead. He can see that the only possible return is a spade: for down one!

Some partnerships play **Reverse Smith Echo** when playing UDCA. Now low-high is encouraging! Be careful, look at the opponents carding scheme.

Foster Echo

This carding procedure was devised by Robert Frederick Foster of New York. He also invented the "rule of eleven."

There are several versions of this convention used primarily against no-trump. One is used when the opening lead is an honor, and the third hand wants to show four cards in the suit headed by an honor.

With four cards, the Foster Echo always begins by following with the third highest card. If the suit lacks an honor, on the second-round partner follows with the fourth highest card, but if headed by an honor, one follows with the second highest. For example, suppose you (third hand) hold:

Hand (1) 8 7 5 2 Hand (2) Q 7 5 2

and partner leads the king with hand (1) you play the five followed by the two (high-low: have no honor); with hand (2) the five is followed by the seven (low-high: have an honor). This version of Foster Echo allows the opening leader to locate the missing honors in the suit and to help choose the right continuation. If you were playing the upside-down carding system, one would discard the eight with hand (1) to discourage and the two with hand (2) to encourage.

Another version (less frequently used) combines an unblocking play with giving count. If the third hand cannot top either the card led or the card played by dummy, he follows with his second highest card; with a four-card holding, on the second round plays the third highest card, next the highest, reserving the lowest for the last round. However, with a three-card holding, on the first-round partner also plays the second-highest card in the suit and on the second round the highest card. This may cause some ambiguity if the suit is headed by two honors. Holding, for example, Q-10-x or J-10x, partner would play the ten on the first round; hence, the leader doesn't know if the higher honor is the queen or the jack against no-trump and the three against a suit contract.

Or playing Foster Echo, one gives count when you cannot beat dummies card. Playing UDCA low-high is even and high-low is odd.

How you play the Foster Echo carding system must be discussed.

Recommendations

When playing bridge defense is often more than half the game since you often defend more that play a hand. What are the worst and best agreements according to Jeff Meckstroth and Andrew Garnett?

To find out I refer you to the recent book **by Andrew Garnett (2016), "Jeff Meckstroth Presents An advanced player's guide to Defensive Communications Leads & Signals", A Bridge Centric book.**

Some of their general guidelines for defending a hand are:

1. Attitude is the primary signal you give on partner's lead. They are made when partner has supported your suit or the first time a suit is lead. The Ace asks for attitude and the King asks for count or to unblock the suit. The Queen also asks for attitude, except in NT from KQ10 it ask partner to unblock the Jack. However, the second time partner leads the suit give remainder count.

2. Give a count signal when dummy leads a suit. However, if partner leads and Ace but if KQJ are in dummy you must give count whenever you cannot beat dummy. With avoid in dummy give a suit preference signal.

3. If you make standard honor leads, lead the highest from two touching honors. The lead of the Queen, Jack, or Ten denies the next higher honor, but promises the next lower one except for the lead of the Q form KQJ.

4. When following to a trick, play the lower of two touching honors.

5. When leading from a doubleton always lead high except when leading trump.

6. Make the Clearest Signal (e.g., your highest or lowest for attitude). Signals may not change mid-stream, only if both count and attitude for a suit are known. If partner leads the Ace, he is looking for attitude, but if KQJ are in dummy you must give count whenever you cannot beat dummy.

7. Lead a major against 1NT-3NT or 2NT-3NT.

8. With no "textbook" lead, and you have no suit of your own, lead a suit bid by dummy.

9. Lead a trump to cut off **known** ruffing power in dummy (e.g., a splinter bid).

10. Lead short suit with long trumps so partner may give you a ruff.

11. Jeff says to always begin with passive lead because he hates to get a bad result because he took a chance on an aggressive lead.

Their comments on some commonly used defensive methods to avoid.

1. Coded 9's and 10's designed to help partner decide which honor to play should be avoided since it gives too must information to the opponents.

2. MUD known as Middle, Up, Down is designed when leading from three small are never used in a suit partner ever supported but are too confusing since it takes too long to discern the information provided by the first discard playing standard methods. This is also the case for the Foster Echo versus NT, partner plays his second highest card in the suit if he cannot beat dummy from three (to show an odd number of cards), except when the third hand has a doubleton, he then plays high-low with an even number of cards.

3. Roman or Odd-Even discards are to be avoided because you do not always have the right card to discard, instead switch to Levinthal. Both apply on only the first discard.

Their comments on some commonly used defensive methods to employ.

1. They prefer third and fifth leads against suit contracts. Recall that 3rd best show odd, lead 3rd from 4 or 6. A 5th best lead shows even low from 5 or 5th from7-cards or low (5th from 5-cards) and low from three cards where the rule of 10 and 12 apply.

2. UDCA where low card encourages and high-card discouragement or continue suit.

3. Attitude leads versus NT or Rusinow honor leads. However, recall that they are never used after the opening lead or when leading partners known long suit (one in which he overcalled, opened, or otherwise showed significant length) even if you never supported it. And you must decide if you play it versus both NT and suit contracts.

4. Playing UDCA, Reverse Smith Echo is recommended versus NT or suit contracts where a low tells partner whether they liked their lead. The signal is on the second card played by declarer (not partner) to tell partner about his prior lead.

5. Trump suit preference is used the first-time declarer leads trump. It is a suit-preference signal but requires 3-trumps to be effective.

While the authors discuss standard carding (e.g., 4th best leads with High-Low signals) with Smith Echo versus NT, the authors do not recommend it.

Even if you do not play the conventions recommended, you must be aware of the opponent's carding agreements to effective play a bridge hand.

CHAPTER 12

BRIDGE LEADS

Many books have been written on Bridge Leads, but the two written by David Bird and Taf Anthias (2011 and 2012) called "Winning Notrump Leads" and "Winning Suit Contract Leads", respectively, published by Master Point Press are the most detailed and comprehensive. Advice is based upon 100,000 simulations for both MP and IMP scoring.

While leads are difficult since a contract may be made or fail because of the lead, the most important thing to remember is to listen to the bidding since it may help the most in what one should or should not lead. Then you must decide whether to be active or passive.

In general, an active lead is when you lead honors; however, it may give up a winner. Alternatively, you may be passive, which avoids giving the declarer a trick he does not deserve.

Dick Olson at www.slospin.net provides a very nice summary of basic lead principles. His recommendations follow, Points 1-6.

Standard Leads

(1) Leading a Trump

If you can attack a contract, it is usually best to do so. However, there are times when a trump lead is called for.

Example 1: You have: ♠64 ♥AJ93 ♦AQ105 ♣KJ6

The bidding goes: [1♠ Dbl 2♠ Pass]: [4♠ Pass Pass Pass]

Since leading a side suit is unattractive, lead a trump here – protect those tenaces.

Example 2: The bidding goes: [1♠ Pass 1NT Pass 2♠]

An optimal time to lead trumps is when dummy denies support for a major suit opener. In Example 2, responder obviously has 0, 1, or 2 card supports for spades. This is a good time to lead a trump.

(2) Leads in Suits that include the Ace

Never under lead an ace against a suit contract at trick one.

If you do not have the king, lead the ace only when you are defending against a slam (except 6NT) or declarer preempted, or

Your ace is singleton, or
Your ace is the only unbid suit against five clubs or five diamonds, or
Your side promised length and strength in the suit, or
You have a seven- or eight-card suit.

Lead the ace from AKx (unless you play Rusinow Leads); after trick one, lead the king from AKx.

(3) Short-Suit Leads

Singletons are invariably good choices.

Doubletons are overrated, especially with one honor.

The best time to lead a short suit is with trump control, e.g., A63.

Avoid a short suit lead when you do not need a ruff, e.g., with trump holdings such as QJ9 and KQ10 or when you have trump length. With four trumps it is usually correct to lead a long suit to make declarer ruff (this is called a forcing game).

(a) Basic Leads

In selecting your lead, you must consider your hand as well as inferences from the bidding.

Desirable Leads

Partner's suit, especially if he promised five or six cards. The proper card to lead is the same one you would have led in any other suit. Therefore, lead low from Q63 or K852 (this is called **BOS** "**B**ottom **O**f **S**omething"; however, some lead the top of a suit if partner has bid the suit. It is best to discuss your approach with partner). Top of a three-card (or longer) sequence is **TON** (**T**op **O**f **N**othing) called **BOSTON** leads.

Sequences

It is better to lead top of a sequence than fourth best (or third and fifth against a suit contract)

A sequence must contain an honor (10 or higher)

Against a suit contract, a sequence can be as short as two cards. Lead the king from KQ53 and the queen from QJ64. However, against a no-trump contract, lead low from both holdings.

Partner has Not Bid and there is no Sequence

Prefer to lead a suit the opponents have not shown. In general, try to lead from length against any contract. A lead from Q1074 is more attractive than from Q107. It is acceptable to lead away from a king against a suit contract.

Leading Dummy's Suit

Leading through strength is overrated. Lead dummy's suit only when partner is likely to have length and strength behind him.

(b) Standard Leads Against Suits (3rd and 5th) -Preferred

Sequences:

A K x, **10** 9 x, **K** Q x, K **J** 10 x, Q J x, K **10** 9 x, J 10 9, Q **10** 9 x, K Q 10 9

Length Leads with an Honor (X = honor) - lowest-card lead usually indicates an honor:

X x **x**, X x **x** x (start of high-low), X x x x **x** (start of low-high), X x x x **x** x (start of high-low)

Length leads Without an Honor:

x x, x **x** x (MUD to indicate no honor), x **x** x x (start of high-low), x x **x** x x (start of low-high), x x **x** x x (start of high-low)

Primary signals:
Count is usually first option
Attitude is given if count doesn't make sense
Suit preference is given if neither count nor attitude makes sense (some always give attitude first).

(c) Standard Leads Against Suits (4th Best) – Not preferred

Sequences:

A **K** x, 10 9 x, K Q x, K **J** 10 x, Q J x, K **10** 9 x, J 10 9, Q **10** 9 x, K Q 10 9

Length Leads with an Honor (X = honor) - Lowest-card lead usually indicates an honor:

X x **x**, X x x **x**, X x x **x** x, X x x **x** x x

Length leads Without an Honor:

x x, x **x** x (MUD to indicate no honor), x **x** x x (MUD), x x **x** x x (MUD), x x **x** x x x (MUD)

Primary signals:
Attitude is first option
Count is given if attitude doesn't make sense
Suit preference is given if neither attitude nor count makes sense

(4) Standard Leads against No-trump

Length Leads ---> 4th best

x x, x **x** x (MUD), x **x** x x (MUD if no honor), x **x** x x x (MUD if no honor), **10** 9 x,
K Q x, K **J** 10 x, Q J x, K **10** 9 x, J 10 9, Q **T** 9 x, K Q 10 9

A **K** x x (x) – only against no-trump; K asks for attitude

A K J x (x) – only against no-trump; A asks to unblock honor; if no honor, then give count

Primary signals: attitude then count

(5) Journalist Leads – "Ten Promises and Jack Denies" (Non-Standard)

Usually against no-trump, though some play it against suit contracts. Purpose is to promise or deny one of the top three honors. Whenever the opening lead is a 10, the leader promises the A, K, or Q and an interior sequence. Whenever a jack is led, the leader denies having the A, K, or Q and shows a sequence headed by the jack. Note a lead of the queen always promises the jack or a singleton, never lead from Qx.

Used when you have:

A high honor with an interior sequence – leads the 10 which indicates having the A, K, or Q. An "interior sequence" is defined as QJ10x, J109x, or 109xx (98xx is not considered a sequence here).

An interior sequence with nothing above it – 10 which denies having the A, K, or Q

Typical hands where a 10 is lead ("Ten Promises")

AJ109(x), AJ10x(x), KJ109(x), K1098(x), Q109x(x) ----- lead the 10

but for the sequence QJ109(x) or QJ10x(x) ----- lead the Q

Typical hands where the J is lead ("Jack Denies")

J109x(x), J10x(x) ----- lead the J

Other leads that deny holding an A, K, or Q

1098(x) or 109x(x) ----- <u>lead the 9</u> (can't lead the 10) which promises either the 10 at the head of a sequence with no high honor or a doubleton 9x.

(6) Rusinow Leads (Non-Standard) normally used against suit contracts and only on the opening lead. Primary purpose of these leads is to remove the ambiguity when using the king lead from AK.

The most difficult play in bridge is the lead. To become proficient, you must listen to the auction. Rules are only helpful when you have limited information. Let's look at an example found in Bridge with the Abbot (David Bird), in the September 2009 issue of the "Bridge Bulletin," page 59.

		♠	753		
		♥	742		
		♦	AQ764		
		♣	83		
♠	QJ1062			♠	94
♥	5		N	♥	983
♦	K95	W	E	♦	J103
♣	9742		S	♣	KQ1065
		♠	AK8		
		♥	AKQJ106		
		♦	82		
		♣	AJ		

The bidding:

West	North	East	South
			2♣
Pass	2♦	Pass	2♥
Pass	3♥	Pass	3♠
Pass	4♦	Pass	6♥
All Pass			

As west, what do you lead? The natural lead is the ♠Q (top of a sequence), but if you listen to the bidding, what have you learned? Clearly, south has a control in spades and north has a control in diamonds. And a trump lead gains nothing; in general, it is not a good idea to lead a singleton trump. The lead that has a chance of setting the contract is a club lead; lead the club 9. Leading away from the king of diamonds when the opponents are strong in the suit is never a good idea.

For more advice on bridge leads, one may also consult books by Mike Lawrence (1996), "Opening Leads," Los Alamitos, CA: C&T Bridge Supplies and Sally Brock (2007), Leading Questions in Bridge", Master Point Press.

Bridge leads Do's and Don'ts

The most difficult task in bridge is the opening lead. It often results in a top or a bottom. You cannot be correct 100% of the time, but there are some does and don'ts. I will go out on a "limb" with the following general guidelines.

Don'ts

1) Don't lead away from a King if you have another option.

2) Don't lead trump.

3) Don't lead an Ace in suit contracts.

4) Don't lead a singleton when you have a better alternative.

5) Don't lead your partner's suit if he has not shown a good suit or you have trump control.

6) Don't lead the unbid suit when the opponents have jumped to game in no-trump.

7) Don't lead fourth best in no-trump when your hand is weak or your suit has bad intermediates.

8) Don't lead doubletons.

9) Don't lead from broken honor sequences.

The above are general guidelines, of course there are exceptions. Never say never in the game of bridge.

Do's

1) Lead fourth best in no-trump contracts with very good intermediaries when you have bid your suit and the opponents have bid no-trump. If not, better to lead low from and honor or top of nothing.

2) Lead partner's suit, even if you have a good 5-card suit as an alternative, unless you also have an outside entry.

3) When the opponents are in a major suit contract, lead the other major unless you have an alternative lead in a minor suit.

4) Lead the unbid suit in no-trump or a suit contract if the opponents reached the contract slowly.

5) When you have a choice between two suits, lead the one with the strongest secondary cards.

6) When partner has bid two suits, lead his second suit. Or, lead a singleton if you know partner has values.

7) When the opponents have bid their suit aggressively, it is time to be passive.

8) Lead an ace against preempts if you have one.

9) When you have a weak defensive hand lead an unsupported honor in partner's suit.

10) Lead a trump when you have five trumps or when partner's double shows good trumps.

The does and don'ts assume that the auction was uninformative. For example, the bidding may go 1x – 1NT.

(1) Suppose the bidding goes: (South) 1♠ - Pass -4♠ - All pass and as west you hold the following hand:

♠ 7 ♥ K873 ♦ KJ53 ♣ K985

You have no information. What do you lead?

Clearly a trump lead is passive and gains nothing for the defense. Do not use the adage "When in doubt lead trump"!

Leading away from your kings in general will give up a trick; do not close your eyes and hope for the best! Observe that by leading a club or a heart will establish at most a single trick. However, if partner were to hold the queen of diamonds, then leading a diamond may set up two tricks.

Hence, you must lead the ♦J or the 3.

(2) The bidding goes (South) 3♠ - Pass - 4♠ -double – All pass and as west you are on lead with the following hand. What do you lead?

♠ AQ7 ♥ J5 ♦ 10987 ♣ K653 what do you lead?

The immediate raise to four spades suggests that dummy has a solid suit, and your partner has doubled. You have no information, lead the trump ace and after seeing dummy you can decide on your switch to reach partner. Do not guess.

As the opponents' bidding becomes stronger, your opening lead should become easier.

The guidelines may help with no information, but there is no substitute for Listening to the Auction!

Leads against 3NT

The bidding has gone 1NT – 3NT and you hold the following cards:

(1) ♠ Q105 ♥ KQ853 ♦ K83 ♣ 82
(2) ♠ 953 ♥ Q53 ♦ 762 ♣ J842
(3) ♠ QJ976 ♥ K5 ♦ J7632 ♣ 7
(4) ♠ AQ97 ♥ AQ54 ♦ 10987 ♣ 7
(5) ♠ 73 ♥ A54 ♦ Q1087 ♣ Q753
(6) ♠ 532 ♥ AQ754 ♦ QJ103 ♣ Q
(7) ♠ 973 ♥ K4 ♦ 876543 ♣ K7
(8) ♠ 972 ♥ AJ1094 ♦ 76 ♣ 543
(9) ♠ Q97 ♥ AJ7 ♦ KJ2 ♣ 8763
(10) ♠ AQ97 ♥ AQ54 ♦ 10987 ♣ 7
(11) ♠ K9852 ♥ 7 ♦ QJ1064 ♣ 73
(12) ♠ A7 ♥ A53 ♦ A76 ♣ 65432

With each of the above hands, you have no information about, what do you lead?

(1) Clearly your best suit is hearts. Lead 4th best, the ♥5; or the ♠5, may be partners suit. They have denied a 4-card major.

(2) You have a weak hand and should try to fine partner's best suit. Leading an unbid major is usually always better than leading an unbid minor. You have values in hearts, lead the ♥3 or ♠3.

(3) You have five spades to the Queen and five diamonds to the Jack. It is usually better to lead a strong four card suit instead of a weak five card suit. Lead the ♥Q.

(4) You do not want to lead from your AQ tenaces, hence, lead the ♦10. Playing coded 9's and 10's it conveys zero or two of the top three honors.

(5) You have two nice 5-card suits; lead the fourth best from the stronger suit, the ♦7. Or lead the ♠3 since a major has been denied.

(6) You have two strong suits, one 5-card and one 4-card. Lead from the stronger 5-card suit. Lead the ♥5, fourth best.

(7) You have two weak suits, spades, and diamonds. You will not develop a trick in diamonds. Lead the ♠9.

(8)   Lead the ♥10 to show zero or two of the top honors in hearts.

(9)   You have a great hand, lead top of nothing or the ♣8. Partner when he gets in will switch to another suit.

(10) Protect your tenaces and lead the ♦10.

(11) You have two suits of equal length, lead from the stronger suit. Lead the ♦Q.

(12) You have three entries to your club suit, lead the ♣6.

How did you do?

SUMMARY when the bidding goes 1NT- 3NT. Almost always lead a major even if you have a long minor. If you have four cards in one major and a singleton in the other, lead the singleton.

If you have two majors, a 4-card, and a 3-card major, lead the shortest.

For more on winning no-trump leads, see the book by David Bird and Taf Anthias (2011) called "Winning No-trump Leads" published by Master Point Press.

In our examples we had no information from the bid, however with more information, the easier the lead. Let's consider an example. Suppose you hold the following hand:

♠ J987 ♥ 853 ♦ J83 ♣ A75

And the bidding goes:

West (you)	North	East	South
Pass	1♦	Pass	1♠
Pass	3♦	Pass	3NT
Pass			

Do you have any clues? First, you know that North has a strong diamond suit and that the defense has spades.

Partner did not overcall one heart over the bid of one diamond so that suggests that you should not lead a heart, he does not have first or second round control. However, he might have a club holding and since the opponents stopped at the three level, may have some values in clubs.

You best lead is a low club – not the ace!

The bidding goes:	North	South
	1♠	1NT
	3♥	3NT

You as west hold the following cards:

♠ A7 ♥ 1098 ♦ J754 ♣ J654

What do you lead?

South has not bid either of the minor suits and did not support the majors bid by his partner. The lead of the 4 of either minor form the Jack is in general not a good lead in no-trump, the opponents have the minors. Lead the ♥10. Or lead the space ace. Always listen to the bidding!

Winning Bridge Leads

One of the most important and hardest tasks in the game of Bridge is the Lead. This Bridge Tip sets out some simple Rules you must remember.

Leads depend on the contract: No-trump; Suits; Slams; and No fit

No Trump Leads playing 15-17

In general, you want to make an aggressive lead when playing in no-trump. However, the bidding may determine the lead!

In General:

1. Partner has bid a suit. You should then lead his suit, low from and honor or top of nothing.
2. Your long suit is one the opponents have bid. You should choose your longest un-bid suit, or a suit dummy has bid, lead through strength.
3. Your long suit has three or more touching honors (KQJx, QJ10x, AQJ10x, J109x, etc.). You should lead the top honor to be sure you force declarer to win with the highest card possible. DO NOT lead 4th best.
4. Leading from three cards is better than leading from four cards with a weak hand.
5. When leading an un-bid suit at no-trump with four cards not headed by an honor, it is too misleading to lead low which shows strength. It is better to lead your highest or next highest card. If you highest card is an eight or lower, lead high. If your highest card is a nine or a ten, lead your second highest card. Lead the 8 from 8543 but lead the 6 from 9642. Lead the 7 from 10732 if you want another suit returned.

If the bidding has gone 1NT-3NT, only lead 4th best major with a 5-card major suit; otherwise ALWAYS lead your shortest major even if you have a 4-card major. Yes, and even if you have a 5-card minor. This also applies if the opponents are playing in 1NT.

If the opponents have transferred into a major after 1NT, lead the other major.

If the bidding goes 1M-1NT, lead the other major.

The bidding has got 1NT-2NT-3NT or 2NT-3NT, make a passive lead. Never lead 4th best; lead a MAJOR.

Against 6NT, be passive by leading spot cards. Never lead away from A, K, or Q and do not lead a sequence with touching honors.

A/K/Q leads against NT

A/Q asks for **Attitude** (with Ace leads we are looking for the Queen – best to unblock, but do not unblock with a Queen lead).

K leads asks for **count**. The King lead is usually from a broken sequence (KQJ.., KQ10...), or a strong suit headed by the ace and king (e.g., AKJ10, AKJ93, and AKQ104). It asks you to unblock any high honor.

Lead of the jack against NT

The jack is usually the top of a sequence, with nothing higher. The jack may also be led from QJ9..., asking partner to play the 10 if he has it. When partner cannot see the 10, he will think the lead is from a jack-high sequence.

Lead of the 10 against NT

The 10 lead usually shows strength: an interior sequence headed by the jack or 10, or a QJ10 sequence. It can also be the right lead from (e.g. AQJ10, KJ10.., AJ10.., AQ109.., AK109.., K109.., A109.., Q109.., QJ10.., AQJ10.., etc.)

Lead of the 9 against NT

The lead shows no higher honor.

Leads of the 7/8 against NT

Usually, a worthless sequence

Suit Leads

In general, you want to make a passive lead when playing in a suit contract. However, the bidding may again determine the lead!

In General:

1. Lead a singleton or doubleton, even if partner has bid a suit.
2. Lead a suit the opponents have not bid.
3. If all suits have been bid, lead through strength.
4. Your long suit has three or more touching honors (KQJx, QJ10x, AQJ10x, J109x, etc.). Lead top honor.
5. If partner has bid, lead low from three and high from two.
6. Do not lead from A, K, or Q; instead lead a trump. And with three trumps, lead low holding the Ace of trump.

If the bidding has gone 1M-2M-4M or 1M-4M, lead an unsupported ace. And do not lead away from an honor, lead trump. Or lead a singleton or doubleton. With Kx or Qx in a suit, lead low –you are more likely to find partner with an honor.

If the opponents have splintered and reached game, lead your weakest side suit. Do not lead trump.

Leads against a major part score 1M-2M. Lead top of sequence but prefer a singleton led to a sequence lead. Lead trump instead of leading away from an honor. With Qxx lead low or lead high from a worthless doubleton.

If the opponents have sacrificed, it is best to lead partner's suit, NOT the OPPONENTS.

Leads against Suit Slams

Be **passive** not aggressive, side suit singletons are best. But do not lead a singleton with a natural trump trick.

In match points lead an ace, but not in IMPS; do not lead an ace if the opponents have indicated a side suit ace. Better to lead a worthless doubleton.

Only lead a trump, when any other lead forces you to lead away from an A, K, or Q.

An Ace lead is less likely to gain two tricks in the suit if the opponents used cue bidding to reach their slam, more like if Blackwood was used.

Only be aggressive with touching sequence honor leads (QJxx, KQx, AJ109xx, etc.).

Trump Leads

Never lead trump if the opponents have a misfit or partner is marked with a singleton.

Lead trump with a strong trump sequence (KQJ, QJ109) avoid leading away from A, K, or Q in all other suits.

In general trump leads are poor unless you are trying to protect tenaces or the opponents have splintered.

CHAPTER 13

Wrap Up

By adopting the philosophy of the Modified Optimal 2/1-Club System, what have we learned and what have we given up by dumping both "traditional" 2/1 and Precision?

First and foremost, opening bids must be counted using **HLD** points with bidding decisions restricted to 3-point increments: 7-9, 10-12, 12-14, 15-17, 18-20, 21-23, 24-26, 27+. All 1-level bids have at most 2 intervals with at most a **6HLD** point range, and all 2-level bids are within a 3-point range to ensure "bidding safety". All strong hands require 18+**HLD** points and are opened 1♣*, all 1-level suit bids require 12-17**HLD** points, and 1NT is defined by 15-17**HLD** points. Yes, partners no longer need to bid with 5H points and may pass with less than 7HL points without the fear of missing a game.

Secondly, one must account for fit and misfit points **for all suits and NT contracts** and eliminate terrible bidding practices like responding 2NT to 1NT, 4NT quantitative bids, and opening NT hands with 6-card minor suits.

Weak major suit 2-level bids in all opened with a 12/14**HLD range, not 6-10** because this wider range is outside the bidding safety zone, a 3-point range. And conventions like Drury and Two-Way Drury are not needed. And 3-level bid show 6/7 card suits.

Playing 2/1 and opening 2NT with 20HCP, you are already too high. Goren's original recommendation was to use 22-24 HCP points since it provides more protection. We solved this problem by opening all hands with 18+**HLD** points 1♣* where a rebid of 1NT=18-20**HLD**, 2NT=21-23**HLD,** and 3NT=24+**HLD** points.

One must always make competitive bidding adjustments to account for the impact of the number of cards one has in the opponents suit and honors cards both within and outside the overcall suit to accurately reflect a hands Offensive or Defensive nature and to make 1/2 level overcall bids. Adjustments must also be made for an alone King in any 3/4 card suit and an alone J in any suit when contemplating a 1NT overcall for balanced hands. These are termed the Adjusted Optimal Count (**AOC**) points.

The Modified Optimal 2/1-Club System allows one to "trash" a host of prior learned Rules like the rule of 9/N, rule of 15, rule of 20/22, rule of 44, rule of 26 (LTC), rule of 44, and many more including the Law of total trumps since the alternative approach to bidding provides optimal accuracy which in turn leads to improved bidding judgement and hence better results at the bridge table for all levels of players.

Overview of the Modified Optimal 2/1-Club System

1♣*	Artificial 18+ **HLD** points any distribution
1♦*	12-17**HLD** artificial with 0-2 diamonds
1♥/1♠	12-17**HLD** and 5+ Majors
1NT	15-17**HLD** All Seats with Crawling Stayman
2♣*	15-17**HLD** 5/6+ Clubs (may have a 4-card major)
2♦*	15-17**HLD** 7+diamonds
2♥*/2♠*	12-14**HLD** 6+cards
2NT*	12-14**HLD** 5-5 in the Minors
3♣*	12-14**HLD** 6/7+clubs
3♦*	12-14**HLD** 6-diamonds
3♥*/3♠*	12-14**HLD** 7-cards
3NT*	GAMBLING solid 7+ minor suit (AKQxxxx)
4♣*/4♦*	NAMYATS

* Indicates forcing alert bids

(1) 1NT* Forcing Convention over Majors

Over 1♠	1NT* (13+**HL/HLD**=flatness)

2♣*	Minimum hand 12/14
2♦	5♠ - 4♦ 15/17
2♥	5♠ - 4♥ 15/17
2♠	6♠ 15/17
2NT	5332 balanced 15/17
3♣	5♠ - 4♣ 15/17
3♦	5♠ - 5♦ 15/17
3♥	5♠ - 5♥ 15/17
3♠	6♠ - 4♣ 15/17

Responder over the Minimum bid of 2♣* may bid 2♥/2♠/2NT/3♣/3♦ as natural bids
2♦* is an artificial shape ask bid with the following responses by the opener

2♥	5♠ - 4♥ 12/14
2♠	6♠ - 4♥ (since 6♠ & 12-14 weak 2-bid opening)

2NT	5332 balanced 12/14
3♣	5♠ - 4♣ 12/14
3♦	5♠ - 4♦ 12/14
3♥	5♠ - 5♥ 12/14

Over 1♥	1NT*

2♣*	Minimum hand 12/14
2♦	5♥ - 4♦ 15/17
2♥	6♥ 15/17
2♠	5♥ - 4♠ 15/17
2NT	3532 balanced 15/17
3♣	5♥ - 4♣ 15/17
3♦	5♥ - 5♦ 15/17

Responder over the Minimum bid of 2♣* may bid 2♥/2♠/2NT/3♣/3♦as natural bids

But 2♦* is again a shape asking bid as above

2♥	6♥ - 4♠ 12/14
2♠	5♥ - 4♠ 12/14
2NT	5♥332 balanced
3♣	5♥ - 4♣ 12/14
3♦	5♥ - 4♦ 12/14

For both the OPC 2/1 method and Traditional 2/1 the strong NT zone is 15-17; hence, the 12-14 zone may be considered a "weak" NT zone.

If the opening bidder has 15/17**HLD** points after the forcing 1NT* bid, game is likely if responder has **12HLD** points. However, if opener has 12/14 without a majors suit fit, game is less likely if responder has <14**HL** points, so there is nothing to prevent responder from passing.

(2) The sequence 1♥-1♠-1NT=12/14 and 1♥-1♠-2NT=15-17

After the bid 1♥-1♠ =7+**HLD** one bids:

1♥	1♠
1NT	3532 12/14
2♣*	Minimum hand 12/14 unbalanced
2♦	5♥ - 4♦ 15/17
2♥	6♥ 15/17
2♠	5♥ - 4♠ 15/17

2NT	3532 balanced 15/17
3♣	5♥ - 4♣ 15/17
3♦	5♥ - 5♦ 15/17

Responder over the Minimum bid of 2♣* may bid 2♥/2♠/2NT/3♣/3♦ as natural bids

But 2♦*	**is a shape asking bid**
2♥	6♥ - 4♠ 12/14
2♠	5♥ - 4♠ 12/14
2NT	5♠ - 5♥ 12/14
3♣	5♥ - 4♣ 12/14
3♦	5♥ - 4♦ 12/14

(3) Rebids after 1♥/♠-2NT*= Modified Jacoby with 16+HLD

Rebids by Opener	**Suit Length**	**HLDF**
3♣*	Club Singleton/Void	12-14
3♦*	Diamond Singleton/Void	12-14
3♥*	Heart Singleton/Void	12-14 with Spades as trumps
3♠*	Spade Singleton/Void	12-14 with Hearts as trumps
3♥*	No Singleton/Void	12-14 with Hearts as trumps
3♠*	No Singleton/Void	12-14 with Spades as trumps
3NT*	Spade Singleton/Void	15-17
4♣*	Club Singleton/Void	15-17
4♦*	Diamond Singleton/Void	15-17
4♥*	Heart Singleton/Void	15-17 with Spades as trumps
4♥*	No Singleton/Void	15-17 with Hearts as trumps
4♠*	No Singleton/Void	15-17 with Spades as trumps

(4) Responses to 1♣* 18+HLD

1♦*	0-6**HLD** points or 13+**HLD** pts
1♥*	Transfer bid for 5+♠ with 7-12**HLD** pts
1♠*	Transfer bid for 1 NT 7-9**HLD** pts
1NT*	Transfer bid for 5+♣ with 7-12**HLD** pts
2♣*	Transfer bid for 5+♦ with 7-12**HLD** pts
2♦*	Transfer bid for 5+♥ with 7-12**HLD** pts.
2♥*/2♠*	6+ card suit with 7-9**HLD**
2NT*	10-12**HLD** balanced no 5-card major/minor

(a) After Negative: 1♦* 0-6 HLD

Opener Rebids after 1♦*:

1♥/1♠/2♣/2♦ Natural forcing one round with 5/6 cards, unbalanced and 18+**HLD**

1NT* 18-20 balanced

    Responder Bids

        Pass   0-4 **HLD**/Garbage Stayman
        2♣   5+**HLD**, Stayman
        2♦/2♥   Jacoby Transfer
        2♠   The Minors

    Opener Bids

        2NT   Prefer Diamonds
        3♣   Prefer Clubs

2♠* shows 5+cards and 21-23**HLD** or 21+**HLD**, forcing one round

2♥ shows 5+cards and 21-23**HLD** or 21+**HLD**, forcing one round

    Responder bids 2♠ (ask)
        2NT 22-23 and balanced
        3NT 24-26 and balanced
        3X = Natural (4/5 cards) with 22+**HLD** and 5+ hearts

2NT* 21-23**HLD** balanced

    Responder Rebids
        Pass   0-2 **HLD**
        3♣   3+**HLD**-Stayman
        3♦/3♥/3♠ Jacoby Transfers (5-card suit- H/S/Clubs)
                  May correct to 4♦ over 4♣-transfer bid
        4♣   Expert Gerber
        4♦   transfers to hearts (6-card)
        4♥   transfers to spades (6-card)
        4♠   transfers to clubs (6-card)
                  Or correct to 5♦ over 5♣-transfer bid

3NT* 24+**HLD** balanced

> Responder Rebids
>> Pass 0**HLD**
>> 4♣   Expert Gerber
>> 4♦   transfers to hearts
>> 4♥   transfers to spades
>> 4♠   transfers to clubs (with correction to diamonds)

(b) After Positive Transfer Responses to 1♣* Opening--Positive Transfer Responses **to 1♣*** are 5+ card suits. Opener must have 3+ card supports to accept transfer.

To transfer to a minor, you need **7-12HLD. Opener will accept again with 3+- card support even though he may have a 5-card major.**

Bids of **1NT=18-20, 2NT=21-23, 3NT=24-26 show NO-FIT**

(c) After 1♠* (7-9 HLD) === Positive Transfer and relay to 1NT by Opener

After opener accepts the suit transfer responder next tells opener about his controls

First Step 0-1 control (K=1), next step = 2 (1Ace/2kings) etc.

> TAB (trump asking bid) Opener may next bid the Trump suit at lowest available level if he wants to ask about responder's trump suit

>> 1st step Five or more trumps with no top honor (A, K, Q)
>> 2nd step Five with one top honor
>> 3rd step Five with two top honors
>> 4th step Six or more with one honor
>> 5th step Six or more with two honors
>> 6th step Five/Six or more with three top honors

> CAB (control asking bid) Opener next may bid any non-trump suit if he wants to ASK for controls in that suit

>> 1st step No Controls (Qxx or worse)
>> 2nd step Second round Control (K/singleton)
>> 3rd step First round Control (A/void)

(d) Responder bids 2♥*/2♠*/3♣*/3♦*shows singleton in bid suit (7+HLD)

Opener Rebids:

3♥/3♠	1430 for bid major
4♣/4♦	1430 for bid minor
4♥/4♠/5♣/5♦	To Play

(e) Responder's bid of 2NT* 10-12HLD, balanced/semi-balanced

Opener Rebids

3♣*	Ask bid
	Responder bids 4-card suits up the line (3♦/3♥/3♠) 3NT* show clubs
3♦/3♥/3♠	Natural bids show 5-card suit
3NT*	Asking Bid
	Responder bids

         4♣*=14 points

         4♦*= 15 points

            After 4 clubs and 4 diamonds, opener bids 4-card suits up-the-line or bids 4NT (to-play)

         4♥*/4♠*/5♣*/5♦*=16+

4♣	Expert Gerber Ace ask

(5) 1♦*- Auctions

Recall that the bid 1♦* has the bidding range 12-17**HLD** points like major suit bids (with two bidding zones 12-14 and 15-17), however, the bid is **artificial** and may have 0-2 diamonds, so it is forcing.

Partner knows you do not have a 5-card major, that your hand may be balanced or unbalanced with 4-clubs or 4/5+diamonds, that it may have a 4-card major or be 4-4 in the majors, that it may be 5-4 clubs and diamonds or even a 4-4-4-1/ 4-4-5-0 hand.

Responder ranges are defined:

    (1) Weak with 7-9HLD
    (2) Invitational 10-12HLD
    (3) Strong 13+HLD

XYZ Convention

The convention goes by two names XYZ or Two-Way Checkback and is like but better than Two-Way New Minor Forcing. It is a corner stone convention for the Modified Optimal 2/1 System when opening 1♦*= 12-17**HLD.**

In applies to the following bidding sequences:

Opener	Responder
1♦*	1♥/1♠
1NT	?
1♥	1♠
1NT	?
1♦*	1♥
1♠	?

The system's basic premise is that bids of 2♣* and 2♦* are both artificial. There are three features to the system

1) The 2♣* response to a 1NT/1♠ rebid is a forced relay to 2♦*
2) The 2♦* response to a 1NT/1♠ rebid is an artificial game force (yes even if partner's opening bid was 1♦). It is usually a Major suit Checkback but is occasionally a prelude to showing a forcing bid in a minor.
3) Jump rebids by responder, in any suit, are forcing. They describe good hands or good suit(s) with good values and long suit(s).

The approach to signing off in a minor is as follows. To sign-off in 2♦ responder bids 2♣* - Opener should alert and explain as a RELAY to 2♦*, either to play or the start of some invitational sequence.

1♦*	1♥ (7+**HLD)**	**Responder's Bids**	
1NT	?	Pass	To play
		2♣*	Forces 2♦*
		2♦*	GF
		2♥	To Play
		2♠	Invitational with 4-Spades
		2NT	6+ diamonds
		3♣	Sign-off in Clubs (5-4)
		3♦	5♦-5♥ slam try
		3♥	6+Hearts, slam try
		3♠	4-Spades and 6+Hearts

1♦*	1♠ (7+**HLD**)		**Responder's Bids**
1NT	?	Pass	To Play
		2♣*	Forces 2♦*
		2♦*	GF
		2♥	5+spades – 4+hearts Opener Pass or bids 2♠ - 3♥ not a possible bid)
		2♠	To Play
		2NT	6+ diamonds
		3♣	Sign-off in Clubs
		3♦	Slam try 5-5
		3♥	Slam try 5-5
		3♠	6+Spades Slam try

Using the XYZ convention the auctions may be weak, invitational, or strong.

Weak	1♦* 1♥	1♦* 1♥
	1♠ 2♥	1♠ 1NT
		2♣* 2♦

Invitational	1♦* 1♥	1♦* 1♥	1♦* 1♥
	1♠ 2♣*	1♠ 2♣*	1♠ 2♣
		2♦* 3♦	2♦ 2♥
			3NT

Slam	1♦*	1♠
	1NT 2♦*	
	3♣	3♦
	4♦	4♥
	5♦	7♦

(6) 1♥/1♠ - Auctions

When partner opens a major responder's primary obligation is to show shortness with a fit with an unbalanced hand. This is done with the aid of mini splinters and full splinters. High card points are great for bidding balanced hands. As distribution enters the picture, the location of cards becomes increasingly important. In general, no single bid describes an unbalanced hand better than a short suit bid. Recall the following over a major suit bid.

Mini splinter - 13-15**HLDF** points with 4-card support
Full Splinter – 16+**HLDF** points 4-card support

1NT* - 13+**HLD** points
2NT* - 16+**HLDF** points 4-card fit no shortness

2/1 Bid with 15+**HLDF** points
2M -7-9**HLDF** points
3M – 10-12**HLDF** points
<7 **HLD** Pass

The structure of the responses to the opening major suit are:

1♥ -   1♠ =7+**HL**
          1NT*-One-round forcing
          2♣/2♦ - Natural (10/12)
          2♥ - simple raise 7-9 HLDF pts
          2♠*- mini-splinter in spades with 4 hearts, 13-15 HLDF pts
          2NT* GF – 4-hearts 16+**HLDF**
          3♣* - mini-splinter, short in clubs with 4 hearts, 13-15 HLDF pts
          3♦* - mini-splinter, short in diamonds with 4 hearts, 13-15 HLDF pt
          3♥ - Natural invite 10-12.
          3♠ - full splinter, short in spades with 4 hearts, 16 + HLDF pts.
          3NT – 13-15 3-card support
          4♣* - full splinter short in clubs with 4 hearts, 16 + HLDF pts.
          4♦* - full splinter short in diamonds. with 4 hearts, 16 + HLDF pts.
          4♥ - To play

1♠ -   1NT*--One-round forcing
          2♣/2♦ - Natural (10-12)
          2♠ - simple raise 7-9 HLDF pts
          2NT*- 4-spades 16+**HLDF**
          3♣* - mini-splinter, short in clubs with 4 spades, 13-15 HLDF pts.
          3♦* - mini-splinter, short in diamonds with 4 spades, 13-15 HLDF pts.
          3♥* - mini-splinter, short in hearts with 4 spades, 13-15 HLDF pts.
          3♠ - Natural invite 10-12
          3NT -13-15 3-card support
          4♣* - full splinter short in clubs with 4 spades, 16 + HLDF pts.
          4♦* - full splinter short in diamonds with 4 spades, 16 + HLDF pts.
          4♥* - full splinter short in hearts with 4 spades, 16 + HLDF pts.
          4♠ - To Play

(7) Responses to 2NT*

This bid is like the unusual 2NT bid playing 2/1. The responses go:

All 3-level bids are to play except 3♥* which is an asking bid.

Over 2NT*=12-14 what follow are the responses to the 3♥* asking bid.

3♠*/3NT*	12/13-14
4♣*/4♦*	6♣-5♦/6♦-5♣ min=12
4♥*/4♠*	6♦-5♣/6♦-5♣ max=13/14
4NT*/5♣	6♦/6♣ min/max with singleton ♥
5♠*/5NT*	6♦/6♣ min/max with singleton ♠
5♠/5NT*	7♣-6♦/6♣-7♦min
6♣	7♣-6♦/6♣-7♦max

Optimal Point Count (OPC) - Summary

The Opening bidder considers HLD points and Responder's only HL points where L≤2 w/o a fit except for flatness -1 4333. With a suit Fit, add/deduct F, Semi-Fit, Distribution-Fit, MS: (HLDF).

HONOR POINTS (H)

Ace: 4½ pts	K: 3pts	Q w/A, K, J: 2 pts	Qxx: 1½ pts	Qx=1pt
		J w/A, K, Q: 1pt	Jxx: ½ pts	Jx=0 pts

Value of **10s** vary: 10K=½, 10A=0, 10Q/J=1, 10J=2
No Aces = -1 pt (Only Opener) No Q =-1 No K=-1 (all hands) with Max=-2
3Ks = +1 pt, 4Ks = +2pts, 4Qs = +1pt

For 3 of the top 5 honors (**suit quality-Q**) in a 5-card suit add +1 pt and in a 6-card suit add +2 pts.
For a Singleton honor or for **TWO** Honor doubletons (AK/AQ/KQ/QJ deduct -1 pt
However, DO NOT deduct a point for an AJ/KJ doubleton since they are better than Ax and Kx.

LENGTH POINTS (L)

For a suit headed with at least 3 points (QJ/K) and 5-cards add +1 pt and for 6-cards add +2 pts
Suit Quality (Q). A 6-card suit without 3 points add only +1 pt.

Add +2 pts for **each point** from the 7th-card on in any 7+ card suit – Length alone has value.

DISTRIBUTION POINTS (D)

VOID = 4pts   Singleton= 2 points **ONE** doubleton= 0 pts **TWO** doubletons = 1pt
4333 = -1pt
Singleton in a NT contract = -1pt

Opening Hands are counted in HLD pts. Responding hands count HL with max of 2L initially. They will add D pts once a fit is found. In NT, responder counts HLD points.

SUIT FIT POINTS (F)

8/9/10 card fit= +1/2/3 pts (all suits)

SEMI-FIT (SF)

Add +1 if you hold an honor doubleton Kx/Qx/J10/Jx doubleton (other than the Ace) in partners long suit (5+cards). Both the opener and the responder make the +1-point adjustment with 2-card suit support.

DISTRIBUTION-FIT (DF)

Number of trumps	4	3	2
Void	4pts	3pts	2pts
Singleton	3pts	2pts	1pts
Doubleton	2pts	1pts	0pts

MISFIT POINTS (MF)

Opposite a long 5-card suit deduct -3/-2/-1 for void /singleton/doubleton
With a Fit, add F, Semi-Fit, Distribution-Fit, and MS pts called (HLDF) points.

WASTED HONOR (WH) ADJUSTMENTS where S=Singleton and V=Void

K/Q/J Honors opposite a S/V -2/-3 Non-Honors opposite S/V +2/+3
Ace opposite Singleton= +1

MIRROR HAND/SUIT (MHS) ADJUSTMENTS

For two perfectly mirror hands or two mirror suits deduct -2 points/-1 point.

Adjusted Optimal Count (AOC) - Summary

To open 1M requires 12-17**HLD** points; however, for a suit overcall in a competitive auction one needs 12-17**AOC** points for a 1-level bid and for a 2-level overcall bid one needs 15-17**AOC** points. Evaluation of **AOC** points are a 3-step process:

- (4) **Starting Points HLD**
- (5) **Adjustments for Opponent's suit length and Honors Held in their suit**
- (6) **Adjustments for Honors in 3 or 4 suits Outside the Opponents' suit**

Overcall Suit Adjustments

Deduct -1 point for 3-cards in the opponent's suit
Deduct -2 point for 4-cards in the opponent's suit
Deduct -3 point for 5-cards in the opponent's suit

Add +1 for a singleton in the opponent's suit (i.e., 2D becomes 3D)
Add +1 for a void in the opponent's suit (i.e., 4D becomes 5D)

The opponents open 1♥ open and you hold:

♥xx	No adjustment
♥xxx	-1L point
♥Axx	-1L point = 3.5 points (4.5-1L)
♥Axxx	-2L point = 2.5 points (4.5-2L)
♥Kxxx	-2L point = 1.0 points (3.0-2L)
♥x	+1D so total =3D
♥ -	+1D so total =5D

A second factor that effects an over call bid are **honors in and outside the opponent's suit**. The honors in 3 and 4 card suits and lone honors help to determine whether your hand is more defensive than offensive orientated.

Overcall Honor Adjustments

(4) Honors in Opponent's Suit

Kxx/Kxxx (K alone) deduct -1 point (regardless of position) with KJx or Kx no adjustment

K with Q -1 when before opponents' suit
+1 when after opponents' suit
Qxx/QJx no adjustment

J **without** a 10 -0.5 (e.g., Jxx/Jxxx J alone); otherwise, no adjustment

(5) Honors in 3/4 card side suits

Kxx/Kxxx alone -1 point with Q/J no adjustment
Jxx/Jxxx alone -0.5 with 10 no adjustment

(6) No other honor adjustments

A simple overcall at the one-level requires 12-17**AOC** points for 1-level bid and includes 2 zones 12/14 and 15/17; for a 2-level bid one needs 15-17**AOC** points.

1NT Overcall

When considering a 1NT overcall bid, holding 4+ cards in the opponent's suit is neither a liability or an asset since it may not generate an additional trick or add any additional protection. However, if the opponent's card were in another suit, it would add offensive value to the hand by having 5-cards in a side suit. Hence, one must deduct -1 point for having 4-cards in the opponent's suit; but not 2. And holding 5-cards, while rare, is a greater liability so one must make a -2-point adjustment.

NT Overcall Suit Length Adjustments

Deduct -1 point for 4-cards in the opponent's suit
Deduct -2 point for 5-cards in the opponent's suit

NT Overcall Honor Card Adjustments

Deduct -1 point for a King alone (Kxx/Kxxxx) in any 3/4-card suit
Deduct -0.5 points for a lone Jack in any suit

Completed Convention Card

SPECIAL DOUBLES
After Overcall: Penalty ☐ _____
Negative ☑ thru infinity _____
Responsive ☑ : thru 3S   Maximal ☐
Support. Dbl ☑ thru 2H   Redbl ☑
Card-showing ☐   Min. Offshape T/O ☐

SIMPLE OVERCALL
1 level 12 to 17 HCP (usually)
often 4 cards ☐   very light style ☐
Responses
New Suit: Forcing ☐ NFConst ☑ NF ☐
Jump Raise: Forcing ☐ Inv. ☑ Weak ☐
ROZ X AND XX

JUMP OVERCALL
Strong ☐   Intermediate ☑   Weak ☐

OPENING PREEMPTS
	Sound	Light	Very Light
3/4-bids	☑	☐	☐
Conv./Resp.			

DIRECT CUEBID
	OVER:	Minor	Major
Natural		☐	☐
Strong T/O		☐	☐
Michaels		☐	☑

SLAM CONVENTIONS
Gerber ☐ : 4NT: Blackwood ☐ RKC ☐ 1430 ☑
EXPERT GERBER - MINORWOOD -KICKBACK -ERKCB
DRKCB
vs Interference: DOPI ☑   DEPO ☑   Level: _____ ROPI ☑

LEADS (circle card led, if not in bold)
versus Suits		versus Notrump	
X x	x x x x	X x	X x x x
x x x	x x x x x	x x x	x x x x x
A K x	T 9 x	A K J x	A Q J x
K Q x	K J T x	A J T 9	A T 9 x
Q J x	K T 9 x	K Q J x	K Q T 9
J T 9	Q T 9 x	Q J T x	Q T 9 x
K Q T 9		J T 9 x	T 9 x x

LENGTH LEADS:
4th Best   vs SUITS ☑ vs NT ☐
3rd/5th Best   vs SUITS ☐ vs NT ☐
Attitude vs NT ☑

Primary signal to partner's leads
Attitude ☑   Count ☐   Suit preference ☐

SPECIAL CARDING ☐ **PLEASE ASK**

NOTRUMP OVERCALLS
Direct: 15 to 18 Systems on ☐
Conv. _____
Balancing: 12 to 14
Jump to 2NT: Minors ☐ 2 Lowest ☐
Conv. _____

DEFENSE VS NOTRUMP
vs:	STRONG	BAL
2♣	D	NATURAL
2♦	H	X=CAPP
2♥	S	
2♠	C	
Dbl:	CAPP	
Other	2NT=MINORS	

OVER OPP'S T/O DOUBLE
New Suit Forcing: 1 level ☑ 2 level ☐
Jump Shift: Forcing ☑ Inv. ☐ Weak ☐
Redouble implies no fit ☑
	2NT Over	Limit+	Limit	Weak
Majors		☐	☐	☐
Minors		☐	☐	☐
Other				

VS Opening Preempts Double Is
Takeout ☐ thru 4H   Penalty ☐
Conv. Takeout: _____
Lebensohl 2NT Response ☐
Other: Lebrnsohl Ov Reverses

DEFENSIVE CARDING
	vs SUITS	vs NT
Standard:	☐	☐
Except ☐		
Upside-Down:		
count	☑	☑
attitude	☑	☑

FIRST DISCARD
Lavinthal	☐	☐
Odd/Even	☐	☐
Rev Smith Eco	☑	☑

OTHER CARDING
Smith Echo	☐	☐
Trump Suit Pref.	☑	
Foster Echo	☑	☑

NAMES
_____

GENERAL APPROACH
Optimal Modified 2/1-Club System
Two Over One: Game Forcing ☑ Game Forcing Except When Suit Rebid ☐
VERY LIGHT: Openings ☐   3rd Hand ☐   Overcalls ☐   Preempts ☐
FORCING OPENING: 1♣ ☑   2♣ ☐   Natural 2 Bids ☐   Other ☐

NOTRUMP OPENING BIDS
1NT
15 to 17
to
5-card Major common ☐
System on over X, 2C
2♣ Stayman ☐ Puppet ☐
2♦ Transfer to ♥ ☑
Forcing Stayman ☐
2♥ Transfer to ♠ ☑
2♠ Clubs
2NT Diamonds

3♣ 5-5<10
3♦ 5-5e10
3♥ 5-5<10
3♠ 5-5e10
4♦ 4♥ Transfer ☑
Smolen ☑
Lebensohl ☑ (st denies)
Neg. Double ☑ Cards
Other: _____

2NT 12 to 14
Puppet Stayman ☐
Transfer Responses:
Jacoby ☐   Texas ☐
3♠
The Minors

3NT ___ to ___
Gambling

Conventional NT Openings

MAJOR OPENING
Expected Min. Length	4	5
1st/2nd	☐	☑
3rd/4th	☐	☑

RESPONSES
Double Raise: Force ☐ Inv. ☑ Weak ☐
After Overcall: Force ☐ Inv. ☑ Weak ☐
Conv. Raise: 2NT ☐ 3NT ☐ Splinter ☑
Other: splinters 13-15
1NT: Forcing ☑   Semi-forcing ☐
2NT: Forcing ☑ Inv. ☐   16+ to ___
3NT: ___ to ___
Drury ☐ : Reverse ☐ 2-Way ☐ Fit ☐
Other: _____

MINOR OPENING
			NF
Expected Min. Length	4	3	0~2 Conv.
1♣	☐	☐	☐
1♦	☐	☐	☑

RESPONSES
Double Raise: Force ☐ Inv. ☑ Weak ☐
After Overcall: Force ☐ Inv. ☑ Weak ☐
Forcing Raise: J/S in other minor ☐
Single raise ☐ Other: 12-17
Frequently bypass 4+♦ ☐
1NT/1♣ ___ to ___
2NT Forcing ☐ Inv. ☐ ___ to ___
3NT: ___ to ___
Other 0-2 diamonds - XYZ

		DESCRIBE	RESPONSES/REBIDS
2♣	15 to 17 HCP		
	Strong ☐ Other ☐	5/6 clubs	
	2♦ Resp: Neg ☐ Waiting ☐		
2♦	15 to 17 HCP	7-diamonds	
	Natural: Weak ☐ Intermediate ☐ Strong ☑ Conv ☐		2NT Force ☑ New Suit NF ☐
2♥	12 to 14 HCP	6-card	Feature
	Natural: Weak ☐ Intermediate ☐ Strong ☑ Conv ☐		2NT Force ☐ New Suit NF ☐
2♠	12 to 14 HCP	6-card	Feature
	Natural: Weak ☐ Intermediate ☐ Strong ☐ Conv ☐		2NT Force ☐ New Suit NF ☐

OTHER CONV. CALLS:
New Minor Forcing ☐   2-Way NMF ☐
Weak Jump Shifts: In Comp. ☐   Not In Comp ☐
4th Suit Forcing: 1 Rd. ☑ Game ☐
UN OVER UN -XYZ - HESS CUE BIDS
3-clubs=7, 3d=6, 3M=7 and 12-14

INDEX

227